Choosing Equality

Praise for *Choosing Equality*

"If middle-class parents were unable to choose schools for their children, there would be no need for vouchers. But because they can, America, if it is to be a just society, has two alternatives: it can forbid the middle class to move to the suburbs or use private schools on the one hand, or it can allow poor and working-class parents school choice on the other. Since the former is impossible, the latter is inevitable. Viteritti explains why anyone committed to equality and fairness has to lend a sympathetic ear to school choice. This is a thought-provoking and essential book."

—Alan Wolfe, director, Center for Religion and
American Public Life, Boston College

"Comprehensive and balanced . . . Viteritti does not promote charter schools or vouchers as a cure-all for every inequality, but he does insist that school choice should be available to everyone—not just to those who can afford to pay for it."

—Cheryl B. Henig, *American School Board Journal*

"Viteritti offers a remarkably fresh perspective on the issue of school choice that should shift policy debate in healthy new directions. He argues convincingly that school choice can be a powerful tool for realizing America's long unfulfilled promise of equal educational opportunity by tapping the cultural, social, and, most importantly, religious resources that communities could bring to schooling if given the opportunity by policymakers to do so. Viteritti bolsters this unusually thoughtful argument with a compelling case for its constitutionality and its potential contribution to American democracy—a truly important work of research and scholarship."

—John E. Chubb, coauthor, *Politics, Markets, and America's Schools*

"Passionately argued . . . . To critics, Viteritti retorts that school choice will create healthy competition, inducing public schools to shape up."

—*Publishers Weekly*

"Viteritti dispels the shallow mythology of public education and discloses our shared history of good intention bent by personal motive. The dreams of those who pursue the egalitarian goal of quality education for all will be nurtured by this message. Finally, a roadmap for those who dare to act on the truth."

—Lisa Graham Keegan, superintendent of
public instruction, State of Arizona

"Viteritti presents a case for school choice designed to appeal to liberals and conservatives alike . . . . If there is a more thorough and thoughtful argument for school choice , I am unaware of it."

—Cristopher Rapp, *National Review*

"*Choosing Equality* is in the best sense a troubling book. It will trouble the conscience of anyone who believes America can continue to tolerate the heinous disparities in its public schools and it will trouble the logic of anyone who thinks the poorest students can be saved without radical reform. Calmly reasoned and yet passionately felt, *Choosing Equality* must be reckoned with by all partisans in the growing debate over school choice and vouchers."

—Samuel G. Freedman, Columbia University, author of *Small Victories* and *Upon This Rock*

"*Choosing Equality* is as original and invigorating as it is scholarly. Viteritti has a knack for connecting history with the present. This book is a significant, if not seminal, work in the school reform literature."

—*CAPE Outlook,* Council for American Private Education

"This is the philosophical manual that has the potential to unite more than ever before both the left and the right political constituencies supporting school choice . . . . An intellectual *tour de force* and a must read for all sides in the school choice debate."

—*School Reform News*

"Those who are looking for school alternatives, those who are attempting to provide school alternatives, and those who are attempting to keep public education alive will find this book informative, practical, and frightening in that order! *Choosing Equality* will prove to be current, well-researched, and as unbiased as any book on this topic can be said to be."

—Gail Lennon, *Education Review*

"Viteritti has constructed an argument that is both sensitive—sensitive, in terms of the author's temperate tone on what is easily the education debate's most divisive issue—and sensible, in terms of Viteritti's belief that America's noble public goal of equality through education may best be reached by private means."

—Daniel McGroarty, *Philanthropy*

Preface

THIS BOOK project began several years ago, although I might say that it has been in preparation for more than twenty. My interest in education was piqued in 1978, when my former graduate school professor, Frank Macchiarola, became head of the New York City public school system and invited me to join his newly assembled staff. Since then I have had the privilege to take on temporary assignments with the school superintendents of Boston and San Francisco. But it was during the initial three-year experience in New York, when I was fresh out of graduate school, that I began to develop a perspective on urban education.

Unlike most of his predecessors, Macchiarola was not a career educator who had worked his way up through the ranks of the public schools. Neither he nor most of the people who surrounded him identified with the system they now managed. Our view of the sprawling bureaucracy that dominated education in the city was entirely functional: either it would become an instrument for implementing new policy, or it would be dealt with as an insufferable impediment to important changes that needed to be made.

Our education agenda became more clearly defined when the late Ron Edmonds took a leave from Harvard to join the team as senior adviser on instructional matters. At the time, Ron was in the midst of a national campaign that became known as the effective schools movement. He was quite agitated by the first Coleman report, which suggested that family background was the key determinant of educational achievement in children, and he was bound to demonstrate that schools do make a difference in determining how well children learn. His assertion that "all children can learn" became not only a motto for the new school administration in New York, but also a philosophical statement that was espoused by reform-minded educators throughout the United States.

Ron had a clear understanding of what was needed to promote educational excellence and equity. If we want to upgrade the condition of education in America, he urged, we must begin by improving the opportunities of those students who are the lowest performers. Just do that well, and the rest will fall into place. Ron was one of the first black educators in America to speak out against busing as a mechanism to advance educational opportunity—not because he didn't support desegregation, but because he thought it was more important to have effective schools within the communities where black and poor children live.

Returning to academia after three years of public service in the nation's largest public school district provided me with a chance to write about what I had learned. My key observation, and the theme of an ensuing book that appeared in 1983, focused on the basic dichotomy that existed between the school system's political constituents and its clients. As viewed from the office of an urban superintendent bent on change, it was evident that the powerful constituents to which the school system and its appointed officials were accountable had little in common with the clientele that actually attended the schools. Very often these influential groups claimed to be speaking on behalf of students and parents, but their interests are not always in accord. The division between powerful constituents and politically weak clients defines a political paradox that makes it difficult to pursue an equitable agenda on behalf of those children who are underserved. This is a dilemma that holds true today not just for New York but for nearly every urban school district in the nation.

Despite these political observations, I emerged from my experience in New York thoroughly persuaded that big-city school districts were manageable, that with commitment and perseverance it would be possible to make these large bureaucratic systems responsive to the needs of all children. This claim has not withstood the test of time. By and large, big-city school systems have not done a very convincing job of educating their least-fortunate students. Like moving a giant boulder up the side of a mountain, progress always comes in short and easily reversible steps. The old bureaucratic structure weighs heavily on those dedicated educators who work day in and day out to humanize a system organized around impersonal rules and regulations.

To achieve educational and social equality in the United States, we need to empower poor parents to act in the best interests of their children and offer them alternatives to failing schools. My objective in this book is to explain how and why school choice in the form of charter schools and vouchers for the poor can advance equality. There are few issues that provoke as much passion in policy circles as choice. I enter the debate with some trepidation, knowing full well that what I propose will manage to arouse the disfavor of people on both the political left and political right. I will argue, nonetheless, that school choice can be enacted in pursuit of political and social values that are the lifeblood of the American democratic system, and for that reason it is worthy of wide support across the political spectrum.

I incurred numerous debts in the preparation of this manuscript. Parts of chapters five and six appeared in slightly different form in articles that were published in the *Yale Law and Policy Review* (1996) and the *Harvard Journal of Law and Public Policy* (1998). At the Brookings Institution Press, Bob Faherty and Nancy Davidson embraced the project early on, while Chris Kelaher saw it through to completion. Gary Kessler provided helpful editorial advice, Inge Lockwood proofread the pages, and Susan Fels indexed the book.

I am extremely fortunate for having so many friends, colleagues, and associates who were willing to share their expertise and read all or parts of my work in its various stages of development. Among those who I especially want to thank are David Armor, John Chubb, Jack Coons, the Reverend Floyd Flake, Howard Fuller, William Galston, Steve Gilles, Michael Heise, Jim Jacobs, Tom James, Frank Macchiarola, Bruno Manno, Susan Mitchell, Dick Netzer, Michael McConnell, Diane Ravitch, Christine Rossell, and my wife, Rosemary Salomone, who was selflessly supportive at a time when she was deeply buried in her own book project. I want to thank my research assistant, Kevin Kosar, and my administrative assistant, Joyce Kong, for their hard work and endurance. I also want to express my gratitude to the John M. Olin Foundation and the Achelis and Bodman Foundations for their generous support. I, of course, accept full responsibility for the contents.

This book is dedicated to my son, Andrew, who reminds me daily that our children are our most precious gift.

For Andrew

Contents

CHAPTER ONE

Debating Choice

NEARLY HALF A CENTURY has passed since the parents of a little black girl from Topeka, Kansas, entered a federal court room to argue that every child in America has an equal right to a decent education. Since then the political process has conjured up a re-markable array of schemes to demonstrate the nation's commitment to that ideal, but the results have been unimpressive. We have sent children on long bus rides into hostile environments; we have poured tons of money into faltering programs; we have tinkered on the edges of institutional reform; and we even have experimented with several forms of school choice—some to promote racial integration, and others to improve the academic opportunities available to disadvantaged children. Notwithstanding Linda Brown's courageous efforts to fulfill the promise of equality and a range of well-intentioned government actions, race and class remain the most reliable predictors of educational achievement in the United States.

Over the last decade, several new approaches to choice have been introduced, emboldening the campaign to upgrade the quality of education. The most popular of these involves charter schools—a form of choice limited to public schools that has been adopted in thirty-six states and the District of Columbia, raising hopes that a new supply of innovative institutions will appear across the educational landscape. The most controversial approach to choice is school vouchers, which would provide government funding for families to send their children to private and reli-

1

gious schools. A modified version of vouchers has been implemented in Milwaukee and Cleveland that is targeted to benefit children whose families meet specific criteria of financial need. Florida passed a statewide voucher plan in the spring of 1999 aimed at students who attend chronically failing schools.

The common feature of all choice programs—whether public or private—is that they are designed to increase the range of educational options available to students beyond the public schools normally found in their school districts. Most choice advocates of today believe that empowering parents to select the schools their children attend will promote competition and provide an incentive for all schools to improve. The choice concept, however, has a diverse and complex lineage.

Social scientists trace the idea to a provocative voucher proposal put forward by economist Milton Friedman in the mid-1950s, where the Nobel laureate envisioned a system of schools that was publicly financed but privately run.[1] The Friedman plan, designed to significantly reduce the role of government in elementary and secondary education, was especially well received by free market advocates, and until today stirs the imagination of many who gravitate towards a more conservative political agenda.[2]

Different forms of voucher plans appeared in the early 1970s. They were put forward by people like Theodore Sizer, Christopher Jencks, John Coons, and Stephen Sugarman,[3] individuals whose writings were more commonly associated with a liberal social agenda. Their respective proposals focused on the educational needs of underserved communities and bear a striking resemblance to the programs more recently enacted in Milwaukee and Cleveland.

Support for charter schools has also emerged from different segments of the education community. One of the first proponents of the idea was Albert Shanker, the late president of the American Federation of Teachers, who saw charters as a way to upgrade the quality of public schools.[4] Among the most articulate champions of charters today are Arizona Education Commissioner Lisa Graham Keegan and former Minnesota school teacher-turned-researcher Joe Nathan—one a proponent of vouchers, the other vigorously opposed.

School choice means different things to different people. Never wholly owned by either the political right or the political left, choice can be adopted to advance a variety of policy objectives depending on how it is designed. My goal in this book is to explain how choice might be applied—crafted, if you may—to advance the goal of equality. I will take as my starting point the enunciation of the principle as it was pronounced in the landmark *Brown* decision. That awesome mandate handed down by the Supreme Court in 1954 was an ambitious proposition even by today's standards, pledging not only equality of educational opportunity for blacks, but full partnership in the American experiment—including its legal, social, economic, and political structure. The opinion was a perceptive discourse on the critical role that education plays in a free society, and I hope to build on its insights and the constitutional tradition from which it was fashioned.

Much can be learned from the rich experience that we have had with various forms of school choice. There is encouraging evidence to suggest that, if properly constructed by policymakers, school choice can function to upgrade the educational opportunities of all children, and, in the process, that it can strengthen the health of American democracy. Some of the evidence remains cloudy. We cannot fully anticipate the outcome of a proposition that has not been fully tried. But we do know that the present situation in education is intolerable. We are also aware of the measures that policymakers have taken to alter the pattern of educational inequality thus far; and it is clear these approaches have proven unsatisfactory.

I do not mean to suggest that school choice, in any form, will serve to cure the lingering inequality that has afflicted America for so many years. Nor do I feel obliged to make such a claim in order to justify its application as part of the treatment for what ails our schools. Unlike scientists in the medical profession, education researchers have never discovered the equivalent of a miracle drug to deal with education's most daunting maladies, and they probably never will. We are well advised, therefore, to administer prescriptions that may help alleviate some of the immediate pain and show promise of contributing to a long-term remedy. School choice, when properly formulated, can fit the call.

To properly determine the contribution that school choice can make to improve education, we must have a better sense of the prevailing condition. This kind of diagnosis does not come easy in education, because there is not a clear consensus among professionals about the nature of the problem, its gravity, or whether a problem exists at all.

It is difficult to fault Americans for lack of commitment when it comes to their schools. Since 1970 per capita spending on education has risen by 63 percent.[5] Increased spending has not been translated into a commensurate improvement in academic performance. Even though we spend more money per student than all but two members (Austria and Switzerland) of the Organization for Economic Cooperation and Development, students in the United States consistently score below their peers in other nations on international assessments.[6]

In the United States, per capita spending on elementary education is $5,300, compared to an international average of $3,310; for high schools, the American amount is $6,680, compared to $4,340 elsewhere.[7] Despite the higher spending, in 1996 American eighth graders scored right smack in the middle on the Third International Math and Science Test. A report released in 1998 showed that in comparison to students in twenty-one other countries, our high school seniors scored eighteenth in math and science, just ahead of Lithuania, Cyprus, and South Africa.[8] Taken together, the scores suggest that American students fall further behind their international peers as they move through the grades.

Some scholars challenge the validity of the above comparisons, and rebuff claims that American education is not doing well.[9] They point out that at least part of the spending disparity can be explained by the overall higher cost of living in the United States. Several of our competitors—Canada, Denmark, and Sweden—actually spend a higher proportion of their domestic national product on education than the United States does. Mindful that for generations Americans have tolerated the practice of leaving the country's poorest unschooled, some commentators remind us that we now educate a larger portion of the school-age population than ever before, and that students tend to remain in school longer. Never before, they explain, have schools been asked to deal with a more destitute population, overwhelmed with poverty, social decay, and unfamiliarity with the American language and culture. All the while, they point out, Americans enjoy a level of technological comfort that is unsurpassed in the rest of the world, and our economy remains among the strongest, as the rest of the globe recoils from crisis to crisis.

In an attempt to offer a balanced perspective on our current condition, Lawrence Stedman has made several observations that speak more directly to the central issue of this volume.[10] Stedman believes that there actually has been little decline in the knowledge base of American students over the past thirty years. The problem, he points out, is more nuanced: a stagnation in knowledge and skills over time when the demand for them has escalated, and a persistent gap in achievement defined by race and class. While it was once possible for an unskilled person to make a respectable living without possessing a high school diploma, the prospects have become more difficult for the postindustrial economy of the twenty-first century. The lack of a decent education places people on the margins of life, with little chance for betterment. The change in the structure of the economy has severe repercussions for those who lag behind academically.

The test score gap between blacks and whites was the subject of a recent volume edited by Christopher Jencks and Meredith Phillips. In their comprehensive introduction to the research findings, Jencks and Phillips explain that although some strides have been made in closing the performance gap since 1970, the typical black student scores below 75 percent of his or her white peers on most standardized tests and below 85 percent on some national assessments.[11] A subsequent volume edited by Susan Mayer and Paul Peterson presents a number of studies indicating that the gap in basic skills evidenced by test scores goes a long way in explaining the disparity in earnings among racial groups.[12] Additional evidence suggests that educational and earning disparities are associated with racial differences in crime, health, and family structure. This leads Jencks and Phillips to propose, "If racial equality is America's goal, reducing the black-white test score gap would probably do more to promote this goal than any other strategy that commands broad political support."[13]

Who Wants Choice?

Phi Delta Kappan, a magazine widely read by educators, has been conducting a Gallup poll on public attitudes toward schools for more than thirty years. In 1994 pollsters began to ask whether respondents would support a proposal that allows parents to send their children to a public, private, or parochial school of choice, with the government paying all or part of the tuition. When the question was first posed in 1994, only 45 percent favored the idea, but since then the balance has shifted. In 1996 support declined to 43 percent. Then for the first time a slight plurality of those questioned in 1997 (49 percent versus 48 percent) expressed support; and support has been gradually mounting ever since.[14] Beneath the evenly divided totals within the general population is a more dramatic dichotomy between certain population groups. Those most sympathetic to the idea of vouchers are blacks (62 percent to 34 percent), nonwhites (61 percent to 36 percent), people in the $20,000 to $30,000 income bracket (55 percent to 43 percent), people in the $10,000 to $20,000 income bracket (53 percent to 42 percent), and manual laborers (53 percent to 44 percent). Those opposing vouchers tend to cluster among suburban residents

(51 percent against to 45 percent for) and people in the $50,000 or above income bracket (57 percent to 41 percent).[15]

These findings, indicating a racial and class divide in attitudes towards vouchers, are replicated in a 1997 study by the Joint Center for Political and Economic Studies in Washington. Its authors found that 57.3 percent of blacks and 65.4 percent of Hispanics supported vouchers, while whites were more evenly divided (47.2 percent in favor, 47.4 percent opposed). The data represented a significant increase in support for vouchers among both blacks (10.6 percent) and whites (4.8 percent) over the short period of a year.[16] The latter study also shows that the attitudes various subgroups had toward the voucher question were at least casually related to their respective levels of satisfaction with local public schools. While a majority of whites (60 percent) rated their local schools excellent or good, only 34.3 percent of blacks and 39.4 percent of Hispanics did the same.[17]

The polling results are not stunning. Although some suburban school districts have taken on many of the negative characteristics commonly attributed to their urban neighbors, most suburban parents are content with the public schools that their children attend, as they should be. Their schools are relatively safe, well financed, physically attractive, and educationally effective. Located in smaller districts, where relationships with administrators and teachers can be more personal, it is easier for suburban residents to feel connected to the institutions their children attend. Choice, even in its more moderate forms, might actually impose new burdens upon these communities. By allowing students from more troubled inner city districts to cross boundaries into their schools, choice might force many suburban parents to confront social and educational problems they thought they were escaping by relocating out of the city. By and large, there is not as strong a motivation for middle-class suburbanites to attend private schools; and even if there were, nonresidential day schools are more commonly located in or near the city.

For all the reasons that white suburbanites resist choice, inner-city parents find it attractive. Safety is a real concern in many urban schools, where students have been known to remain home just to avoid the threat of being assaulted by one of their own classmates.[18] The large impersonal factory model schools these systems inherited from the nineteenth century are difficult to identify with, and their often dilapidated state of repair is an indignity for students and teachers alike.[19] More important, a large portion of these institutions are not academically effective, as evidenced by standardized test scores that are reported year after year.

A study released by *Education Week* in 1998 revealed that most urban public school students around the nation are failing to perform at even the most basic level of achievement.[20] Only 40 percent of fourth and eighth graders who attend city schools scored satisfactorily on national exams in reading, math, and science. In contrast, nearly two-thirds of all students in suburban and rural districts met or exceeded standards. These statistics were based on national trend data taken from the National Assessment of Educational Progress (NEAP), which reflects the performance gap defined by race and the concentration of minority children in urban districts. While 24 percent of all students in the United States attend urban schools, 35 percent of the poor and 43 percent of racial minorities do. It should not be surprising, therefore, that minority parents seek to expand the educational options available for their children.

Another national survey was completed in 1998 by Public Agenda in cooperation with the Public Education Network.[21] Once again, black parents expressed strong support for school choice, with 60 percent saying they would switch their children from public school to private school if money were not an obstacle. What is more noteworthy about the latter is its documentation of a strong consensus between black and white parents concerning what they want from their public schools. This study built on research that Public Agenda had been conducting over a period of several years. In 1994 the large majority of black (91 percent) and white (95 percent) parents agreed that ensuring safety, maintaining order, and teaching the three Rs are the hallmarks of a good education.[22] What drew attention to the 1998 report was the admission by black parents (80 percent) that they wanted schools to place a higher priority on raising academic standards than on the achievement of social goals such as racial integration. When asked further, 77 percent of those black parents emphasized the need to raise and enforce academic standards in failing schools so that students receive passing grades only when they have learned what they are supposed to learn. Many felt that teachers ignore their children or set low expectations for them simply because they are black. Most (60 percent) believed that underachievement among black students is not confined to inner cities, and more than half (54 percent) said that the problem affects students regardless of family income.

Education researcher Lisa Delpit insists that there is a serious cultural dissonance between many white educators and minority parents who have different aspirations for children. While the former emphasize the "humanized" open classroom and a more fluid approach to assessment, black reformers seek to focus more on the development of basic academic skills that will eventually grant children entrée into the mainstream of society. Black parents want to see their children perform well on standardized academic tests so that they can demonstrate beyond a doubt that they deserve an opportunity to enjoy the full benefits of living a middle class existence. As Delpit explains:

> Many liberal educators hold that the primary goal of education is for children to become autonomous, to develop fully who they are in the classroom setting without having arbitrary outside standards forced upon them. This is a very reasonable goal for people who are already participants in the culture of power and who have already internalized its codes. . . . But parents who don't function within the culture often want something else.[23]

White parents interviewed in the Public Agenda survey seemed to agree that black children do not have the same educational opportunities as their own, but the white parents expressed less urgency about correcting the situation. When asked, 54 percent admitted that black children do not attend good schools, but 63 percent believed that a majority of white students do. While 54 percent of black parents said that the problem of educational inequity is "a crisis that must be addressed quickly," only 33 percent of whites saw it that way. A total of 74 percent of blacks and 57 percent of whites thought that giving more money and resources to failing public schools is an excellent or good idea, but there was widespread concern among both groups that measures must be taken to ensure that the additional money be used well. While 54 percent of the black parents supported the idea of giving a private school voucher to students attending failing public schools, only 36 percent of the whites did. An equal percentage (55) of blacks and whites supported the implementation of charter schools.

Although scholars may argue back and forth about the efficacy of the American educational system, one fact is evident: we have not done a good enough job educating the children of the poor, a disproportionate number of whom are blacks and Hispanics living in urban environments. The poor seem to know this better than anyone else. For too long, the so-called debate about education reform has been a conversation among middle-class actors—politicians and professors, journalists, and jurists—about how to elevate the position of the least advantaged members of society.

Policymakers who aspire to achieve educational equality can no longer avoid listening very carefully to what the poor and underserved have to say. Many, frustrated with the status quo, are ready to move beyond the old remedies and to try something different. Like the victims of a chronic health crisis, those who suffer the harshest pain are most inclined to try new medicine. Having the least to lose and the most to gain, they are prepared to accept risk of experimenting with a different treatment. Nevertheless, as many professionals are wont to advise, the risks inherent in change may be real, especially when improperly formulated; and they cannot be dismissed lightly.

Reasonable Doubts

The implementation of choice programs has provoked a considerable amount of anxiety and criticism within the scholarly community, much of it well founded.[24] The principal arguments commonly registered by those concerned generally fall into three broad categories: educational, constitutional, and civic. Although the three are interrelated, for now we will take each in turn.

Respected research on both public and private choice programs suggests that parents who take advantage of school choice tend to be better educated and more astute than those who do not.[25] There is a suggestion here that poor parents are not as well informed about the educational options available for their children or aware of the advantages that certain schools may hold over others. Such unevenness in the ability of parents to make intelligent decisions could result in a sorting process that leaves the poor behind in failing institutions, while better prepared students exit to choice schools that are academically superior. Under these circumstances—often referred to in the literature as "skimming" or "creaming"—low-performing institutions could grow worse as weaker students remain concentrated in them. Given the strong correlation between race, class, and performance, this sorting process could actually contribute to segregation and aggravate the problem of educational inequality.

The scenario considered here grows even more bleak when vouchers are introduced. Once the principle is established that dollars will follow students, it is predicted that a disproportionate number of middle-class families will remove their children from public schools and place them in private or parochial institutions. An evacuation by the middle class would effect not only low-performing schools, but the entire public school system. The transfer of tax dollars from public to private institutions would create financial stress for school districts, many of which are already faced with severe fiscal problems. The loss of a middle-class constituency to nonpublic institutions would motivate political leaders to further divest funds from public schools.

The worst outcome envisioned by skeptics is a form of educational apartheid, with middle-class children attending high-performing private institutions and poor minority students trapped in an inferior system of public education. Skeptics point out that the free market has not served poor people well in other consumer areas, and there is no guarantee that newly emerging private schools will do so either. Just take a quick walk through some inner-city neighborhoods, and you find that the supermarket, drugstore, or movie house that was once there has either closed down or moved on to greener pastures, where the income base is more promising.

Notwithstanding the educational arguments that are often made against voucher proposals, some of the most significant challenges that stand in their way are legal in nature. Constitutional scholars contend that government aid to parochial schools or tuition assistance to the students who attend them violates the Establishment Clause of the First Amendment.[26] On more than one occasion, their position has been upheld by the Supreme Court of the United States.[27] Legal constraints are further complicated by a federalist system that allows each of the fifty states to set its own legal standard for the separation of church and state. Many of the states have "Blaine amendment" provisions in their constitutions that lay down more prohibitive criteria for separation than those found in the First Amendment.[28] This is why most of the legal challenges launched against voucher programs over the last five years—such as those in Wisconsin, Ohio, Vermont, and Maine—have been fought in the state courts.

At the heart of these constitutional concerns is a deep appreciation of the role that education plays in preserving the health of our democratic institutions.[29] For more than a century, the public school has been a principal vehicle for conveying the values that define the American civic culture, a unique mechanism for carving a single people out of a diverse population of groups and individuals brought together by historical accident. Critics question how choice might compromise this cohesive process. They fear that choice would ultimately be divisive and would allow schools to become places that accentuate our differences, with different religious, ethnic, cultural, and ideological clusters setting up separate academies. Both charter schools and vouchers could provide a mechanism for radical organizations, religious or other, to use tax money to establish schools that promote intolerance and undermine the principles of American democracy. If allowed to flourish with abandon, school choice could ultimately have a detrimental effect on civic life, our sense of citizenship, and our viability as a free people.

So why, if it is so dangerous, toy with the idea of choice at all?

The Case for Choice

From the material that has been presented thus far, it is apparent that discussions on the merits of school choice operate on two different levels. As intellectuals engage in esoteric discourse on the abstractions of distributive justice, market dynamics, religious liberty, and civil society, the poor understand on a more visceral level that it is their children who are trapped in inferior schools. The intuition of the latter, for whom the stakes are more immediate and personal, is evident in the polls. The discussion bespeaks an illuminating insight on the issue, underscored by the fact that choice already exists for many if not most Americans.

Most Americans have the economic wherewithal to live in or move to communities where the schools are at least adequate,[30] and quite a large number have the means to afford private or religious schools that reflect their own values. The poor do not have ready access to the same kinds of institutions. In a survey released by the National Center for Education Statistics in 1997, one in five American parents indicated that they exercised choice in selecting their child's school, and an additional two in five suggested that the quality of schools in particular neighborhoods was a factor in deciding where to live. Among parents whose children attend assigned public schools, 60 percent of those with incomes of $50,000 or more said that school quality was a factor in choosing a residence, as opposed to 40 percent of those with an income of $15,000 or less.[31]

As a group, poor people exercise relatively little choice when it comes to deciding what schools their children attend. Beyond the social science evidence, we know that to be true because it is inconceivable that so many parents would send their children to the kinds of schools the poor typically attend if they had an alternative. From the perspective of educational equality, these are the most compelling arguments for choice: the fact that some Americans have it and some do not; the realization that the availability of choice is very much a function of economics and social class; the sad admission that the lack of choice has consigned an entire segment of the population to schools that most middle-class parents would not allow their sons and daughters to attend; the constant reminder in the polls that many of those who do not enjoy choice really want it for their own children.

In the past, we have provided poor children with access to better schools by putting them on buses and sending them to other neighborhoods for an education. That kind of choice is no longer acceptable. In a later chapter, I will explain why I believe that policy was ill conceived and detrimental to the disadvantaged, as well as to their communities. For now, let us stay with the choice issue.

The available data depicting who chooses under the current system sheds important light on issues that were raised earlier, in anticipating the negative effects of a public policy that would extend choice to a wider population. Especially when viewed in conjunction with information on parental satisfaction, the material suggests that concerns about the evacuation of public schools by the middle class may be overstated. Public education is doing a lot better than the evacuation thesis implies. According to the Gallup poll cited above, 64 percent of all American parents give their child's school a grade of A or B, with another 23 percent assigning a grade of C.[32] As already noted, satisfaction is even higher among middle-class and suburban families. There is little reason to expect that choice would prompt a wide exodus by satisfied parents, especially since many have found a way to exercise choice under the current arrangement.

Viewing the evidence as a whole—assessments of school performance, feedback on parental satisfaction, and the polling data on school choice— it is reasonable to predict that minority, poor, and urban parents are more apt to utilize the exit option if choice is extended as a deliberate form of public policy. Thus fears of a "skimming" effect may also be exaggerated. This is not to say, however, that other problems will not arise that need to be addressed in the context of policy design. Strapping dollars on the backs of departing students will indeed bleed school systems of precious dollars. However, limiting the amount of a voucher to the per capita cost of educating the child in his or her home school district could assure a net financial result that is neutral. There is no justification for a fiscal policy that either rewards or penalizes children who exercise choice.

The anticipated exodus of students from low-performing urban school districts—while a positive development for the underserved—could present other complications. One is capacity, the availability of space in desirable institutions to accommodate students seeking alternatives. Notwithstanding constitutional issues that will inevitably arise, the capacity problem is an argument for extending choice to nonpublic schools. Capacity could also be enhanced by adopting a vigorous charter school plan that serves as a mechanism for creating a large number of new institutions within the public domain.

Under normal circumstances, leaving an inner-city public school to attend a private or parochial institution would allow minority students to be educated in a more racially integrated environment than that to which they generally are accustomed. Under certain circumstances, the large transfer of underserved students to newly opened charter schools could result in an overrepresentation of poor and minority students in charter institutions. Some observers would classify the latter result as a form of segregation. We might argue over the terminology. It is unreasonable, nonetheless, to equate the once horrible situation that existed prior to *Brown* with the recent development of charter schools. One involved the exclusion of children from institutions on the basis of race; the other involves the voluntary inclusion of children in institutions to advance their educational goals. One was determined to limit opportunity, the other to expand it.

Whether or not school choice gets implemented as a broad-scale strategy to improve education, there will always be some parents who are more informed, more alert, and more aggressive at finding the best schools for their children. We see it now within public education. Some parents are just more adept at calling up appropriate information and working the system to ensure that their children get access to the best schools possible. It is reasonable to assume that a disproportionate number of those who fit the description are better educated themselves and enjoy a number of other social advantages. The question before us is whether a comprehensive system of school choice will alleviate the existing inequities or exacerbate them. The worst-case scenario envisioned by choice critics is a stratified system of education in which white and middle-class students attend the most desirable schools, while minority and poor children are left behind in failing institutions that nobody else wants to attend.

It might be sobering to note that the terrible nightmare imagined by choice opponents is not a far cry from the situation that now exists, more similar perhaps than most Americans would care to admit. Choice can help to turn things around, if it is designed to do so. Education policy cannot in the short run change the dynamic that occurs when more advantaged parents work the system for the benefit of their own kids. But it can change the system so that the economic impediments that stand in the way of disadvantaged parents are removed, or at least lowered. If school choice is to be adopted as a mechanism for reducing inequality, then public policy must be designed specifically to benefit poor children who attend inadequate schools. The long-term goal must be to enhance the educational options available to disadvantaged populations so that their opportunities more closely resemble the opportunities that pertain to the middle class.

The best way to guarantee that no child is left behind in a failing school is to adopt a policy that does not tolerate the perpetuation of failing schools. Of course, nobody wants failing schools. The problem is that we some-times pretend that we do not know what to do with the children who attend such schools when it is suggested that we close them down; so the typical response is to leave them there and try to do better. It does not work very well for those unfortunate kids left behind.

A more reasonable response to the problem would be to give these children access to more schools: regular public schools, charter schools, private schools, and parochial schools. Poor parents may not be as sophis-ticated as their middle-class counterparts, but they seem to know what they want for their children, and it is not very different from what others want: safe learning environments with high academic standards. As Milton Friedman told us long ago, giving more parents the power to choose the schools their children attend could provide a needed incentive for regular public schools to do a better job at educating all children. Releasing public dollars from the hold of moribund systems could also offer an impetus for new schools, public and private, to come into existence.

The plan I have in mind, described fully in chapter 8, borrows from those that have appeared before. Because it is specifically targeted to help the poor, it has a great deal in common with the redistributive social poli-cies usually identified with a liberal public agenda. Like the plans put forward by Friedman and other free market advocates, it places a great deal of hope in the power of competition, assuming that real competition will be encouraged; but rather than eliminate the role of government in education, this plan seeks to change it. In addition to running its own schools, government would have an important responsibility for enforc-ing quality control for all schools, public or private, that participate in a tax-supported choice or voucher program.

The various perspectives introduced from the left and right sides of the political spectrum have more in common than many of their respective proponents would be inclined to believe. In the next three chapters, I will mine the considerable experience and evidence that has gone before to explain why, how, and under what conditions school choice can be enlisted in the campaign to advance educational equality. In the course of that journey, it will become more apparent that the choice debate in America is not just a philosophical meditation, but it is a highly politicized controversy that involves powerful groups with a great deal at stake (substantively or ideologically), all of whom claim to be speaking in the best interests of children. The academy is not removed from these intense battles.

It is impossible to do justice to the choice debate without entering into the perennial, sometimes tedious, methodological and substantive discussions that occupy academicians concerning the relative performance of public and nonpublic schools. I intend to explain why I am persuaded that inner-city parochial schools are more effective in meeting the educational needs of poor children than are typical public schools in the same neighborhoods. Given the fierce arguments on the topic that have divided researchers long before this volume was imagined, I have no illusions of convincing those who are inclined, for one reason or another, to disagree. I would urge them, however, to try to go beyond the empirical quibbles, and to recognize, as many of its critics implore, that choice is ultimately an issue that concerns significant political and legal values that are similarly compelling.

Most empiricists would agree that there is no substantial evidence to suggest that choice would be educationally harmful to disadvantaged students. Given the inequality inherent in the status quo, that knowledge not only limits the risk of further experimentation, it is encouraging—if not obliging—to move the matter forward. I actually am prepared to take the case further, beyond the important issue of test scores. I intend to argue that there are collateral benefits to extending school choice that are germane to the larger questions raised earlier. Which takes us back to the corollary issues of law and civil society, which will occupy the second half of the volume (chapters 5–7). The issues are closely interrelated, for if our Constitution is anything, it is a blueprint for a vibrant democracy. If, in the process of improving education for disadvantaged children, we were to compromise precious freedoms protected by the First Amendment or undermine civil society, we would have achieved a hollow victory.

Once again, I find the criticisms launched by choice opponents, now on different grounds, unpersuasive. In these instances, the threats they alert us to are not just overstated, they are in some respects wrongheaded and counterintuitive. If I may turn the critics' arguments on their heads, I will propose how a carefully crafted system of school choice, while advancing educational equality, could also serve to enhance religious liberty and invigorate civil society. Before doing that, however, we need to have a better understanding of the principles that underlie the Constitution.

The Constitution and Civil Society

Does the Constitution require such a rigid separation of church and state so as to prohibit aid to students who attend religious schools? In truth, the word separation does not appear in the First Amendment. While they rejected the idea of an established church, the authors of the Constitution did not otherwise act as though they perceived there to be a serious legal tension between government and religious organizations, at least not to the extent that strict separationists do today. To the contrary, the document was produced in an age when the productive interaction between government and religious institutions was quite common.[33] At the Founding, the very notion of political community was based on the composition of religious congregations.[34] Education, to the degree that it was conducted in an organized fashion, was overseen by the clergy, usually with the support of local taxes.[35]

While the argument has become commonplace within the American legal profession, translating disestablishment into absolute separation represents a giant conceptual leap, even for imaginative legal thinkers. It is an unusual interpretation of religious freedom among modern Western democracies, especially when applied to education.[36] The legal construct, with all its authority, is a relatively recent judicial invention within our own system of jurisprudence.

So far as education was concerned, the Supreme Court itself did not invoke the famous Jeffersonian metaphor denoting a "wall of separation" until 1947.[37] It was much later, in the 1970s, that the wall was raised to such an extraordinary height that any incidental aid to sectarian schools was proscribed, regardless of the larger benefits that might have ensued. The prohibitions required by these decisions led one distinguished constitutional scholar to comment that the Supreme Court had begun to confuse freedom of religion with freedom from religion.[38] It appeared that religious institutions were being singled out for exclusion from government-sponsored programs that had been made available to others on a universal basis, raising other constitutional questions.

This rigid notion of separation has been relaxed by the Rehnquist Court. Applying First Amendment reasoning (the Free Exercise clause specifically) and the Equal Protection provision of the Fourteenth Amendment, the Rehnquist Court on several occasions has ruled that religious institutions cannot be discriminated against in determining eligibility for participation in government programs, effectively joining free exercise and egalitarian considerations.[39] As late as 1998, the Supreme Court refused to hear an appeal of a state court decision in Wisconsin that upheld the constitutionality of the Milwaukee school choice law providing public funds for children to attend parochial schools.[40]

The Supreme Court has recognized a significant analytic distinction between financial aid that is given to religious institutions, which is generally suspect, and aid that is appropriated to individuals who attend these institutions, which is generally permissible. This is not a recent conceptual innovation. The distinction dates back to a decision handed down in 1930,[41] and it has been applied throughout the modern history of the Court.

As the U.S. Supreme Court appears to be moving in an accommodationist direction on funding, the state courts have become a more intense battleground for the legal struggle on school vouchers, where opponents are increasingly reliant on more restrictive Blaine amendment provisions within the state constitutions. The conflict between national and state standards on the issue of separation raises some interesting questions concerning American federalism and has the makings of a genuine constitutional crisis.

Our system of federalism permits the states, using their own criteria, to define rights more broadly than the national government does; but they cannot apply their own rules—either by constitutional provision, legislation, judicial decree, or administrative action—to abridge protections contained within the United States Constitution. Imposing strict standards of separation to prevent children in religious schools from taking advantage of publicly funded choice programs raises serious concerns regarding the free exercise and equal protection guarantees of those affected. As with other restrictions on choice, such rigidity is most burdensome on the poor, who cannot afford a religious education when they desire it. Although choice proponents have taken comfort from the Supreme Court's refusal in 1998 to hear the Wisconsin case, the rights of some individuals remain in a precarious position until the Court sets clear standards for the states that are consistent with its own.

Blaine amendment provisions, found in more than half the state constitutions, are a notable illustration of the kind of inverted logic that has influenced church-state relations for more than a century. While many strict separationists point to the Blaine amendment as a legal mechanism to protect religious freedom, an examination of Blaine's history shows that it was borne out of a spirit of religious bigotry and intolerance directed against Catholic immigrants during the nineteenth century. It was not conceived in the spirit of the First Amendment but to impose restrictions that its advocates thought were missing from the Constitution and Bill of Rights. The ugly politics that produced Blaine provide a dramatic illustration of the dangers inherent in a situation where government institutions maintain a legal monopoly over funding for elementary and secondary education.

The meaning of the First Amendment, and the proper balance between its two religious clauses, is best understood in a larger constitutional context. The Bill of Rights was written to protect individuals from excessive government by delineating the legal boundaries of personal freedom. The thought of employing it to narrow the range of choices available to individuals appears to be somewhat self-defeating. The legitimate constraints imposed on government by the Establishment clause[42] must be measured against an array of political values that are essential to a free society. The most obvious of these contending values is found in the Free Exercise clause of the same First Amendment. Less apparent, but similarly compelling in a twenty-first century civilization, is the value of an equal opportunity for every person to receive a decent education. This value is not explicit in the Constitution, but it was stipulated by the Supreme Court in *Brown* on the basis of the Fourteenth Amendment as instrumental for a broader political, economic, and social equality so essential to democracy.

While strict separationists are inclined to draw upon the wisdom of Jefferson in interpreting the Constitution, it may be more enlightening to consult with Madison, whose model of political pluralism shaped the design of the document and the government that it produced and whose vision of political pluralism was a strong foundation for the egalitarian ideal that we still strive to achieve. Neither of the two men were consistent in their writing on religion. However, Madison was more appreciative of the role that religion could play in fostering a healthy democracy; his insights would later be echoed by Tocqueville and confirmed in a substantial body of research performed by contemporary social scientists.[43]

Neither Madison nor Tocqueville could have anticipated that by the nineteenth century the common school would play such a crucial role in melding a diverse people into one nation. They would have been equally surprised, however, by a secularist mentality that held that only public schools could foster the values essential for democratic government. There is no evidence to support such an assumption. To the contrary, the record suggests that parochial schools in the United States have been quite effective in preparing their students to assume the responsibilities of democratic citizenship.[44] There is nothing inherent in a religious education that is anathema to the ethos of democracy, whether it is paid for by parents or with the assistance of public funding.

It may be that some extremist religious groups would seize upon vouchers as an opportunity to establish schools that undermine principles so dear to a free society. They, along with radical political groups, may also view charters as an avenue for advancing a public agenda that is harmful to American democracy. The appropriate way to deal with such threats is through proper public vigilance, not by denying choice to the great majority of faith-based communities or others who cherish the American way of life. Imposing strict standards of separation to prohibit government funding for those who desire a religious education for their children can create severe burdens for deeply religious people, the very ones that the First Amendment was designed to protect.

Once again, in anticipating the risks inherent in change, we must come to terms with the intrinsic limits inherent of the status quo. With all the talk about how school choice or vouchers might weaken the social fabric of American democracy, the level of civic involvement that has thrived under the current educational arrangement is wanting. "Bowling alone" has become a popular metaphor for American attitudes towards community.[45] The public lacks confidence in government institutions and political leaders; participation in elections and community life is in decline; and, most disturbing from the perspective of this book, the social capital needed for meaningful participation is unevenly distributed.[46] To state the issue more precisely, educational inequality is a corrosive correlate to political inequality. If we are committed to bolstering the health of American democracy, it is essential to replenish an interest in civic life, and it is imperative to find ways for involving those who are disaffected. But we must start by providing all citizens with a decent education. Religious institutions can be instrumental on all of these counts.

Over the last several decades policymakers have engineered a variety of plans designed to strengthen the voice and influence of poor people in the political process. They have attempted to work around the deficient education that serves to cap the political power of the poor. While well meaning, many of these schemes were out of touch with both the needs and strengths of the very people they were trying to help. Decisionmakers failed to recognize that improving education was an essential first step to meaningful participation in public life; nor did they fully appreciate how the church could be such a valuable resource for improving education and invigorating public life.

One of the great paradoxes of the policy process is that decisions made on behalf of the weak are rarely made by those who are supposed to benefit from them. The cultural dissonance that Lisa Delpit points to in the classroom often shows its face in the realm of public policy. Separation of church and state is a white, middle-class legal and social construct that is out of step with the ethos of the black community and undermines the black community's most significant local institution. In no American community since the Founding has the church played such an essential role in civic life.[47] During slavery the church was the only institution in their midst through which blacks could develop a sense of self apart from their frightening surroundings. The black church was also a major organizing force within the civil rights movement of the 1950s and 1960s.[48]

In more recent years religious congregations in both black and Hispanic neighborhoods have assumed an important role in community development efforts to provide jobs, housing, and social services to those in need.[49] The church is not just limited to a spiritual function. It is the most significant force for social change available to poor people. Some innovative ministers within urban congregations have begun to start their own church-affiliated schools as an alternative to the failing public schools in their communities. They understand the importance of a good education as a foundation for all other forms of social progress, and they see the religious mission of their schools as a strong antidote to the social decay that surrounds them. Alongside these church-run schools, one also finds a new sector of black independent schools, many of which were started by the clergy but which no longer have a church affiliation.

The expansion of black religious and independent schools has been inhibited by the absence of public assistance for poor parents who cannot afford the tuition. In the meantime, precious tax dollars are invested in government-run institutions that fail generation upon generation of disadvantaged children. While they wait for local public schools to improve, parents are encouraged, under the banner of racial balance, to send their children to other communities to acquire a suitable education. There can be no real hope for improving the quality of civic life in poor communities so long as public policy prevails that inhibits the power of the church or denies children access to decent neighborhood schools.

What Follows

In chapter 2, I will examine several competing definitions of equality and discuss their relevance to education policy. Then I will consider a number of ways in which the goal of equal educational opportunity has been pursued since the *Brown* decision of 1954. The methods explored include racial integration, increased spending in the form of compensatory education programs and school finance reform, and political empowerment. A review of the research literature regarding each of these approaches shows that they have had a minimal effect on the academic performance of poor and minority children, and in the end serve as ineffectual proxies for the enhancement of educational opportunity.

Chapter 3 explores various kinds of school choice programs and their relevance to the goal of educational equity. I will critically consider these approaches, explaining the significant differences between various voucher proposals and an assortment of public choice programs that have been tried, such as magnet programs, controlled choice, interdistrict choice, and charter schools. Each approach speaks to a different conception of equality. A close review of these programs and their implementation indicates that many were designed in ways that compromised the wants, needs, and interests of disadvantaged communities.

Chapter 4 will focus on the role that nonpublic schools—private and religious—can play in advancing the educational opportunities of underserved populations. Here I will consider the complex political alliances that shape various choice and voucher programs. I will review the relevant social science research on nonpublic schools, the experience with voucher experiments in Milwaukee and Cleveland, and the evolution of privately supported voucher programs throughout the nation. Thus far the evidence on these programs remains encouraging but inconclusive. Nonetheless, given our chronic failure to address the educational needs of disadvantaged communities, the information we have offers no reason to discourage further experimentation.

Chapter 5 will focus on the constitutional issues. I will begin with an examination of the principles that shaped the writing of the Constitution, comparing the influential perspectives of Jefferson and Madison and explaining why the latter is more useful for understanding the First Amendment. I will then discuss how, in the context of a strong secularist philosophy that dominates the public school curriculum, legal prohibitions against vouchers impose a particularly heavy burden on poor people with a strong religious identity who may want to educate their children differently. A review of First Amendment jurisprudence will show that the more accommodationist position assumed by the Rehnquist Court on the question of state aid to parochial school children is in keeping with a long-standing American constitutional tradition. This reading of the Constitution has significant implications for advancing the goal of equal opportunity in education.

Chapter 6 will deal with state constitutional law, which in recent years has become a more significant legal obstacle to the implementation of school choice programs than the First Amendment. Here I will trace the evolution of state jurisprudence and its connection to the common school movement. The legal prohibitions that followed continue to set the parameters of the choice debate in many states. A review of the cases currently working their way through several state judicial systems reveals a fundamental tension between federal and state standards of separation in need of remedy by the federal courts.

Chapter 7 explores the connection between education and civic involvement. It begins by reviewing the research on the present state of community and political life in the United States. Then it examines the role that inner-city churches can play as a resource for addressing the related problems of educational and social inequality that afflict poor communities.

Chapter 8 will serve as a conclusion, drawing on lessons learned from the preceding chapters to propose a set of policy recommendations to further the goal of equal opportunity in education. This agenda is premised on the need to break the empirical connection between academic achievement and the demographic markers of race and class.

CHAPTER TWO

Defining Equality

A BELIEF IN HUMAN EQUALITY is the foundation of a free society. It is the basic assumption on which the American nation was formed. The Jeffersonian notion of equality that endows each of us with divinely bestowed inalienable rights is biblical in origin. The New Testament teaches that we are all equal in the eyes of God, and as God's creatures, we share similar claims to the enjoyment of human dignity.[1] We celebrate this egalitarian ethos each time we recite the Declaration of Independence.[2] It is an essential part of our civic culture; yet as a practical consideration for governing our daily lives, equality defies the senses. It is difficult to reconcile with what we really know about ourselves and each other.

Ask anyone who has ever seen Michael Jordan fly through the air, or listened to a Mozart symphony in a great hall. Can it be denied that the same Creator who endowed every person with the essence of human dignity also graced each of us with distinct gifts and talents that bespeak our overall inequality? No matter how hard I practice, I will never get anyone to pay me large sums of money to toss a basketball, nor will my tinkering on a piano ever draw a crowd to Carnegie Hall. Recognizing our inherent differences, should we all expect to be treated the same by our fellows, or to derive the same benefits from life? What role should the state play in moderating our natural advantages to ensure the equality we so cherish as part of our democratic heritage?

23

Jefferson's objective in drafting the Declaration was not just to liberate citizens from the force of an oppressive foreign government, but also to set forth a view of political equality requiring that all people—free men to be exact—be treated in the same manner before the law.[3] Jefferson's was a limited notion of equality, however, not just for his obvious omission of women and slaves from public life, but for his failure to consider political equality within a larger social context. Even if the rights of citizenship were guaranteed to all on an equal basis, might those who had been born to wealth be afforded innumerable advantages for exercising influence in the political arena?[4] Certainly, legal equality cannot be equated with political equality in a society where individuals are born into widely different social circumstances, not to mention the unique aptitude each of us possesses for pursuing our interests through political activity.

Tocqueville was one of the first observers of the American scene to appreciate how the spirit of equality would shape our civic culture, and the effect its evolution would have in transforming our government from a limited to an activist state. Accustomed to the aristocratic ways of the European continent, the Frenchman was struck by the "passion for equality" that incited Americans. But he was also wary of how this drive, when taken to an extreme, could diminish human liberty. He warned of a "depraved state of equality," which he feared "impels the weak to lower the powerful to their level, and reduces men to prefer equality in slavery to inequality in freedom."[5] Tocqueville's thoughts on how democratic nations display "a more ardent and enduring love of equality than of liberty" would have a profound effect on the way Americans came to perceive themselves.[6] His juxtaposition of liberty and equality would shape a perennial debate among intellectuals in this country. The struggle pits proponents of the modern liberal state, who would employ public authority to promote social equality, against champions of political freedom, determined to limit the role of the state as a guarantor of life's benefits.[7]

Contemporary social theorists generally perceive the ongoing disagreement over the appropriate state role in terms of varying conceptions of equality, all of which are implicit from the previous discussion and will be employed throughout the remainder of the book. Legal equality, of the sort identified with Jefferson, represents the least ambitious form. It casts the state in a neutral role among citizens and simply requires that each individual is treated the same in the distribution of honors or favors.[8] Here priority is given to the protection of personal freedom, usually through the stipulation of legally defined rights; but little concern is paid to how one's talents or social status influence the exercise of those rights. Equality of opportunity is closely related to legal equality. It differs in the sense that it considers how individual ability or privilege practically affects one's competitive advantage over others. It is similar in the sense that its philosophical adherents do not concede any governmental role in mediating such advantages. Commonly associated with the concept of "career open to talent," these egalitarians resist public intrusions into the personal affairs of citizens as a serious violation of individual liberties.[9] Economists of this persuasion, such as Milton Friedman, are more comfortable with the prospect of letting the market moderate competitive interactions rather than compromising political freedom.[10]

Aristotle had assumed that social stratification among classes resulted from a natural order of talent and virtue that enables the most able to govern society in the public interest.[11] Liberal democratic theorists do not quite see it that way. For them, politics is a contentious enterprise through which individuals and groups seek to satisfy their own needs and wants. Social stratification is a function of privilege that gives certain people an advantage over others. True political equality cannot be attained merely by guaranteeing all citizens equal treatment before the law. For the ideals of democracy to be realized, government must play a positive role in ensuring that each individual possesses the minimum social requisites to participate effectively in public life, even to the point of reallocating wealth and privilege among the various classes. Whether it be through the enforcement of preferential treatment, the disbursements of the welfare state, or other aggressive forms of social spending, the objective of government action is to strive for, if not achieve, an equality of outcomes.[12] In the liberal state, such equality would take precedent over the individual liberty valued by Tocqueville, and in the end would serve to guarantee genuine political freedom for all people. Providing all with a sound education would play a large part in the balancing process.

Brown's Promise

Brown v. Board of Education[13] was the most important Supreme Court decision of the twentieth century. In terms of its immediate objective—the desegregation of the races in education—the decision might originally have been perceived as rather modest in scope. At least in light of our multilayered understanding of the equality principle thus far, its goal of ensuring that each child is given the same legal access to public schools regardless of skin color, can hardly be deemed morally ambitious. But *Brown* would eventually become much more than a tool for achieving legal equality. To begin with, school desegregation in the South would require the radical restructuring of a society that had been built around a consensus of apartheid since the time of slavery. As a matter of constitutional law, *Brown* was the instrument through which the Supreme Court embraced the Fourteenth Amendment to impose a new racial order on the states.[14] It resulted in an aggrandizement of judicial power that had been unparalleled in America before this time, and it recast federalism so that the national government would become a significantly more powerful partner in relation to the states.[15]

Brown provided legal precedent for subsequent decisions by the Warren Court that would apply the Equal Protection clause to outlaw discrimination in a variety of public facilities outside of education, including parks, golf courses, beaches, airports, libraries, and other public buildings.[16] *Brown* also set the political stage for Congress to pass legislation, beginning with the Civil Rights Act of 1964, that would prohibit discrimination in public accommodations, education, and employment. Title IV of the act authorized the attorney general of the United States to initiate litigation on behalf of people who were victims of discrimination, providing black people who could not afford legal counsel with an important ally in the courts. Title VI denied federal assistance to any school district engaged in racial segregation, a serious threat to localities at a time when the federal government was gearing up to accelerate spending on education. In 1965 the Voting Rights Act was passed, removing legal barriers to participation in elections that had long constrained the possibility of black political equality in the South.[17]

Coupled with a series of significant Supreme Court decisions, the legislative program pursued by Congress worked to make litigation on behalf of minorities a more effective instrument for remedying past wrongs.[18] The full impact of *Brown* in advancing political and social equality was nothing less than revolutionary. At the center of this revolution was a thorough understanding of the indispensable role that education plays in a free society—as a wellspring of civic virtue, acculturation, economic prosperity, and, ultimately, full equality. Listen to its words; they are worth quoting at length:

> Today, education is perhaps the most important function of state and local governments. Compulsory school attendance laws and the great expenditures for education both demonstrate our recognition

of the importance of education to our democratic society. . . . It is the very foundation of good citizenship. Today it is the principal instrument in awakening the child to cultural values, in preparing him for later professional training, and in helping him to adjust normally to his environment. In these days, it is doubtful that any child may reasonably be expected to succeed in life if he is denied the opportunity of an education. Such an opportunity, where the state has undertaken to provide it, is a right that must be made available to all on equal terms.[19]

Brown's promise was to realize racial equality through educational opportunity, declaring decent schooling to be nothing less than the right of every American. How this promise might be translated into concrete public policy turned out to be a more daunting challenge than anyone at the time could have imagined.[20] For better of worse, university-based social scientists would become key participants in the recurring conversation among policymakers to determine the effect segregation had on the education of blacks and how these effects might be reversed.

The Civil Rights Act of 1964 had required the United States Office of Education to undertake a comprehensive survey to measure "the lack of availability of equal educational opportunities for individuals by reason of race, color, religion or national origin" among public school students throughout the country.[21] In pursuit of that mandate, Education Commissioner Francis Keppel engaged Professor James Coleman to conduct what was then the largest social science survey in national history. It involved a sample of five hundred and seventy thousand school children, sixty thousand teachers, and four thousand school buildings. It correlated achievement levels with a demographic profile of students as well as a variety of educational inputs, such as staff, spending, and facilities. The "Coleman Report," published in 1966, was both controversial and profound.[22] Its author would emerge as the key figure in education research throughout the next three decades of his life. Here he found that:

—Most black and white children attend segregated schools.

—The measured characteristics of schools, that is, their facilities and resources, are similar among black and white institutions.

—The academic achievement level of blacks is significantly behind that of whites and increases with each year of school attendance.

—The measured characteristics of school inputs have a minimal effect on student achievement.

—Family background is the key variable in determining student outcomes.

—The presence of students from affluent backgrounds is positively related to achievement levels in particular schools.

From a policy standpoint, the implications of the report were far-reaching on a number of points. At least in terms of inputs, it suggested, along the lines of the *Plessy* Court, that blacks and whites were educated in separate but equal school systems.[23] The finding of de facto segregation provided a rationale for the rigorous enforcement of desegregation; the correlation between family background and school performance was a strong evidentiary foundation for the pursuit of integration. The most discouraging assertion of the report was that schools do not matter in determining how well students learn; that performance is more a function of social class and home environment. By taking his investigation beyond the usual consideration of school inputs to a concern for pupil achievement, however, Coleman effectively reshaped the discourse on educational equality. Thereafter, educational equality would no longer be discussed as a mere matter of opportunity; it was now couched in terms of outcomes and results.

In 1972 Christopher Jencks and a group of researchers from Harvard completed a reanalysis of the Coleman data.[24] Once again it was found that school conditions have little effect on student performance. It was becoming apparent—to some social scientists at least—that educators, for the most part, do not know what to do to raise student achievement, and, furthermore, that increased public spending on education would not bring about the results sought. Jencks and his colleagues argued further that it would require nothing less than an economic restructuring of the nation to bring about the educational and social advancement of blacks.[25] This line of reasoning seemed to pose a chicken and egg kind of puzzle regarding the relationship between education and social equality.

False Starts

The "schools don't matter" attitude that grew out of the Coleman and Jencks studies elicited a rigorous response from some education researchers who had produced evidence demonstrating that schools are capable of improving the performance of poor and minority children when they are properly run and organized. Ron Edmonds was one of the first educators in the nation to speak out. Edmonds's research focused on identifying the institutional characteristics that define high-performing schools in low-income districts.[26] He toured the country widely to urge school administrators in minority districts to replicate the conditions he found in his studies on effective schools. Beyond the data, Edmonds was not prepared to accept such a deterministic view of minority schooling, nor did he believe that black children had to sit beside white children to be properly educated. Coleman, Jencks, and Edmonds aside, the nation embarked on a campaign to promote racial integration among students and to put huge amounts of money into education programs.[27] A search was under way to discover how educational equality could be translated from principle to policy.

Equality as Racial Integration

The "all deliberate speed" standard announced in the second *Brown* case[28] created the initial impression that the Supreme Court would move slowly and cautiously in implementing desegregation, as it did for some time. Southern school districts interpreted the words as an invitation for obfuscation and delay. By 1957, the year of the dramatic confrontation in Little Rock, southern states had enacted at least 136 laws and constitutional amendments to undermine desegregation. By 1964 the number had grown to 200.[29] The District of Columbia stood alone as the only jurisdiction in the South to implement a serious plan.[30] With the slow pace of progress recorded, the Court began to assume a more aggressive posture.

One way in which school boards thwarted progress was to close down their public schools and provide funding to parents for the establishment of "choice" academies. The practice was particularly popular in Georgia, Mississippi, Alabama, Louisiana, and Virginia. Many of these private institutions, supported by tuition grants to parents, either outwardly discriminated against black children or conjured administrative hurdles to prevent them from enrolling.[31] In 1964 the Supreme Court, declaring that "the time for 'mere deliberate speed' has run out," determined that the practice of using these academies to preserve segregation offends the Constitution.[32] In 1968 the Court ruled against another "freedom of choice" plan and found that school districts with a history of de jure segregation had an "affirmative duty to take whatever steps might be necessary to convert to a unitary system."[33] Thus began an important strategic transition in which the federal judiciary moved from a policy designed to end discrimination to a policy for promoting racial balance.

The Burger Court handed down its first desegregation decision in 1971. The unanimous ruling assumed broad remedial powers for the judicial branch that far exceeded anything the authors of *Brown* could have imagined. The *Swann*[34] decision established a framework that applied racial quotas as a starting point for crafting a remedy, and instituted the practice of busing as a means to achieve them. Within a short period of time, litigation initiated by civil rights groups began to work its way north.[35] Now the terms of the discussion were radically changing. Beyond achieving legal equality for children who had been purposely excluded from attending certain public schools because of their race, the Supreme Court was now beginning to define equality in terms of results—results that would be measured by whether black and white children did indeed attend the same schools, regardless of whether the pattern was the outcome of intentional public policy.

There is no public issue that has so deeply divided the American people along racial lines than school busing. Busing violated one of the basic institutions of community life, the neighborhood school. It imposed burdens on white lower- and middle-class families in the North that had never perceived themselves as culpable for the centuries of racial inequality that *Brown* had meant to correct.[36] Even scholars who had supported desegregation seriously questioned the wisdom of a policy that would presume to compromise the individual prerogatives of some citizens in order to advance the cause of racial integration.[37] Public reaction to busing in the North was sharp and often violent. Its greatest victims were those children who themselves were required to break the racial barriers that an older generation had constructed. More often than not, it was black children who were forced to ride the bus to promote integration. It became their problem to resolve. Few people who lived through the experience will ever be able to erase the ugly mental image of black children being pelted with rocks and anger, as they sat waiting in yellow buses outside of South Boston High School in 1974 to carry out Judge Garrity's famous order.[38] Twenty years earlier, psychologist Kenneth Clark had persuaded the High Court that segregation imposed severe psychological damage on minority children. Now what damage had been done in the name of social progress?

In 1975 sociologist James Coleman completed a second major study, this time depicting trends in school segregation that he followed between 1968 and 1973.[39] It showed that desegregation efforts were a significant cause of white enrollment declines in public schools, thereby increasing separation between the races. Once again Coleman's discoveries provoked wide controversy in policy circles, this time for giving birth to the "white flight" thesis. Social scientists who had identified themselves and their reputations with busing attacked the methodology of the report and accused Coleman of betraying the cause of desegregation. Coleman's detractors—and there were many within academe—dismissed the connection between busing and white migration patterns, arguing that many whites would have moved to the suburbs anyway.[40] But the methodological debates could not mask the seething anger. At one point, the president of the American Sociological Association proposed censuring Coleman for publishing a study that would undermine the credibility of a policy position so dear to the members of that society.[41]

Notwithstanding the harsh reaction, Coleman's report was eventually endorsed by a number of other notable social scientists who had been studying the same problem, some of whom had initially contested Coleman's findings.[42] Since then, the white flight thesis has become widely, though not universally, accepted, giving credence to the idea that aggressive forms of integration have actually undermined their own objectives.[43] In the most comprehensive survey extant, David Armor cites studies indicating that between 1968 and 1989, the proportion of white students enrolled in large public school systems declined from 73 percent to 52 percent.[44] Combined with the unpopularity of forced busing, white flight theory made voluntary choice plans a more politically attractive way to achieve racial balance.[45] Research had begun to demonstrate that such voluntary programs and a variety of magnet school options are actually more effective.[46]

In 1972, shortly after the Supreme Court approved busing as a remedy for racial integration, Congress passed the Emergency School Aid Act, which appropriated funds to assist school systems in implementing desegregation.[47] Heated congressional debate on the bill reflected a growing public consensus against busing. Two years later, the Equal Educational Opportunities Act was signed into law, declaring that all school children "are entitled to an equal educational opportunity without regard to race, color, sex, or national origin."[48] This time Congress and the president wanted to communicate that equal educational opportunity does not necessarily include extraordinary governmental action to mix students by race. The act stipulated that failure to achieve racial balance is not illegal. It prohibited busing as a remedy for segregation before other, less intrusive approaches had proven ineffective. And it was resolute in prescribing that "the neighborhood is the appropriate basis for determining public school assignments."[49] Between 1974 and 1980 it became a common congressional practice to amend appropriation bills by adding riders to discourage the practice of transporting children great distances to achieve school integration.

The legislative die was cast against school busing as a form of social policy, and Congress's doubts about overreaching intervention in school district affairs seemed to be echoing loudly in the judicial branch. As early as 1974 the Supreme Court had refused to endorse an interdistrict integration plan involving suburban districts in Detroit, because it could not be demonstrated that the suburban jurisdictions had any hand in producing racial isolation in the city.[50] In 1991 the Court ruled in an Oklahoma City case that judicial supervision of desegregation is only a temporary measure and could be terminated if a school district shows a good faith effort to comply with the law and eliminate the vestiges of past discrimination "to the extent practicable."[51] A year later the Court issued a unanimous decision holding that a suburban district in Georgia could not be held responsible for correcting racial imbalance that had resulted purely from demographic factors.[52]

The change of heart now apparent on the Supreme Court seemed to signal a return to the approach originally outlined by the Warren Court in *Brown*, finding legal discrimination as a violation of the Constitution, while hesitant to target racial mixing as an appropriate social objective.[53] There is, however, a deeper philosophical disagreement between the Rehnquist Court and its predecessors, trumpeting perhaps the former's reflection of contemporary public sentiment. While the Warren and, to a lesser extent, the Burger Court had proceeded on the assumption that racial isolation was inherently harmful to minority students, whether or not it is state imposed, the Rehnquist majority is reluctant to accept the premise that sitting next to white students holds intrinsic advantages for black students. Associate Justice Clarence Thomas remarked in a separate opinion in the Kansas City case, "It never ceases to amaze me that the Courts are so willing to assume that anything predominately black must be inferior."[54] As a matter of public policy, concerns for quality education have trumped racial integration. Equality of opportunity is being redefined.[55]

The Missouri decision was of enormous symbolic value, since the case itself highlighted so much of the thinking that surrounded the policy of aggressive school integration.[56] After twelve years of deep judicial involvement, a busing program, and the expenditure of $1.8 billion, Kansas City schools remain racially segregated and the achievement level of black students continues to be dismally low.[57] The more restrained mood on the

High Court has spurred school officials—in places such as Indianapolis, Denver, Minneapolis, Cleveland, Pittsburgh, Seattle, and Wilmington, Delaware—to extricate themselves from the supervision of federal district courts. Some have been more successful than others in ending forced busing and replacing it with either voluntary choice programs or a return to the neighborhood school.

Indianapolis officials have argued that after seventeen years of judicial intervention, the burden of busing still falls entirely on fifty-five hundred black students who are sent to outlying suburbs, taking with them $2,000 per capita that could be invested in their own communities. When a district court turned down their initial plea, they eventually obtained relief from an appellate panel. After more than a decade of involvement, a federal court has refused to relieve New York State of financial liability for desegregating the Yonkers School District. While racial discrimination has been eliminated in every public school in the district, many local observers agree that the overall effort has been a failure. Because of white flight, minority enrollment in the district has increased from 47 percent to 70 percent, while black and Hispanic students continue to score more than two grade levels below their white peers. The sorry episode in Yonkers prompted Kenneth Jenkins, the president of the local NAACP, to comment nearly a decade after its onset that busing has "outlived its usefulness," since the district spends $13 million per year transporting black and Hispanic pupils from one predominately minority school to another rather than using the funds to improve educational programs.[58] Mr. Jenkins's remarks stirred a national debate within his organization and eventually led to his firing.

The NAACP continues to take an aggressive position in support of school integration. Black parents, much as white parents, prefer to have their children attend neighborhood schools. Although a majority of black parents view desegregation as a worthwhile social objective, most do not want to have their children transported out of their communities just to achieve racial balance.[59] In the national survey conducted by the Public Agenda Foundation in 1998, 80 percent of black parents said that they would prefer schools to focus on achievement rather than integration. The study noted a "distinctive lack of energy and passion for integration."[60] Black legal scholar Derrick Bell has criticized the NAACP for pursuing a racial agenda that is unpopular with minorities, while neglecting the more important issue of quality education. He explains the contradiction as an internal tension within the organization, which, on the one

hand, litigates on behalf of poor black parents and, on the other, is accountable to middle-class whites and blacks who provide financial support and are deeply committed to racial integration as a symbolic
battleground of racial politics.[61]

Equality as More Spending

The resource enhancement approach to equality took root as a result in
two distinct forms of public policy, one initiated at the federal level, the
other largely by the states. The former was characterized by an aggressive
program of compensatory spending, designed to improve the educational
opportunities of disadvantaged populations; the latter was meant to equal-
ize spending for educational services between the rich and the poor. The
Elementary and Secondary Education Act (ESEA) of 1965 was a corner-
stone of President Lyndon Johnson's "War on Poverty."[62] In just one year,
it doubled federal spending on education from $1 billion to $2 billion, and
increased the amount to nearly $3 billion by the end of the decade. Under
Titles I and II of the act, funds were provided to distinct populations of
children identified on the basis of economic need. The legislation declared:

> In recognition of the special education needs of children of low in-
> come families and the impact that the concentration of low income
> families have on the ability of local education agencies to support
> adequate educational programs, the Congress hereby declares it to
> be the policy of the United States to provide financial assistance . . .
> to local educational agencies serving areas with concentrations of
> children from low income families.[63]

ESEA explicitly guaranteed that children attending private and parochial schools would not be excluded from consideration in determining
eligibility. Although funds would be administered through the public
schools, educationally and economically deprived children attending
nonpublic schools were permitted to participate in programs through au-
diovisual devices, television and radio programs, mobile teaching units,
and dual enrollment programs. No part of the funds, however, would be
permitted to flow directly to private or parochial schools or to compensate their teachers. ESEA very consciously represented a legislative enactment of "child benefit theory," drawing a conceptual distinction between
benefits accrued by students and benefits provided to institutions, and
confirming a legal principle that was central to the voucher debate.[64]

Politically, this allowed Congress to gain the support of parochial school constituents without losing the backing of the public school lobby. Legally, this presumed to allow Congress to respond to all impoverished children in a nondiscriminatory way, while at the same time accommodating First Amendment considerations of separation. Of course, in reality, no children received direct aid, and only government-run schools were permitted to administer the programs. The legislative precautions were remarkable in light of other existing programs—most of which did not involve primary and secondary education—that permitted direct funding to secular institutions. Prior to ESEA, federal assistance was disbursed to religious institutions under the GI Bill, the National Defense Education Act, the National Science Foundation Act, the National School Lunch Act, and the Hill-Burton Hospital Reconstruction Act.[65]

The administration of ESEA-sponsored programs became unduly burdened in 1985, when the United States Supreme Court ruled that public school teachers could not be sent into parochial schools to provide remedial instruction.[66] Consequently, public school districts were required to rent additional space. In some cases, this meant setting up trailers outside of school buildings, where instructors would conduct classes. The requirements imposed by the 1985 decision not only led to wasteful spending, it proved to be extremely disruptive to parochial school children who had to leave the comfort of their own school buildings for remedial services. In the meantime, classrooms within the building were left vacant. In New York City, where the order was eventually challenged in federal court, excess costs amounted to $16 million annually.[67] These practices remained in force until 1997, when the Supreme Court reversed its previous decision.[68]

The immense outpouring of dollars, however well intentioned it might have been at the outset of Lyndon Johnson's Great Society program, did not prove to be effective in closing the achievement gap for disadvantaged children. Study after study has demonstrated that Title I is a remarkably expensive failure. The first longitudinal study, completed in 1984 after $40 billion in aid had been spent, showed that while children served by the program gained at a slightly faster pace than their peers, this progress was not sustained over time.[69] Thirteen years and $78 billion later, researchers from Abt Associates completed another major study involving forty thousand students. They were unable to discern any difference in performance between program participants and a control group.[70] A companion study attached to the latter showed that in those exceptional cases where funds were invested in tried and true programs at the school level, notable gains were achieved.[71] But these indeed were rare exceptions to the general rule, where moneys indiscriminately got tangled in the morass of the intergovernmental bureaucracy that stood between Washington and the classroom. While the program was supposedly designed to help disadvantaged children, many poor students do not benefit from it because they are not in Title I schools. Aid is distributed to institutions rather than to individuals.

In the spring of 1999 the U.S. Department of Education issued an optimistic report on Title I, noting that fourth graders in the highest poverty schools had made notable progress on national reading tests between 1992 and 1998, and in math between 1990 and 1996.[72] It had failed to note, however, that the 1996 reading scores were the equivalent of what they had been in 1990. The same National Assessment of Educational Progress (NAEP) scores showed that nearly 70 percent of the same students were "below basic" in achievement, as were nearly 60 percent in math.

The federal government continues to support ESEA at a rate of more than $14 billion a year, while another five-year evaluation is under way. In the meantime, as Congress prepares to reauthorize the program for four more years, debate soars in both chambers about how to reshape it to better accommodate the needs of the poor.

Generosity remained a powerful lever for federal intervention in state and local affairs. So long as Congress could attach terms to its funds, the national government would have a tool for imposing its will on school districts, regardless of whether Washington could boast any record of accomplishment. This said, it is worth pointing out that even in 1980, at the peak of federal spending, only 9.8 percent of all education dollars originated in Washington. By the mid-1990s, the federal share had dwindled to below 7 percent.[73] If money were to remain a significant factor in the equity equation, attention would have to be directed to the state and local levels. By the early 1970s, a substantial research literature had begun to emerge showing disparities in funding between property-rich districts and poor districts.[74] It became apparent that the major determinant of school spending within particular districts is the value of taxable property, tempered by the complex formulas written in state legislatures. Much of the disparity observed could be explained in dramatic differences between suburban and urban districts. The growing knowledge of these disparities gave rise to calls for fundamental reform in the way education is financed.

In 1971 a state supreme court invalidated the school finance formula of California, finding that it discriminated against the poor and thereby violated the Equal Protection clause of the Fourteenth Amendment.[75] The

Serrano decision seemed like a reasonable interpretation of the U.S. Constitution in the wake of *Brown*, which had deemed equality of opportunity a fundamental right. This sentiment would be echoed by Congress in 1974, when it passed the Equal Educational Opportunities Act. *Serrano* had sped the hopes of reformers throughout the nation, but their jubilation was short lived. In 1973 the U.S. Supreme Court rejected the Fourteenth Amendment argument that the state judiciary had accepted in striking down the school finance formula of California. The High Court reasoned that "the Equal Protection Clause does not require absolute equality or precisely equal advantages" in education.[76] In reaching its conclusion, the Court noted "the absence of any evidence that the financing system discriminates against a definable category of 'poor people.'"[77]

The *Rodriguez* decision proved to be both confusing and disheartening for school finance reformers. On the one hand, the decision left the door open for the presentation of factual proof of discrimination in future litigation. On the other hand, the Court appeared to be stepping back from *Brown*. In writing for the majority, Justice Powell confirmed the growing reluctance of his colleagues to employ judicial power to meddle in the affairs of the states, cautioning that "every claim arising under the Equal Protection Clause has implications for the relationship between national and state power under our federal system."[78] But if the allocation of resources was not germane to the calculus of educational equality, what was? Since most litigators and legal scholars read *Rodriguez* to mean that the federal judiciary was excusing itself from the equity fray—an interpretation with which I am not entirely comfortable—that question would be passed on to the states.

Less than two weeks after *Rodriguez* was delivered, a state supreme court struck down the school finance plan of New Jersey as a violation of the "thorough and efficient" clause of the state constitution. Based on a historical analysis of the reasoning behind the clause's original adoption and considerable speculation, the court determined, "We do not doubt that an equal educational opportunity for children was precisely in mind."[79] Perhaps it was a matter of timing, but the New Jersey decision had the immediate effect of propelling school finance litigation deeply into the state courts, forsaking the hope that relief to the problem of fiscal equity would ever again be a matter of federal law. Before *Rodriguez*, five cases had been brought challenging the school finance formulas of states based on the Equal Protection clause of the federal Constitution.[80] All subsequent litigation, involving thirty-three states to date (as of this writing), has been crafted around state constitutional arguments. In California, the *Serrano* case was reheard and affirmed on state constitutional grounds.

Of the thirty-three suits that have been initiated in states thus far, sixteen have resulted in decisions ordering jurisdictions to reform their financing mechanisms.[81] The overall effect of the litigation has been mixed and limited. Several studies in California, for example, indicate that equalization policies enacted there actually reduced per pupil spending.[82] A more comprehensive survey of sixteen thousand districts located in states where litigation took place between 1972 and 1992 is somewhat more encouraging for would-be reformers.[83] The latter found that court-ordered reforms resulted in better parity, with spending rising in the poorest districts by 11 percent and in median districts by 7 percent. Most of these increases are explained by leveling-up strategies enacted by state legislatures through increased state spending rather than through an actual redistribution of funds or a fundamental restructuring of the revenue stream flowing from local property taxes. As a result, actual spending by richer districts remained approximately the same. Very little change was found in those states where the courts did not get involved in mandating reform. Because of the state-specific nature of the remedies enacted, there has been virtually no adjustment in the substantial spending inequities that exist among states on a national level.

After two decades of political and legal contention, Michigan stands alone as the only state that has restructured its financing scheme into a uniform system funded mostly by sales tax revenues as opposed to property taxes. Although the new plan has resulted in higher levels of spending for small rural districts, poorer urban districts, including Detroit, actually suffered a loss of net income.[84] On the whole, disparities in spending between urban and suburban districts persist in many places across the country.[85] Rural districts suffer similar disadvantages.[86] In the final analysis, unevenness prevails across states, across districts, and even across schools within districts.[87] While judicial intervention may be a necessary condition for meaningful school finance reform, it is by no means sufficient. The real power to enact changes in revenue and spending policies resides in the legislative branch. Be reminded that state legislatures are the authors of the original funding schemes being challenged in the courts, and the plans in effect are often a reflection of the political architecture that shapes legislative decisionmaking. It should come as no surprise, therefore, that mandates passed down by the judicial branch often end in political deadlock after they are taken up by the legislature.[88]

In all fairness to the political bodies on which the responsibility falls to find a solution, school finance is a complex enigma in which equity claims can be entertained from a variety of perspectives. As the empirical research suggests, school funds can be redistributed in one of two ways. First, the legislature may level up by spending more money and funneling it into poorer districts. While this approach is the less aggressive of the two from the viewpoint of wealthier districts, it is limited by the capacity of the legislature to raise additional revenues through taxation and other means. It rarely results in parity. The second, a Robin Hood approach, would decrease spending in richer districts to redirect funds into poorer communities. It is obvious why this method, which penalizes powerful suburban districts, is politically unpopular. Its opponents have legitimate concerns that cannot be passed over lightly in a discussion about equality. Why should wealthy citizens who desire to invest their own money in the education of their children in public schools not be allowed to do so without constraints imposed from higher levels of government? At what point does redistributive politics carried out in the name of equity begin to bunk up against the liberty and property rights of those who are required to make a greater personal sacrifice?

The choice between the two approaches is a classic illustration of Tocqueville's dilemma. Both, in actuality, represent a form of redistributive policy. It is just that the latter is painfully obvious and more reaching than the former. Liberty claims come into play as we move our social agenda from a definition of equality based on opportunity to one that is geared towards results. While the latter is politically unpopular, Americans exhibit an extraordinary tolerance for such presumptions. As Tocqueville told us, we are instinctively egalitarian to the point of being eccentric. We are especially so inclined when it comes to education, because, as *Brown* reminds us, we really do believe that education is an essential good that all people must be able to enjoy. Even many of those egalitarians who are not results oriented perceive a decent education as being so fundamental to any view of opportunity that all manifestations of generosity are worthy of consideration, if not actualization. But what is a decent education?

By the late 1980s, following decisions handed down by courts in Montana, Kentucky, and Texas, legal scholars began to detect a "third wave" of litigation that went beyond the more vague equal-protection claims formerly argued in federal and state courts; it focused more specifically on the concept of adequacy.[89] If it were not politically feasible to ensure that every child benefits from the same level of spending as the children of the wealthy, then perhaps it might be possible to guarantee that every child at least has a chance to acquire an adequate education.[90] Is this not too much to ask from a society that has at times championed education as a fundamental right to which all are entitled? Judges and scholars have made noble attempts to define what constitutes an adequate education, but they have had only moderate success. The first major decision of this kind was handed down by a Kentucky court in 1987. It not only invalidated the school finance formula for the state, it found that the entire educational system was inadequate and therefore unconstitutional.[91] In an attempt to define what in fact constitutes an adequate education, the court determined that schools must focus on student development and show progress in seven basic capacities, ranging across such diverse areas as student achievement scores, high school graduation rates, per-pupil spending, and teacher salaries. More recently, in 1997, North Carolina's highest court drew a distinction between equal funding and a sound basic education that is of high quality, chiding:

> An education that does not serve the purpose of preparing students to participate and compete in the society in which they live and work is devoid of substance and is constitutionally inadequate.[92]

Chief Justice Burley Mitchell went on to explain what particular objectives he and his colleagues had in mind for children in their pursuit of quality. It included such goals as the ability to read, write, and speak in English; knowledge of fundamental mathematics and physical science to function in a complex and rapidly changing society; knowledge of geography, history, economics, and political science to make informed choices on issues; and academic or vocational skills to successfully engage in higher education or to work in contemporary society. All were reasonable objectives that coincide with the expectations parents usually recite when asked about the kind of education they want for their children. The opinion was unusual, however, not only because of the level of judicial intervention that it implicated into education decisionmaking, but because it was constructed around outcomes. The court's mandate was focused on what people expect their children to get from education, rather than inputs or resources that educators and their lawyers so regularly emphasize. But the North Carolina opinion still left the question open regarding how these outcomes would be achieved or measured.

With all the gesturing about adequacy, most equity litigation, even at the crest of the "third wave," resorts to a conversation about money. Fairness inevitably is defined as more spending. New Jersey is a case in point. In 1997 the highest court of that state struck down its school finance scheme for the fourth time in twenty-eight years.[93] Throughout the long saga of this legal contest, New Jersey has experienced a chronic problem of poor performance in its urban districts, several of which have been put into state receivership because of inept management. In the twenty-eight "special needs" districts of the state, where 82 percent of the students are black or Hispanic, only 41.8 percent of these students are able to pass a basic proficiency test.[94] In the 1997 ruling, the court declared that Governor Whitman's plan to upgrade curriculum standards was inadequate without the infusion of more resources into failing districts. Specifically, the court ordered the state to provide dollar for dollar parity between each of the 28 poorest districts and the 120 wealthiest in the state. Since 1990 an allocation of $850 million in extra state funding for poor districts had brought their spending up to 90 percent of the total per capita level of the richest suburbs and above that of middle-income suburbs ($7,300 versus $7,144). Per capita spending in Newark and Jersey City ($8,181), two of the school districts that had been taken over by the state, actually exceeded the average of the wealthiest districts.[95]

In the spring of 1998 the court ordered the state education department to implement a plan that was designed to ensure that additional funds allocated in the special needs districts were applied efficiently and effectively. The plan required the institution of a whole-school reform model for schools in the targeted districts, supplemental activities that included kindergarten and preschool programs, and facilities improvements. This action by the court raised hopes among reform advocates that additional funding for the disadvantaged districts would be translated into higher achievement for students.[96]

Reasonable people might assume that investing greater amounts of resources on behalf of a particular social objective is more likely to result in success than investing less. There is a significant body of educational research indicating that the sensible application of education dollars has a positive effect on student performance.[97] However, there is an equally compelling economics literature indicating that education dollars are not generally used in ways that lead to an improvement in student achievement.[98] This second pattern of spending is often reflected in districts where court-ordered financial reforms have actually resulted in increased appropriations for disadvantaged districts.[99]

Districts that serve poor populations are not any more responsible in spending their money well than are richer districts. In fact, the opposite is often true. Large urban districts are notorious for wasting resources on overhead and administrative functions, while classrooms are denied basic materials such as textbooks, and school buildings rot in disrepair. It does not benefit students very much to funnel more dollars into places like Newark or Jersey City, where management has been so corrupt or incompetent that the state has taken over the running of the schools. The problems inherent in these districts go beyond dollars. Very often school finance attorneys lose sight of who the real victims are when large city districts post failing test scores year after year. Settlements that award these districts more money resemble a reckless driving case where the court offers compensation for the driver to purchase a bigger car, rather than address the losses of the injured party. But these lawyers, many of them well meaning, represent school systems, not school children, and the consequences of their efforts cannot be fully appreciated until they are considered in the context of other alternatives.

Since 1950 per-pupil costs for public education at the elementary and secondary level in the United States have quadrupled, even after adjusting for inflation.[100] A number of factors explain this enormous leap. They include the enactment of compensatory education programs for economically disadvantaged children, the growth of spending for services to children with disabilities, the implementation of school desegregation initiatives, and the leveling up of state expenditures in response to school finance litigation. This dramatic increase in costs has not been accompanied by any notable improvement in pupil performance. When all is said and done, the preponderance of the research evidence continues to support the findings that Coleman uncovered more than thirty years ago: there is no consistent relationship between education spending and student achievement.[101]

While money could matter, if applied appropriately, it is difficult to make a convincing case that investing more funds in failing systems would have a positive effect on student performance, especially in bureaucratic urban districts, where a disproportionate number of poor children are found. Given the dynamics of legislative politics, it is not feasible to expect a major redistribution of funds in the states where disparities between urban and suburban districts are greatest.

Equality as Political Power

Another aspect of Lyndon Johnson's Great Society program that reached deeply into the core of city life spoke more directly to politics than to money, although the two were intricately connected. The Voting Rights Act of 1965, originally designed to remove legal obstacles from the electoral process in the South, had been largely irrelevant in the North. The constraints on black participation in the city were more subtle, a function of political organization rather than law. The old Democratic party machines that controlled the entry points of local politics were bastions of white ethnic influence, not particularly receptive to newcomers who might compete for the spoils of their labors.

Most identified with the antipoverty program, the theme "maximum feasible participation" was bound to completely reshape the contours of urban politics and, in the process, the discussion about schools. The idea was born on the Lower East Side of New York in 1963, with the creation of a social experiment called the "Mobilization for Youth" (MFY). Carrying the endorsement of the Kennedy administration in Washington and financial support from the Ford Foundation and a host of other private organizations, the experiment was designed to overcome the alienation of inner-city youths by encouraging them to become active participants in the life of their communities. Based on the opportunity theory formulated by sociologists Richard Cloward and Lloyd Ohlin, MFY involved young people in a variety of social and political activities, including voter registration drives, rent strikes, school boycotts, and a number of militant demonstrations against city agencies.[102] MFY was the precursor of the Economic Opportunity Act, which was signed into law in 1964, and it defined a political dimension of the law that went beyond the mere allocation of federal funds to fight poverty. As Daniel Patrick Moynihan explained it:

> Community action in both its conservative and radical formations was a product of New York. The war on poverty was a product of Washington. The one deeply concerned with society, the other preoccupied with government; the one emotionally no less than ideologically committed to social change, the other profoundly attached to the artifacts of stability and continuity; the one fascinated by racial, ethnic and religious diversity, the other still fiercely loyal to the Republic and still trying to fashion a nation out of a continent. It was a contrast between ideas and information, between brilliance and endurance, between innovation and preservation.[103]

The architects of the Community Action Program (CAP), devised under the Economic Opportunity Act of 1964, were determined to create a new political culture in cities by making the poor and racial minorities serious players in the governmental process. Their strategy was to bypass the traditional governmental institutions elected citywide and to funnel money directly into communities where new units of power, elected by community residents, determined how resources are to be dispersed. As two close observers of the program commented, the "hallmark of the Great Society" was "the direct relationship between the national government and the ghettos, a relationship in which both the state and local governments were undercut."[104] A product of Democratic party politics in Washington, the overall approach of CAP was a direct assault on the traditional Democratic party base in northern cities, much as desegregation and voting rights had been in the South.

Local chief executives finally grouped their forces in reaction to these developments at a meeting of the U.S. Conference of Mayors in 1965. There, Mayors John Shelly of San Francisco and Sam Yorty of Los Angeles sponsored a resolution accusing Sargeant Shriver, director of the U.S. Office of Equal Opportunity (OEO), of fostering class warfare in urban areas. The conference then formed a committee under the chairmanship of Chicago Mayor Richard Daley with the resolve to urge OEO to recognize only city hall-endorsed agencies as the proper channel for community action funds. The mayors eventually took their arguments to Congress, which responded in 1967 by amending the law. The new version of the Economic Opportunity Act gave local governments sole authority to set up community action agencies. Similar terms were set for the Model Cities Program that was enacted the prior year.[105] But these legislative attempts to correct the disjuncture between Democratic party politics and the social agenda of an emerging black leadership did not serve to quell the growing racial animosity that had already been sown in urban areas.

Aside from the distributive advantages that result from participatory politics, democratic political theorists of the period had become enamored with the inherent benefits of civic involvement.[106] It was a legitimate consideration in the context of a national dialogue on political and social equality, especially for a community that had been left on the fringe of public life. Participation was perceived as an end in itself, which was fine. The idea, however, became romanticized, almost to the point of naïveté. *Brown* had defined education as "the very Foundation of good citizenship," a qualifier for meaningful participation in public life. CAP and other programs sought to jump start participatory politics before the opportunity for an equal education was realized. The impulse to do so was commendable and impatience with the pace of progress was understandable, but the outcome was predictable.

Generations of political scientists had demonstrated the inseparable connection between political efficacy and such social variables as education and class.[107] The experience with community action programs followed suit. In most cases, fewer than 5 percent of those eligible bothered even to vote. The experience also showed that black political activists were no less inclined toward corruption than white activists; and the low participation rates of those populations that were supposed to benefit from the new money gushing into local communities created opportunities for corruption that would have delighted any political boss of an earlier era.

It was inevitable that education would become a battleground for the new politics. By the mid-1960s, more militant leaders in the black community had soured on the missteps of racial integration and had decided that their energies would be better spent by trying to gain political control of their own neighborhood schools. This tactical change fit well within the program of an emerging black power movement that was already gaining momentum in cities across the country.[108] Now it was a matter of racial pride. As Supreme Court Justice Clarence Thomas would object three decades later, there was no reason to believe that black schools had to be inferior schools. If only people could gain control of their own educational destiny, there was hope in the community. But urban school systems were still run by large government bureaucracies that historically had been unaccountable to the clients they were supposed to serve. Structural decentralization became the focus of local plans to actualize community control.[109]

The governance of urban schools represented a particular challenge for proponents of participatory democracy. While municipal institutions had been created on the premise of representative government, urban school systems deliberately had been designed to remove education from the political process.[110] Organizationally, they were closed systems. In fact, school boards were set up as an antidote to local politics, which the progressive architects of reform rightly perceived as corrupt and unworthy. Although the school board allowed for some semblance of democratic control, it originally was conceived as a sacred trust to protect the upper class's vision of the public good, rather than as a representative body that would provide channels of access to school clientele.

The durability of this system through the twentieth century resulted in a hierarchical managerial structure controlled by a professional class of educators who were remote from and inaccessible to the families whose children populated the classrooms.[111] By the mid-1960s, it was apparent to leaders in black communities that these rulers and the huge bureaucracy they commanded were out of touch with the educational needs of their clients. The old factory model schools that had processed millions of European immigrants through the gateway of industrialized cities was incapable of preparing the most recent arrivals from the rural South and Latin America for life in the postindustrial economy of urban America.

In no place was the clash between the Progressive model of governance and the rising black demand for power heard so loudly as in New York. It was here, the home of the largest, most incorrigible education bureaucracy in America, where the ideology of participation had been born.[112] By the time the Great Society had been launched in Washington, New York had experienced a decade of failure in its attempt to better integrate its public schools. Study after study had demonstrated that blacks were attending separate and inferior schools.[113] Changing demographics not only made integration unachievable, it accentuated the fact that a predominantly black and Hispanic school system was being run by a white-controlled bureaucracy more preoccupied with its own preservation than with the welfare of students.

New York was especially ripe for a new struggle over who would run education. Unlike many other cities whose leadership was wed to the old ethnic politics of the past, New York's young Republican mayor, John Lindsay, an outsider himself, had cast his lot with the new politics of community control.[114] This, the last of the "Great School Wars" of New York City, would prove to be one of the most racially divisive episodes in modern times, with the white, predominantly Jewish, teachers union pitted against black militants.[115] The outcome of the battle was the most radical school decentralization plan in the country. With the exception of Detroit, which also instituted political decentralization,[116] most urban school districts had responded to the community revolution of the 1960s with administrative decentralization, devolving decisionmaking down to lower levels of management within the school bureaucracy. New York took matters a step further in 1969 with political decentralization, granting citizens and parents the power to elect community boards with authority to make decisions about schools within newly drawn districts. Even in New York, however, community power was circumscribed by the bureaucracy, and in the end the plan was a failure.

If the power of the central school bureaucracy was compromised in

New York by decentralization, this did not happen because authority was ceded directly to parents whose children attended the schools. Authority was shared with a new middle layer of decisionmakers that stood between the schools and the central board of education. Yes, the middle layer would be elected, but by whom? Presented to the community as an opportunity to become active in local school decisions, it soon turned out to be political quicksand for anyone who was trying to get the system to respond to the needs of their child. In a private or parochial school, parent participation is a transaction that takes place between mothers or fathers and those teachers or administrators who deal with the child on a daily basis. Politicians do not have a role. School decentralization kept the opportunity costs of participation high for poor parents who were not accustomed to politics and who did not possess social requisites to be successful political players. Once again the jump start to power politics skipped right past the opportunity for a decent education and rendered the goal more improbable than ever before.

Community school board elections in New York are controlled by local interest groups, and many districts have become havens of corruption and political patronage.[117] Turnout in these contests has been alarmingly low since their inception, recorded at 5.2 percent of those eligible to vote in 1996. In that same year, the state legislature amended the decentralization law to provide the chancellor of schools with veto power over the selection of community superintendents, marking a conspicuous turn toward a recentralization of power without any attempt to create opportunities for meaningful parental involvement. In the meantime, the elected school boards were left in place to preside over a system that has been associated with dramatic increases in spending and a continuing spiral downwards in student achievement.[118]

In 1988 reformers in the city of Chicago pushed the community power envelope a major step further when they persuaded the Illinois legislature to enact a new education governance law that created local councils for each and every school in the city.[119] Chicago had a long history of community activism that even predated the radical politics promulgated by its famous son, Saul Alinsky.[120] By the late 1980s, most local observers had agreed with a highly publicized statement made by former education secretary William Bennett that the city had the "worst school system in America."[121] Student test scores in reading and math were hovering near the thirtieth percentile. The high school dropout rate was 43 percent systemwide, and it exceeded 50 percent for black and Hispanic students.

A political consensus had developed placing a large share of the blame for the system's low academic performance on the central school bureaucracy and school-level professionals.

Unlike New York, which achieved decentralization by creating a middle level of bureaucracy, the agreement negotiated by lawmakers and activists in Chicago resulted in a radical transfer of decisionmaking to the school level. There, authority was placed in the hands of local boards, each chaired by a parent and composed of six elected parents, two elected community members, two teachers, the principal, and a student. These councils have formal power over the hiring, evaluation, and firing of the principal; approve the budget; and participate in the development and monitoring of a school improvement plan. The Chicago reform attracted national attention for going further than any innovation in the history of urban education to integrate the goals of structural decentralization, site-based management, and parental control. The results of the ambitious experiment, however, have proven to be uneven and disappointing—at least in its original form.

The Consortium of Chicago School Research has been organized at the University of Chicago to evaluate "democratic localism" as a viable lever for revitalizing public schools.[122] It found that only one-third of the low-performing elementary schools developed strong participatory cultures among parents, community leaders, teachers, and principals, who joined together to institute a systemic approach to school improvement. Other schools were characterized by unfocused change, adversarial politics, or concerted efforts at maintaining the status quo. While the school governance law had required a range of central initiatives to complement local empowerment, the evaluators found that the bureaucracy was slow to cooperate and acted in an obstructive manner. Such bureaucratic resistance is commonly documented in studies of school-based management, especially in cases where the authority of central administrators is seriously compromised.[123]

Most disappointing of all, there is no discernible improvement in student performance that can be attributed to the structural changes that initially were carried out. In 1995 the Illinois legislature, at the urging of Mayor Daley, passed a second School Reform Act. The law, enacted seven years after the original decentralization legislation, still described the Chicago schools as a "school system in crisis."[124] It granted the mayor vast managerial powers over the school system, enabling him to appoint all members of a newly constituted school board designed to impose increased fiscal and educational accountability on the local councils. In 1996 a newly appointed chief executive officer (also chosen by the mayor) announced that 109 of the 557 schools in the city of Chicago were being placed on probation because of their poor academic standing; another twenty-five were identified as candidates for less aggressive forms of remediation and oversight.

In less than three years, the school system has begun to show signs of a turnaround. Social promotion has been ended, remediation programs implemented, incompetent principals removed. Reading and math scores on standardized tests have been on the rise in every grade, dropout and truancy rates are declining, and school enrollments are up. Chicago has also begun to experiment with privatization and choice. Alternative education programs, as well as certain special education and vocational education programs, have been contracted out to private institutions. As of the beginning of 1999, the city also has fourteen charter schools.[125]

While at first blush the events that have unfolded in Chicago may have been discouraging to reformers, the city's second phase of restructuring may point the way to a new approach to big city governance. Combining devolution of power with accountability to a central authority, the architects of Chicago's new plan may have found a new way to carve out a meaningful role for school-based decisionmakers, while at the same time enforcing high academic standards and fiscal controls. If choice, in the form of charter schools and private school options, is expanded, the power of parents will be further augmented, enabling them to vote with their feet when dissatisfied with the quality of services at their schools, thereby imposing a new form of accountability from below.

Still, Separate and Unequal

At the time the Supreme Court handed down its landmark decision in 1954, school segregation was required by law in seventeen states and the District of Columbia. Four other states permitted legal segregation as a local option. All told, eight million white and two and a half million black pupils were being educated under a dual system. The *Brown* order would effectively eliminate de jure segregation in the South, a vast achievement. By 1995, 78 percent of the urban school districts in the country had undertaken either a court-mandated or voluntary program of racial balancing.[126] Nevertheless, most children who attend public school in the United States today do so in a segregated setting.

In his authoritative study of school desegregation, David Armor found that while black-white imbalance improved substantially between 1968 and 1989, there was only a slight improvement in the degree to which minority and white students were exposed to each other in a school setting.[127] This means that although the racial profiles of individual schools now more closely resemble the composition of their respective districts, the opportunity for minority and white students to attend school together has actually improved minimally. Using a "dissimilarity index" that compares school profiles with community profiles, Armor found that the index for blacks improved from 67 percent in 1968, to 51 percent in 1972, to 43 percent in 1980, where it has remained constant. Among Hispanics, the index went from 53 percent in 1968, to 42 percent in 1972, to 40 percent in 1980, where it has remained. "Exposure rates," which measure the percentage of whites in the average minority school, tell a more revealing story. For blacks, these scores fluctuated from 43 percent in 1968, to 54 percent in 1972, to 47 percent in 1989. For Hispanics, it changed from 70 percent in 1978 to 51 percent in 1989.

Using different data sets, Gary Orfield and his colleagues present an even more negative picture of racial balance in American public schools.[128] They found that while the percentage of black students attending predominantly minority schools decreased from 76.6 percent in 1968–69 to 62.9 percent in 1980-81 (a low point), by 1994–95 it had risen again to 67.1 percent. They were especially troubled by what they found to be the steadily increasing isolation of Hispanic students in predominantly minority schools: rising from 54.8 percent in 1968–69, to 68.1 percent in 1980-81, to 74.0 percent in 1994–95. Orfield attributes a perceived resegregation of the races in education to judicial actions that have dismantled and reversed the policies of the post-*Brown* era and urges the federal courts to again focus their sights on racial balance.[129] School profiles, however, largely reflect residential patterns. Therefore, an aggressive assault on de facto racial segregation would have to be advanced at the expense of the neighborhood school.

To date, there is no definitive evidence that sitting next to children of another race serves to improve the academic performance of minority children,[130] nor that it has a positive effect on one's self-esteem. In fact, some studies indicate that blacks attending predominantly black schools enjoy higher self-esteem than their peers in integrated schools.[131] And, as stated before, most black parents prefer to have their children attend neighborhood schools rather than transporting them elsewhere to achieve racial balance.

As things stand now, blacks living in big cities are less likely to attend racially integrated schools than those in rural areas or small towns.[132] On average, students from small towns find themselves in schools where the enrollment is about 50 percent white, whereas the typical big city school is only 17 percent white. Although there is no compelling evidence that racial integration on its own promotes student achievement, the prevailing evidence does suggest that blacks attend inferior schools. This is indicated both by the amount of resources available and by pupil performance.

A study conducted for Congress by the General Accounting Office in 1998 showed that while progress has been made in achieving spending parity between the rich and the poor, gaps continue to exist.[133] A combined effect of compensatory allocations by the federal government and leveling up spending by the states has managed to eliminate significant inequities in sixteen of thirty-seven states where they existed prior to 1991–92. These gains fell short of helping most of the nation's impoverished students, two-thirds of whom live in the twenty-one states where there remains on average a 5 percent funding difference between affluent and poor districts. These differences are not as monumental as one might have expected to find, given the gross disparities that exist in student performance. They suggest, as much of the prior research has argued, that something else is at play in determining the quality of schooling other than money. The great tragedy in American education continues to be the learning gap defined by race.

No matter what their sentiments are regarding racial integration, busing, spending, or the reallocation of tax revenues, most parents would agree that the crucial question in determining the level of educational opportunity afforded to any one group is whether its children are adequately learning. On this count, when it comes to certain populations, our public schools have failed miserably. Although there were some signs—according to both the NAEP and SAT scores—that the gulf between whites and racial minorities was beginning to close during the 1980s, by the end of that decade it became clear that the skill deficit of blacks and Hispanics is static.[134] While it is commonplace for educators to explain away the tragic gap in performance as a function of class, increasing evidence shows race to be independently related to academic achievement. Stephan and Abigail Thernstrom are among the most optimistic observers of America's racial dilemma, and their monumental study on the subject has sparked a firestorm of debate. When commenting on education, their optimism is tempered by the cruel facts of reality:

> Today's typical black twelfth grader scores no better on a reading test than the average white in the eighth grade, and is 5.4 years behind the typical white in science. Blacks in families earning over $70,000 a year have lower average SAT scores than whites from families taking in less than $10,000; blacks with a parent who graduated from college on average score lower than whites whose parents never finished high school.[135]

Test scores for Hispanic students—who now make up 13.5 percent of the school-age population, and who are poised to become the largest ethnic minority in America—are even more discouraging. A report released by the U.S. Department of Education in 1998 shows that the high school dropout rate for Hispanics is three and a half times that of non-Hispanic whites and twice that of blacks. These findings cut across income levels.[136] I do not mean to suggest here that the disadvantages of poverty are insignificant in determining the peculiar education needs of poor populations. The data tell us, however, that the problem of educational failure manifests itself along two patterns that are terribly interwoven—one having to do with class, the other with race. The failure of public schooling in America can be precisely defined as an inability to sever the connection between these two demographic variables and academic achievement. Given the fact that such a disproportionate number of black and Hispanic families live in urban settings, this fundamental dilemma in American education is most dramatically apparent in our cities.

If we were to believe the "schools don't matter" claim incarnated by Coleman and others in the mid-1960s, this would be the end of our discussion. We might just reconcile ourselves to the effects of economic or racial determinism and accept the inevitable failure of education institutions in certain social settings. But Coleman's first study, mammoth as it was, limited itself to public schools. His subsequent work would push the boundaries of education research into a broader comparative perspective. It would show that schools that typically serve destitute populations figure prominently in explaining the problem of academic failure. Public schools, especially urban schools, have not only neglected to address the effects of race and poverty, their structure and culture have actually aggravated the condition.

CHAPTER THREE

The Salience of Choice

Economist Milton Friedman first put forward his provocative proposal for a full-fledged system of school vouchers exactly a year after the *Brown* decision was handed down. Friedman's plan would minimize the role of government in education and replace public schools with privately run institutions supported by taxes.[1] A disciple of Adam Smith, Friedman was a firm believer in the power of the market to meet human needs on the basis of voluntary association without interference from public authority. Having earned his professional reputation in economics for his work on monetary theory, the Nobel laureate was convinced that unencumbered competition motivates private entrepreneurs toward high levels of performance and the efficient delivery of goods and services at a reasonable cost.

The distinguished economist was troubled by the dominance of a government-run bureaucracy in education that he believed perpetuated mediocrity and placed private schools at a competitive disadvantage for resources. So long as government-run institutions had an exclusive claim on public dollars, there were relatively few families that could realistically afford to consider private alternatives, and there was little incentive for public schools to improve. Friedman envisioned a more diversified educational marketplace. Some schools would be run by private entrepreneurs for a profit, others would be operated by nonprofit organizations to carry out more specialized educational missions. He offered the possibility that such voluntary organizations as the Boy Scouts or the YMCA might eventually start their own schools. The government would set minimum standards of operation for providers, as it does for the food industry, for example, but would not be directly responsible for running any schools. In the end, the viability of an institution would be determined by its ability to attract customers who would exchange their government-appropriated vouchers for the educational services the school provided.

Several decades ahead of his time, Friedman anticipated not only the voucher debate, but also the rise of private entrepreneurs as education providers, as well as the spread of charter schools—all of which would change the face of American education at the close of the century.[2] Although Friedman expected his idea to provoke controversy, he could never have appreciated the cultural clash that was sparked when he confronted the education profession with the concept of a free market. Most educators were outraged by the notion of school profits. They were uneasy with his language of competition and the drastic consequences it brought to failing schools. But Friedman's provocative proposal was more than a Darwinian formula for survival and extinction. A political as well as an economic tract, it was infused with the philosophy of classical liberalism, and scattered with references to Jefferson, Tocqueville, and John Stuart Mill.

Friedman understood the distinctions between competing definitions of equality.[3] He carefully delineated between equality of opportunity, which he favored, and equality of results, which made him uncomfortable. Like Tocqueville, he warned that if government were to get aggressively involved in guaranteeing the same quality of life for all people, its intervention would inevitably compromise individual freedom. But as one reads further in Friedman's work, the issue grows more complex. The unique status of education in the equality debate becomes increasingly apparent.

The same writer who counseled egalitarians to shy away from considerations of societal outcomes expressed deep concerns that the government monopoly in education effectively denies choice only to those who cannot afford a private education; that the saddest victims of the existing arrangement are inner-city minorities who do not have access to the economically advantaged schools in the suburbs; and that the exclusion of parochial schools from public support especially compromises the religious freedom of poor people who desire to be educated according to the precepts of their faith.[4] The same writer who asserted a minimalist state role in education was unequivocal in his position that government had an obligation to provide decent schooling to all at public expense. Friedman understood, as the authors of *Brown* did, that without fostering equality in educational outcomes, there could be no real equality of opportunity in a larger social context. Education is the irreplaceable link that ties the two together, an essential ingredient for both liberty and equality in a democratic society.

More than a decade would pass before the voucher debate would begin to churn within the mainstream of the education community. The parade of advocates who would step forward over time was wide and varied, each attracted by a nuanced approach to the policy options. In 1968 Theodore Sizer, the dean of the Harvard Graduate School of Education, long identified with liberal causes, put forward a voucher plan that was specifically targeted at economically disadvantaged families. Sizer incorporated his plan in a larger proposal to promulgate a "poor children's bill of rights."[5] He also cautioned that offering vouchers to all children would unfairly favor the middle class and severely damage the public schools.

In 1970 sociologist Christopher Jencks presented a more detailed proposal prepared under contract with the federal Office of Economic Opportunity (OEO), the same administrative entity that had given birth to the antipoverty program of the mid-1960s.[6] Jencks, who had been a respondent to the first Coleman report, was becoming persuaded that public schools were incapable of addressing the needs of America's most deprived children.[7] He perceived vouchers as a redistributive policy mechanism for educating the poor. Unlike Friedman, Jencks endorsed a highly regulated program. His proposal required that participating schools accept all applicants for whom space was available or fill seats on the basis of a lottery, and that schools accept the voucher in full payment of tuition. It also made additional compensatory funding available to low-income children. Jencks circulated his ideas in the *New Republic*, the left-of-center magazine which he served as a contributing editor.[8]

To build public support for Jencks's proposal, the OEO made funding available to operate experimental programs in six cities around the nation. Although all of the cities initially accepted the offer, only one—Alum Rock, California—went through with the study.[9] Even there, the experiment was limited to public schools and proved inconclusive.[10] The other districts withdrew in response to vehement opposition from local education groups. In the meantime, a national coalition, composed of the American Federation of Teachers, the National Education Association, the National Association of Elementary School Principals, and the American Association of School Administrators, began to lobby Congress to defeat the plan. They argued that, with the endorsement of school vouchers, the "original purpose of the OEO—assistance to the poor—has been redirected into an ill-conceived attempt to privatize our social services."[11]

In 1971 another detailed plan appeared under the authorship of legal scholars John Coons and Stephen Sugarman.[12] The two U.C. Berkeley professors were no newcomers to the equality debate. It had been their provocative study of education funding that set off the explosion of school finance reform in California and the nation just a year earlier.[13] It was they who had brought national attention to the fact that an enormous funding gap existed between rich and poor school districts. Now they were taking the point a step further. Rather than merely advocating the reallocation of dollars to property-poor districts, they were now pushing the more radical idea of appropriating funds directly to parents. This would allow underserved populations to decide for themselves what schools were most likely to accommodate the educational needs of their children. The proposal was a poignant juxtaposition of the equity issue and choice, not sufficiently appreciated by researchers or policy advocates at the time, but now gaining more attention among legal scholars.[14]

Although Coons and Sugarman did not share Friedman's faith in the market, their plan did reflect a strong libertarian leaning. Beyond the promotion of educational equality, Coons and Sugarman saw choice as a vehicle through which families could select schools that reflected their own educational values. They conceived parental empowerment in both political and economic terms. They sought to equip poor parents with a range of choices resembling those enjoyed by the middle class, not just to foster competition but to actualize independence and freedom. Like Jencks and Sizer, Coons and Sugarman shared a notion of equity demanding that every child have access to a decent education. But in so much as Coons and Sugarman's plan was also a plea for educational freedom, they were offended by the prospect that a public bureaucracy could wield such unchallenged control in determining whose values might be reflected in the instructional process.

In its wide variety of forms, school choice was beginning to appeal to a diverse, yet small constituency. Free market economists liked choice for promoting competition in a system of education that was monopolistic in character. Liberals liked it because it provided an escape hatch for impoverished children who had been trapped in failing public schools. Cultural and religious minorities, who felt that their values were being undermined by the public school curriculum, saw choice as a way of gaining more control over the education of their children. But it failed to catch on with the wider public. Ballot initiatives for vouchers were handily defeated in Michigan in 1978 and Washington, D.C., in 1981.

As the national political pendulum swung to the right, vouchers increasingly became identified with conservative politics and the Christian coalition. President Ronald Reagan, who enjoyed strong support from the religious right, submitted voucher bills to Congress on three separate occasions—in 1983, 1985, and 1986. While garnished in the stirring rhetoric of privatization, these plans were actually quite timid. The final version gave local districts discretion to determine whether they would participate and whether they would permit the voucher to be used for paying tuition at a private institution. Furthermore, under the Reagan plan, eligibility for a voucher would be limited to children who had demonstrated a need for remediation that was not adequately being addressed at their own public schools.[15]

In 1986 the National Governors Conference issued a statement endorsing the concept of public school choice as a way to "unlock the values of competition in the marketplace."[16] By 1988 President Reagan began to make a strategic retreat on the issue, de-emphasizing talk about vouchers and tax credits, and emphasizing a growing reliance on public school choice as a mechanism for fostering competition.[17]

Public School Choice

Opponents of school choice often identify its genesis with the freedom of choice academies in the South that were created to undermine desegregation. In actuality, the subsequent experience with choice as a tool to achieve desegregation is a more appropriate starting place for informing the ongoing debate. The process started in 1976, after federal district courts in Milwaukee and Buffalo approved comprehensive voluntary plans designed around the magnet school principle. Between 1976 and 1981, the federal government provided $30 million a year for magnet programs; then between 1985 and 1991, it spent an additional $739 million. By 1991 more than 1.2 million school children were enrolled in 2,433 magnet schools in 230 districts. Another hundred and twenty thousand were on waiting lists. More than half the magnet districts and 80 percent of the programs were located in urban areas where enrollment exceeded ten thousand.[18]

The theory behind the magnet concept was that the provision of enriched academic programs would motivate a racially mixed group of students to attend schools outside their neighborhoods and achieve integration. The preponderance of the evaluation research available suggests that these programs had some success in improving racial balance, racial exposure, and student achievement.[19] Critics have found, however, that a disproportionate number of the students who reap the benefits of these initiatives are either white or among the more advantaged minorities.[20] In fact, some would argue that the availability of magnet schools has a negative effect on nearby schools when the best students are skimmed off.[21] This stratification effect is plausible, given that such programs are open to all comers regardless of class. There is no evidence, however, that the sorting process that may take place under magnet programs is any more stratified than that which occurs under normal circumstances when parents select schools for their children.[22]

At times, minority students are denied access to exemplary programs in their own communities so that white students can be brought in to achieve racial balance. In Louisville, black parents recently initiated litigation in federal court to challenge an admissions policy in a local magnet school that denied access to more than eight hundred black applicants to accommodate white suburban students who were in attendance.[23] In Prince Georges County, Maryland, the school board voted to eliminate social controls on magnets in 1996 under pressure from black parents whose children were denied seats reserved for whites for the purpose of integration.

Controlled Choice

Even though voluntary choice programs proved to be more successful than mandatory reassignments or busing,[24] some desegregation proponents were concerned that the level of discretion left to parents did not allow integration to progress as rapidly as it should. Controlled choice was developed as a backup strategy, a halfway approach between real choice and forced assignments. If certain standards of racial balance were not met, students could be told what schools to attend regardless of their wishes. In 1981 Cambridge, Massachusetts, became the first school district to try this approach when it adopted a school assignment policy for "maximizing competition and choice among desegregated schools."[25] To provide students with the most extensive range of options, the district eliminated all assignment zones so that families could rank their selections on a citywide basis, but mandatory assignments remained a possibility in instances where schools were deemed to be out of balance.

The Cambridge plan became a model for sixteen other Massachusetts districts, including Boston. Similar programs soon developed in White Plains, New York, and Montclair, New Jersey, and later in Seattle and San Jose, among other places. Controlled choice was largely an urban phenomenon, where concerns for racial balance and high quality schooling tended to coincide. As a rule, there are no specialized magnet schools built into controlled choice, or, as proponents put it, every school is a magnet school; but in most large systems, incentives were built in through specialized programs, even though they were not specifically called magnets.

The initial evaluations of controlled choice were generally positive, indicating high levels of integration, academic achievement, and parental satisfaction.[26] Further investigation raised a number of concerns. One involved transportation costs, which skyrocketed as students had to travel to far-reaching corners of their school districts. Another was the extraordinarily high cost of specialized teachers, facilities, and additional resources that were designed to attract a racially mixed group of students. The Richmond, California, school district, for example, went bankrupt in 1991 because of the combined costs of busing and specialized programs for their choice schools.[27]

Another major problem observed in controlled choice programs is what desegregation expert Christine Rossell referred to as "not enough choice, too much control."[28] She explains that the major complaint most parents have with this approach is that administrators, not they, have the final word on where a child attends school. As a result, districts using these plans experience about one-third more white enrollment decline than those with voluntary plans. In fact, further analysis indicates that most parents, both black and white, are not supportive of assignment policies that limit their options. When asked in a second study, most parents (including minorities) admitted that they would prefer to have their children attend a neighborhood school. To be more precise, most parents seek to avoid extensive travel unless there is an extraordinary academic benefit derived in the form of a magnet or specialized program, and even then they want it to be their choice.[29] Some urban school districts—for example, Austin, Cleveland, Denver, Oklahoma City, and Savannah—have actually reverted to some version of geographic zoning geared toward neighborhood schools.[30]

Another consideration to keep in mind regarding controlled choice programs is that they are primarily designed to achieve racial balance and only secondarily focus on improving instruction. There is no reason to believe, or evidence to suggest, that moving students around from one school to another, in and of itself, is going to have a positive effect on how well they learn. This is especially true when no magnet programs exist, which is usually the case. Unless programmatic innovation accompanies choice, it is unlikely to result in improved pupil performance. Rossell found that controlled choice reduces the effect of competition. In the end, less desirable schools get saved by mandatory reassignments that were implemented to accomplish desegregation.[31]

There are several lessons that can be learned from the experience with choice as a desegregation tool. It appears that if most parents had their way, they would prefer to be able to choose from a variety of educational options within the proximity of their own communities. Most parents, black and white, seem to value choice as a route to a better education, rather than for racial balancing. As far as the market is concerned, if choice is to function as an instrument to improve the educational product available to the public, then it must include a mechanism to replace underachieving institutions with new ones that are more responsive to student needs. Protecting failing schools is counterproductive. Finally, there is no reason to assume that controlled choice worked any better than magnet schools or traditional assignment processes to reverse the advantage that better informed parents have in selecting high quality institutions for their children.

Choice as Reform: Harlem's Miracle

By the early 1970s, the public outcry for high quality schooling had begun to drown out demands from both blacks and whites for school integration. Choice was now portrayed as the prod for moving schools toward reform. No such initiative would receive more national attention than the public choice program that operated in District 4, the East Harlem community in New York City.[32] Nor would any program be put under such careful scrutiny by proponents and opponents, for this experiment would serve as the nose under the tent for a concept that had received an ambivalent response even among more innovative professional educators. Nurtured by individuals who eventually became associated with the right-leaning Manhattan Institute for Policy Research, the East Harlem Experiment was unambiguously an effort to improve educational opportunity by extending the range of high quality educational offerings made available to underserved populations. There was no focus on integration here, no conspicuous racial agenda of any kind, except that most of the underserved students involved were black or Hispanic.

District 4 was another great anomaly of the choice crusade, enacted in the cradle of urban liberalism, by an organization with strong ties to the Republican party, on behalf of one of the most destitute inner-city communities in the land. It is a dramatic story. In 1973 only 16 percent of the students from East Harlem were reading at grade level. By 1987 the figure leaped to 63 percent.[33] In a manner of speaking, the experiment came about serendipitously when good educational instincts were allowed to carry the day. In a way, it was fortuitous that so many gifted educators— Anthony Alvarado, Seymour Fliegel, Deborah Meier—would show up in the same place at the same time. Each had a distinct philosophical bent on school reform, brought together by a common determination to create effective schools in an otherwise impoverished community.

It all started with the idea of alternative schools: custom-made institutions that would not be cast in the same mold as traditional public schools.[34] There was no central plan for choice at the district level so much as there was an overall philosophy that allowed professionals to innovate, to create small schools built around particular curricular themes: the performing arts, the environment, the humanities, math and science, health and medicine. As with previous experiments elsewhere, traditional assignment zones were eliminated, but real choice grew out of a diverse menu of high-quality options that was unprecedented in an urban setting. And choice was nurtured by a large measure of autonomy that allowed each school to define its own character unencumbered by a central bureaucracy.[35] Soon District 4 would become a magnet for students from all corners of the city, not to mention teachers and other professionals with an appetite for innovation.

District 4 also attracted the skeptics and the cynics who did not believe the success story that had grown out of Harlem. As the theme of alternative education got translated into an argument for choice and identified with conservative politics, District 4 became more controversial. The discussion grew more partisan. Contrary to the claims of choice advocates in the district, several researchers pointed out that there was no demonstrable evidence of a causal link between choice and academic improvement.[36] Others offered their own explanations: for example, the unusual collection of talented educators, excessive spending, smaller school size.[37] One commentator alleged that there was a "hidden selection process" at play to recruit exceptionally skilled students from other neighborhoods.[38]

In 1998 a group of political scientists from the State University of New York completed an extensive evaluation.[39] They found that since 1974, reading and math scores had improved significantly when compared to the thirty-one other school districts in the city, even after controlling for socioeconomic variables. They identified choice as the key causal factor. They found that parents who had opted for choice schools were no better educated than those who had not, and that the key characteristic attracting minority parents to choice schools is the quality of the schools' academic programs. They also found that the existence of choice schools in the district did not have an adverse effect in the neighboring schools and, instead, may even have contributed to their improvement. The same group found, in a separate study involving District 4, that poor parents are intelligent shoppers. When they are given the opportunity to choose, they tend to select schools that reflect their own personal values.[40] Notwithstanding the generally positive assessment of the program that they studied, the District 4 experience would also serve to highlight the limits of public school choice as a mechanism for reform. Although student performance improved through the mid-1980s, the rise in test scores leveled off and reversed during the 1990s. In 1997 only 42.5 percent of the public school children in the district were reading at or above grade level. This was a huge improvement over 1973 (16 percent), but hardly a satisfactory level of performance after more than twenty years of reform.

Extending Boundaries: Interdistrict Choice

Perhaps the boundaries of the school district are just too confining. Especially in the inner city, where the overall quality of public schools remains wanting, it is difficult to translate choice into opportunity. If the market is to become a factor in promoting excellence for all students and weeding out inferior institutions, the range of choices available to families has to be enlarged. There must be an adequate supply of desirable institutions to accommodate demands.

In 1985 Minnesota became the first jurisdiction in the country to introduce a statewide choice plan that allowed students to move across district lines to attend any school where space is available. Republican Governor Rudy Perpich, a devout supporter of public education, endorsed the idea following a bruising battle in the state over a voucher proposal. Under the plan, per capita state aid follows the student to the district where he or she is enrolled. Minnesota, which boasts a proud tradition of progressive politics, has long been on the cutting edge of school reform.[41] As far back as 1958 its legislature enacted a tuition tax credit for parents whose children attend private and parochial schools. In 1985 the state piloted a plan that allowed at-risk students to exit their own neighborhood districts to obtain remedial instruction in other public and private schools. That same year lawmakers implemented a postsecondary education choice program for qualified high school juniors and seniors to take courses at public and private colleges. Parochial schools were excluded from the remedial program, and sectarian courses were deemed ineligible for the college program. Both programs were strongly opposed by the state teachers union, concerned with the inevitable migration of students and dollars from public school districts where its members were employed.

The Minnesota programs have gotten mixed reviews.[42] Most of the evaluations indicate that both the remedial and postsecondary programs had a positive effect on student achievement. Poor, minority, and inner-city students were well represented in the remedial programs for at-risk populations; middle-class students were overrepresented in the college programs for high performers. Such demographic sorting is predictable to the intelligent observer. One wonders why such common intelligence is not employed in the design of other choice programs that are supposed to improve the educational opportunities of disadvantaged students.

While the remedial and college programs became models for other states, it was the interdistrict option program that attracted the most attention in the education community. By 1991 there were eighty-five hundred students utilizing the open enrollment plan, and there was some evidence that districts that were losing students began to respond with new curricula and program offerings designed to stop the exodus.[43] Since 1987 seventeen states have instituted similar programs; another eleven have implemented open enrollment at a local level.[44] In 1992 the Carnegie Foundation issued a high-profile report that was to give a full account of the nation's overall encounter with the growing phenomenon of school choice.[45] Weighing in very heavily on the negative side of the scale, the widely circulated document found little merit with what had been experienced.

In addition to the usual skimming argument, the Carnegie report noted how interdistrict choice programs funneled money away from economically disadvantaged districts and into wealthier, more desirable districts, severely penalizing those students left behind. It failed to note that while state funds followed students to other locations, home districts were not expected to contribute any support for those of their residents who were being educated elsewhere. In this sense, interdistrict choice made more per capita dollars available for students who remained behind. This kind of funding arrangement helps explain why many school districts are reluctant to accept students from other jurisdictions. At a certain point, the introduction of new students with approximately half the dollars needed to support their education becomes a financial burden.

The Carnegie report cites national data indicating that a large majority of parents in states where school choice exists do not want to send their children to school outside their home district. This is a common assertion in the choice debate, but it has little bearing on the merits of the question. Under open enrollment, people who are content with the schools their children attend are under no obligation to move. The point of school choice is to offer options to those parents who are not satisfied with their schools. Further analysis in the report speaks directly to the issue of why parents hesitate to opt out of their school districts. As Ernest Boyer, the president of the foundation, explained in an essay: most parents prefer neighborhood schools.[46] This, by now, is a familiar message. We heard it in response to busing plans that were implemented to promote racial integration; we read it in the research on controlled choice. One of the vexing problems inherent in statewide choice as a policy strategy is that it presupposes students want to travel long distances to attend school. Most of the evidence tells us that when students are willing to travel long distances for a decent education, it is usually done out of desperation. They don't really want to travel, but this does not mean to say that they and their parents do not want choice. What they may want is localized choice.

Charter Schools

Minnesota responded to the call for education reform again in 1991, when it passed the nation's first charter school law. A year later, California passed a similar law. Colorado, Georgia, Massachusetts, Michigan, New Mexico, and Wisconsin followed in 1993. By the end of 1998, thirty-six states and the District of Columbia had signed on to the charter school concept in one form or another. Charter schools would become the most revolutionary idea in education for the 1990s, a concrete alternative to the factory model of schooling inherited from the nineteenth century.[47] The idea is complex, representing different things to different people: new governance, innovation, competition, choice, opportunity. The underlying premise of the charter school concept was to provide more independence to school-level professionals in exchange for a higher level of accountability. Because charter schools are public schools, their appearance would broaden the political constituency for choice among reform advocates who were philosophically opposed to privitization. Unlike the other forms of choice discussed in this chapter, charter schools deliberately address the supply side of the market equation.

Charter schools can come about in either of two ways. Some are formed when professionals and parents at an existing school are permitted by vote to opt out of the bureaucratic system that governs traditional schools. Others are new schools that are established when educators, nonprofit groups, for-profit entrepreneurs, or parents submit a proposal to a state or local chartering agency. The sponsoring agency may be the state education department, a special board set up by the state to review charter applications, the state university, or a local school board. This charter releases the school from certain legal regulations and establishes a new governing board for the school. Jurisdictions with stronger laws—like those of Arizona, Michigan, Massachusetts, and the District of Columbia—give school-level personnel wide discretion over their budgetary and personnel decisions and release them from all regulations except those that deal with civil rights, health, and safety. This allows school personnel to set such policies as the length of the school day, the ratio of administrators to staff, the amount of funding committed to professional development, dress codes, teaching materials, and the overall theme of the curriculum—all of which are typically determined in the public school system by central administrators who have little to do with the school on a regular basis. Many laws also prescribe a mechanism for meaningful parental involvement in school-level decisionmaking. Once the school is established, it becomes entitled to the funds that would otherwise have been allocated to the school district for its students.

In return for autonomy, the charter stipulates academic, organizational, and financial standards for which the school will be held accountable. If these criteria are not met, the charter may be rescinded. This was the case in 1995 when Edutrain, a school in Los Angeles, had its charter revoked for financial mismanagement. In 1996 Phoenix's Citizen 2000 School was shut down after problems with financial mismanagement and enrollment declines.[48] In 1997 the struggling Marcus Garvey School in Washington, D.C., was allowed to retain its charter only after its board of trustees agreed to replace its principal, but it too was eventually closed.[49] The Chicago Preparatory School was also closed, after local monitors became dismayed with the services being provided to special education students. Charter school critics point to such closings as a flaw in the charter concept; supporters praise these instances as a sign of effectiveness. Few traditional public schools are held to such a high level of accountability. While the Garvey School was forced to close, dozens of troubled public schools in Washington, D.C., were permitted to keep their doors open despite years of academic decline and mismanagement.

According to a report prepared by the Center for Education Reform, a Washington-based advocacy group that supports charters and choice, 30 of the 1,128 (2.6 percent) charter schools that opened prior to November 1998 have been closed. Of these, twenty had their charters revoked by public authorities, mostly because of mismanagement or financial improprieties; six did not have their charters renewed by authorities, due to inadequate enrollments or academic performance; three closed voluntarily because they lacked sufficient community support; and one merged with another institution.[50]

A Matter of Choice

The architects of the charter school concept had learned much from the previous wars over school governance, and, indeed, their vision was a plan to overcome the missteps of the past. In one way the campaign to enact charter legislation in the state legislatures was a result of failed attempts undertaken by innovative educators to capture more autonomy for professionals who work at the school level. These educators wanted to be less encumbered by an overreaching bureaucracy that weighed them down in administrative trivia and preempted sensible decisionmaking. Previous experiments carried out under the rubric of "site-based management" had demonstrated that even those central administrators who gave lip service to local autonomy were quite reluctant to abdicate authority.[51] Devolution of this sort violated the basic instincts of bureaucratic behavior. It could never happen graciously, only through legislative fiat, and even then after much political maneuvering and compromise.

Charter schools could potentially fill the void of meaningful parental involvement that is so elusive in traditionally structured school systems, particularly those located in big cities. But this was a novel approach to parental involvement, at least for public sector schools. Contrary to the decentralization model in New York, which was political and confrontational in nature, the charter school model would be more collegial and cooperative. Reformers were no longer thinking in the antagonistic terms of the 1960s and 1970s. Unlike the participatory model implemented in Chicago, charter schools, while giving parents a significant voice in decisionmaking, are run by professionals. It is almost as if the architects of charter schools had anticipated the problems that grew out of Chicago's first reorganization plan; instead, they coupled local autonomy with centralized accountability as Chicago had done in implementing its revised governance plan. So far as parental power was concerned, the most important premise of the charter school idea was to embolden voice with choice—to provide parents with an exit option from any school with which they were dissatisfied. Empowering parents to carry off public education dollars to another institution was meant to guarantee a level of accountability that did not exist in New York or Chicago, where schools continued to decline.

Localized governance at the school level was deemed essential to advancing real choice. This would allow each school to define its own character. It was hoped that such localism would result in a diverse set of offerings from which parents and children could pick and choose. Charter schools represented a rejection of the cookie cutter, one-size-fits-all approach to education that had become the norm. No student or teacher is assigned to a charter school. All are there on their own accord. Charter legislation has created a path for developing many new institutions that incorporate a rich variety of curricula. By the beginning of 1999, there were nearly twelve hundred charter schools in thirty-five jurisdictions serving nearly two hundred and fifty thousand students.[52] Consider the possibilities.[53]

The Community Involved Charter School in Lakewood, Colorado, has a K–12 college preparatory program that promotes open education, experimental learning, and basic academics. The Renaissance School in Englewood, Colorado, emphasizes personalized multilingual learning. The City on a Hill Charter School in Boston is oriented toward the liberal arts and public service. The Benjamin Franklin School in Franklin, Massachusetts, uses the Core Knowledge Sequence developed by E. D. Hirsch. Aisa Shule/WEB Dubois Preparatory Academy is a basic skills independent learning school in Detroit with an African American focus. Metro Deaf, a school for the hearing impaired in St. Paul, uses American Sign Language to deliver instruction. The New Country School in Le Sueur, Minnesota, offers an individualized, competency-based approach to learning for grades 7 through 12. Beaver Dam Charter School uses individualized instruction and work experience to reach at-risk middle and high school students in Wisconsin.

Charter schools provide a way to channel institutional and community resources into education through organizations that might not ordinarily be directly involved in teaching and learning. In Detroit, the U.S. Drug Enforcement Administration helped found the Woodward School, a residential academy for at-risk adolescents. The Boys and Girls Club of Mesa, Arizona, runs the Boys and Girls Academy, which is focused on the arts. The Ford Motor Company has opened the Henry Ford Academy of Arts and Sciences in Detroit. In Wilmington, Delaware, a medical center has collaborated with four local corporations to launch a High School for Science. In Houston, the Medical Center Charter School serves 130 K–5 pupils, where local residents attend school with the children of employees from the Texas Medical Center. Boston University operates a residential high school that caters to students in foster care. Such partnerships can and do occur with regular public schools, but they are not part of the standard design as they are with charters.

Charter legislation has also provided a way for private entrepreneurs to become involved in the delivery of educational services. The most conspicuous illustration of this phenomenon is the Edison Project, a venture begun with considerable fanfare by communications executive Chris Whittle.[54] By 1998 Edison was operating fifty-one schools in twelve states and twenty-five cities and was serving twenty-four thousand students. Its own reports indicate that 76 percent of the students who attend Edison schools are racial minorities, and 62 percent qualify economically for the federal lunch program. A majority of the schools qualify for Title I aid.[55]

Edison's arrival on the education scene was controversial to say the least, especially in light of the spectacular disasters suffered by one of its key competitors in the newly emerging for-profit education sector. At about the same time Edison came into being, Educational Alternatives Incorporated (EAI) got involved in high-profile contractual arrangements to take over the management of the faltering Hartford public school system in Connecticut and to operate six inner-city schools in Baltimore. Both plans proved to be ill conceived, and high hopes came tumbling down in 1995, when officials in the two cities canceled the contracts.[56]

Edison's experience thus far has been dramatically different. Edison has adopted a more cautious approach that involves planning, curriculum development, staff development, and evaluation. Thirty-four of its schools are operated in partnership with local districts either under contract or through the granting of a charter; seventeen were created through the issuance of state charters. After two years of operation, an evaluation based on standardized tests, absentee rates, and measurements of parental and student satisfaction proved quite positive, although its findings have been contested in a report distributed by the American Federation of Teachers.[57]

Since 1995 the corporation has invested $70 million of its private funds in public education. The fact that its executives are answerable to private shareholders adds a dimension of accountability to the venture that is not present in an ordinary public school. In this sense Edison's fortunes, for better or worse, epitomize the competitive stakes that shape the dynamics of the market approach. Edison schools, however, like all charter schools, are public institutions. They are financed by public dollars, are open to all on a first come, first served basis, and are ultimately accountable to a public authority that can revoke the charter. Thus it is important to note the significant definitional distinction here between a fully privatized system regulated solely by the market and a contractual arrangement that is negotiated between a public authority and a private provider for operating a public service.[58]

In May 1998 Edison received a $25 million gift from the Fisher family, owners of the Gap Clothing Company of San Francisco, to be used by California school districts that wish to hire Edison to operate schools under an expanded charter school law. Edison announced that the funding would allow it to open fifteen new schools.[59] This is not the first time that the for-profit corporation was the beneficiary of a private donation. In Denver, several foundations and corporations had earlier raised $4 million to rehabilitate an old school building to house a new Edison school opening in the fall of 1998.

Not all new openings would come so easily to the New York-based corporation. Edison has received serious opposition from powerful teachers unions. In the spring of 1998, the National Education Association successfully defeated a proposal by the superintendent of schools in Dayton, Ohio, to turn over the management of five underperforming schools to Edison. Union representatives expressed concern that the corporation might require teachers to work longer days and extend the school year in order to affect a turnaround. The president of the local union affiliate pledged, "We did not want to turn our classrooms into corporate classrooms."[60]

Politics vs. Reform

As with most changes in educational governance, charter school legislation did not come about without a struggle in the state capitols. Local school boards that stood to lose power, students, and money did not take well to the new concept. Teachers unions expressed concern that charter school laws would relieve prospective teaching personnel from certification requirements and other regulations, and they were especially troubled by the prospect of having teachers and schools reach contractual agreements outside those negotiated between the union and local school districts. Many of the state and local regulations from which charter advocates sought relief had originally been drafted at the behest of school boards and teachers unions. Some of these political battles were more heated than others.

In 1994 the Michigan state teachers association and other education groups brought litigation to prevent the charter law from being implemented after it was enacted, arguing that charter schools were loosely regulated private schools that are not entitled to public funding. While they successfully pleaded their case at the trial and appellate levels, the education groups were finally rebuked by a 5–1 majority of the Michigan supreme court in 1997, which held that charter schools are public institutions.[61] The controversy over charters took a more ugly turn in the sleepy harbor town of Marblehead, Massachusetts, where parents who had organized to open a new charter school complained that they and their children had been threatened and harassed by public school employees.[62] In a more detailed study of charter schools in Massachusetts, Loveless and Jasin found repeated incidences of hostility toward charter school organizers, parents, and students by school district personnel, as well as a refusal to make student records and other information available.[63]

An interesting debate enveloped the Benjamin Banneker School in Cambridge, Massachusetts, the original site of local choice initiatives. Banneker, whose founders included Harvard Law Professor Charles Ogletree and his wife Pamela, its director, is a K–5 school intended to provide individualized instruction to disadvantaged children who are having difficulty in traditionally structured schools. While enrollment in the school is based on a lottery, most of the students applying happen to be black. When some critics expressed concern that the new school would promote racial isolation, Ms. Ogletree, who is black, responded that she was more focused on providing a new opportunity to children who are not well served by the Cambridge public schools. School district administrators complained that the transfer of students to Banneker would cost them $1.4 million in state aid during its first year of operation and up to $2 million annually thereafter.[64] A similar dispute broke out in North Carolina, where the law requires that the racial composition of the student body in charter schools must "reasonably reflect" the demographics of the school districts they serve.[65] Apparently, twenty-two of the schools in the state are out of compliance, largely because of oversubscription by black children who are fleeing other public schools. At the behest of the teachers union, civil rights groups, and some black legislators, the state education department was urged to close down these schools. It is an ironic turn in a state where blacks have been the object of racial discrimination for so long. Now, forty-five years after *Brown*, racial criteria were about to be used again to deny black students access to schools of their choice.

Despite the commotion it caused in the education profession, the tide in favor of charter schools was irresistible. For Democratic politicians aligned with teachers unions and other education groups, it represented a convenient compromise on choice: no funding for private schools, no church-state entanglements, a mechanism for increased accountability. President Clinton, an early supporter of public school choice, found the idea appealing and pledged that by the year 2000, there would be three thousand charter schools in the United States. In 1995 Secretary of Education Richard Riley announced that $5 million in federal grants would be awarded to eight states to help set up charter schools. An additional $2.1 million was set aside to conduct a four-year evaluation of charter schools, to be performed under contract with the Education Department by RPP International, a research organization in Berkeley, California.[66] This will provide the first comprehensive national survey of student performance in charter schools.[67]

Six months after Riley's announcement, the National Education Association, a one-time opponent of the idea, announced that it was investing $1.5 million over a five-year period to assist its local affiliates in setting up charter schools in five states.[68] Shortly thereafter, the American Federation of Teachers (AFT) issued its own report on charter schools, cautiously endorsing the idea, and warning of the need for greater attention to the protection of employee rights and high academic standards.[69] It seemed now that the controversy over charter schools was about to come to an end. In reality, the debate was transformed, less fixed on the question of whether such laws should be enacted and more focused on the particulars of what these laws would entail. Charter school advocates like to distinguish between real charter school provisions and Potemkin bills that pretend to be serious reforms but lack the essential ingredients of strong laws.[70] Then there is the other side. The AFT report mentions Rhode Island as having a "good" charter law. It is one of the most restrictive in the nation. It limits charters to existing public schools, and allows them to convert only with the approval of two-thirds of the teachers and half the parents, after which all teachers remain employees of the school district. While the law has been in place since 1995, as of 1998 only two charter schools existed in the entire state.

With charter schools too, the devil is in the details. If charter schools were going to thrive and compete with traditional public schools, they would have to be furnished with adequate resources and financial support. If charter schools were going to distinguish themselves from other institutions, they would need sufficient autonomy to develop their own character. If charter schools were going to redefine the educational options available to parents and impose market competition on existing institutions, their supply would need to be abundant. So long as local school boards would be allowed to play a key role in determining the number of charter schools permitted to exist, and the kind of managerial discretion they would enjoy, then the prospect for developing a robust system of alternatives would be quite modest. In the end, all charter school laws are the product of negotiations that take place in the state legislative arena, where potential opponents such as teachers unions and other education groups wield a considerable amount of influence.

The Evidence Thus Far

RPP International has released two reports based on the national surveys it completed for the U.S. Department of Education. The most recent data are derived from an examination of statutes that existed in twenty-nine states and the District of Columbia by September 1997, as well as telephone interviews with 428 schools (89 percent response rate) and site visits at ninety-one locations where charters existed during the 1996–97 school year. The researchers found that there is "no such thing as a typical charter school," describing them as being "extraordinarily diverse."[71] These schools used a variety of pedagogical approaches, some more traditional than others.

One characteristic of charter schools that stands out, however, is their small size.[72] Their median enrollment is about a hundred and fifty students, compared to the median enrollment of five hundred for regular public schools in the districts where charters are found. More than 60 percent of charters enroll fewer than a hundred and fifty students, compared to only 16 percent of the other public schools. Approximately 62 percent of the charters are new institutions; the remainder are conversion schools that were preexisting public (25 percent) or private schools (13 percent).

When asked why they started charter schools, the majority of those who founded new institutions said they did so to realize an alternative educational vision or to serve a special target population of students whose needs were not adequately being met in existing schools. Most of those involved with public school conversions said that they wanted to achieve more managerial autonomy, while private school conversions were motivated by the availability of public funding and the opportunity to attract a broader range of students. More than 70 percent of the schools had waiting lists of students.

In response to concerns that charter schools might have a skimming effect on public school districts, the RPP team examined demographic data on students in attendance. They found no evidence that charter schools as a group served a disproportionate number of white or economically advantaged students when compared to other schools in their states. On a district level, they estimated that 60 percent of the charter schools were not racially distinct (within a range of 20 percent) from other public schools. About one in three, however, served a higher percentage of minority students, and of these, about two-thirds served a distinctly higher percentage of poor students. Only 5 percent had populations with a higher percentage of white students than other public schools in their respective districts.

Many charter school parents who participated in focus groups expressed serious dissatisfaction with the public schools their children previously attended, registering such concerns as low academic standards, a dehumanizing culture, student safety, and unresponsiveness to serious parent involvement. When charter school operators were asked what characteristics they believed attracted parents to their institutions, they focused on similar factors: nurturing environment (93 percent), safe environment (90 percent), value system (88 percent), quality of academic program (84 percent), high academic standards (83 percent), small class size (73 percent), clear goals for each student (73 percent), structured environment (71 percent), adaptive environment (69 percent), central parent role (68 percent), and dress/behavior code (50 percent).

A second national study, performed by the Hudson Institute with support from Pew Charitable Trusts, was completed in June 1997. The two-year effort involved site visits to forty-five schools in thirteen states. Its findings were strikingly similar to those that appeared in the RPP reports. It also provided a detailed portrait of students, parents, and teachers who were directly involved with charter schools and their assessment of the experience thus far. The researchers found that charter schools are "havens for children who had bad educational experiences elsewhere," including low-income children, at-risk children, minority children, and children with learning disabilities or behavior problems.[73] They explained that since charter schools were open to all comers and commonly filled their seats by lottery, there were no inherent biases built into their recruitment patterns.

When asked why they decided to send their children to charter schools, most parents offered concrete educational explanations: small school size (53 percent), higher standards (45.9 percent), educational philosophy (44 percent), and better teachers (41.9 percent). Over two-thirds of the same parents indicated that the charter schools were better on these counts than the schools their children previously attended. Three-fifths of the students expressed higher levels of satisfaction with the charter schools. When teachers were asked what attracted them to charter schools, most identified factors associated with the character and climate of the school: educational philosophy (76.8 percent), new institution (64.8 percent), like-minded colleagues (62.9 percent), good administrators (54.6 percent), and class size (54.2 percent). Over 90 percent of the teachers said that they were satisfied with their new schools, and three-quarters expressed satisfaction with the level of input they had in decisionmaking at their schools.

Throughout the history of the school choice debate, skeptics have wondered whether poor parents have the wherewithal to function as intelligent shoppers when it comes to finding appropriate schools for their children, often making the implicit point that it is better to let others make such decisions for them. The Carnegie report published in 1992, for example, questioned whether disadvantaged parents would be capable of gathering relevant information to identify institutions that match their children's needs.[74] Others have questioned whether disadvantaged parents have the motivation to do what is required to move their children into better schools. The research on charter schools suggests that poor parents have precise educational goals in mind for their children that they are capable of acting on when given the opportunity to select a school.

The pattern of behavior exhibited by poor parents whose children attend charter schools is consistent with observations made by researchers studying public school choice in New York. Schneider and colleagues found that while, on average, low-income parents have little accurate information about objective conditions in schools, they know enough to enroll their children in schools that reflect their own educational priorities.[75]

Although parents have demonstrated a capacity to take advantage of the opportunities made available by charter schools, lawmakers in state capitals have not demonstrated an equal capability to make the hard decisions that would allow the charter concept to realize its potential as a tool for reform. Many, if not most, statutes in existence are remarkably weak. In most states that have charter school laws, approval by the local school district is required to set up a charter, there is a limit on the number of schools allowed, and funding is inadequate. When asked to identify the major difficulties they had in developing and implementing charters, practitioners responding to the RPP survey identified the following key factors: lack of start-up funds (57.6 percent), inadequate operating funds (41.1 percent), inadequate facilities (38.6 percent), lack of planning time (38.4 percent), state or local board opposition (23.1 percent), district resistance or regulations (18.3 percent), state department of education resistance or regulations (14.8 percent), and union resistance (11.3 percent). These concerns were confirmed by participants in the Hudson survey.

These complaints may sound like the usual carping we hear from educators all the time, but the truth is that charter schools operate with peculiar disadvantages. To begin with, unless they are converted from preexisting institutions—and fewer than 40 percent are—charter schools do not start out with a building in which to function. And since there is usually no funding available for start-up costs, these schools are planned and designed on a voluntary basis. Once charter schools are operating they usually do so with less than 100 percent of the resources allocated to other public schools.

Under the typical law, the charter school is entitled only to a portion of the per-pupil local operating expenditures and is rarely given resources to cover capital costs. The local district often gets to keep a portion of the local funding for a resident pupil who left it, and sometimes the local district gets compensated by the state for the state funds that follow students who have opted out.[76] This not only establishes a windfall for the home district, but also sets up an unfair competitive situation for the new school. It penalizes the winner and rewards the loser. Unfortunately, as we saw earlier, this type of arrangement is not altogether unusual with public school choice programs. It is the product of the kind of horse trading that takes place in state legislatures before innovation is permitted to occur.

Although the charter concept may have great promise as an impetus for school reform, it remains flawed in the way it has been designed and implemented in most states. In 1998 the University of California at Berkeley published a study concerning the effect of charter schools on school districts. This study was based on 200 interviews with public school administrators and teachers from twenty-five districts in eight states and the

District of Columbia.[77] The sample deliberately included a random mix of urban, suburban, and rural districts with charter schools, but none of the respondents were people who worked in charter schools. Overall, the study found that charter schools had a minimal effect on other schools or their districts as a whole, especially in large urban jurisdictions.

Respondents in fourteen of twenty-five districts indicated that they experienced no "felt-loss" of financing, and in only five did district personnel assert that they experienced significant losses. Many urban districts had simultaneously experienced such significant enrollment increases that the opening of a few charter schools did not have a serious effect on either head counts or funding. Beyond that, lawmakers were careful to ensure that school district constituents were held harmless throughout the process of educational experimentation. As one district superintendent candidly explained:

> I'd suggest that perhaps typically the legislators found a way to leave the extreme rhetoric hanging out there and create a reality that's almost 180 degrees the other way. Because, in fact, we haven't lost a nickel. The legislature has found ways to supplement our state aid.[78]

Respondents in a majority of the districts indicated that they had gone about business as usual, with no significant changes in educational programs or a notable effort to compete for students. In fact, few superintendents or principals admitted to using the new charter schools as educational laboratories from which they could learn to emulate successful practices. Most expressed little interest in having anything to do with charter schools. Many perceived charter schools as a way of getting rid of disgruntled students who had a long record of disciplinary and academic problems. One superintendent in Massachusetts claimed, "Charter schools skimmed off the loudest gripers, and gave us a relative breathing space to begin to turn one of our schools around." A school board member in Arizona exclaimed, "The district was glad to see these guys shuffling off to Buffalo and leaving them alone."[79]

On the positive side, the Berkeley study confirmed the findings of the previous reports to show that charter schools do not skim off the better students. To the contrary, as indicated in the previous reports, the Berkeley study suggests that charter schools have served as a form of relief for traditional public schools and for the students with which they have been mismatched. In this sense, choice seems to be working to expand alternatives available to students and parents who are not adequately being served.

On the negative side, the Berkeley study indicates that until now, charter schools have had a limited effect in promoting more widespread school reform. The number of charter schools that exist, especially in large urban school districts, is too limited to create real competition.

As noted above, these limitations are most often a function of the laws themselves. Laws have been written in such a way as to protect traditional public schools from any financial penalty that could be brought about through market-like competition. Therefore, school administrators in traditional public schools do not feel the pressure to experiment or innovate as a result of charter school laws as they are written now.

There are exceptions to the general rule. Arizona, which has one of the most liberal charter school laws in the country, sets no limit on their number. As a result, this state accounted for 25 percent of all charter schools in the country by 1998 (271). When California passed its statute in 1992, the limit was set at 100. In 1998 the California legislature raised the ceiling by adopting an amendment that allows it to add 100 new charter schools annually. By the end of that year, it counted 156 charter schools. There is preliminary evidence in both states indicating that charter schools are having a positive competitive effect on other public schools, encouraging them to implement innovative new programs and adopt other kinds of reforms.[80] Michigan, with 139 charters as of 1998, also shows some promise. These states, however, remain exceptions among thirty-five jurisdictions that set stringent limitations on the number of new institutions permitted to bloom.

Limits of Government Action

In the previous chapter, we considered how government has responded to the call for equal opportunity by adopting policies that represented a variety of proxy measures—racial integration, increased spending, and a redistribution of political power. None of these could be attached to notable progress in closing the learning gap that continues to afflict disadvantaged populations; such progress has yet to occur.

In this chapter, we examined a number of ways in which the government has implemented public school choice. The experience has been mixed, yet informative. On the whole, we found that parents are willing and able to move their children from one school to another when they perceive there to be a distinct educational advantage to doing so. But we were also cautioned by the evidence on magnet schools and interdistrict programs that, under certain conditions, there is a strong possibility that middle-class students would reap greater benefits from such experiments than poor students. There is nothing inherently wrong with expanding the educational opportunities of the middle class. It does not help, however, address the problem of educational inequality that occupies us here, and may in fact exacerbate it. To a large degree, such programs often replicate a pattern of self-selection that occurs under the ordinary enrollment patterns that govern public schools.

The evidence on controlled choice programs is somewhat more telling. It reinforces the notion that parents want choice, but it further suggests that they want to be able to exercise it in the communities where they live. This appears to make an awful lot of good sense. Most parents would not have much difficulty understanding the instinct expressed. What's more, a policy that begins with the presumption that certain children must leave the communities where they live to acquire a decent education seems to undermine the egalitarian principle that it supposedly is designed to advance. When considered together, the records on magnet schools and controlled choice underscore the fact that in order for choice to be meaningful for parents, it must provide them with real alternatives to the ordinary menu of programs available to their children.

Charter schools, at least in theory, possess many of the institutional characteristics required to promote real choice. They are autonomous and diverse. Many are neighborhood schools. While they are open to all children, they have functioned to provide a significant alternative to underserved populations. The limited experience we have had with charters indicates that poor parents want choice and they are capable of using it to their advantage when given the opportunity to do so.

The design of charter school laws has functioned to limit their power to promote such opportunities. In the course of the legislative process, charter laws have been subject to a process of political bargaining in which the interests of students are severely compromised. Many charter laws have been written to put the demands of local school districts before the needs of children. To limit competition, the number of charter schools permitted to operate has been severely restricted. As a result, most charter schools have long waiting lists of children who remain confined to institutions they no longer want to attend. Many charter schools are encumbered by regulations imposed by these same political and bureaucratic actors that are threatened by their existence, such as state and local school boards.

Charter schools are usually handicapped by inadequate funding. Financially, they are put at a competitive disadvantage with traditional public schools—assuming full responsibility for the instruction of children who choose to attend them, but often receiving only partial funding to cover the costs. In the meantime, school districts retain a portion of the dollars allocated for children who have gone elsewhere in pursuit of a better education. This has been a perennial problem with several types of public school choice. The cost of extracting reform legislation from the political process often involves an "opportunity tax" that benefits school districts and denies children adequate support. In the end, the overall design of charter legislation in many states serves to undermine competition and minimize the incentives for change.

Public
Schools
and Private
Schools

IT WAS 1981. Six years had passed since sociologist James
Coleman wrote his provocative report warning the nation
that school busing was contributing to the further segregation of the races,
nearly two decades since he had set off thunderous debate by suggesting
that schools had a minimal effect on the academic performance of students. With a third major work, the University of Chicago professor would
define another area of discourse within the education profession. This
time he completed a comprehensive national study comparing public, private, and parochial schools.[1] The new investigation, commissioned by the
National Center for Education Statistics, was based on data that appeared
in High School and Beyond (HS&B), a national longitudinal survey of
secondary schools. The survey reached sixty thousand students in 1,016
schools across all sectors of education. Among the major conclusions were
the following:

—Private schools produce better cognitive outcomes, even after controlling for the family background of students.

—Private schools provide a safer, more disciplined and structured learning environment.

—While non-Catholic private schools have lower student/teacher ratios than public schools, Catholic schools have somewhat higher ratios.

—While private schools enroll a smaller proportion of blacks than public
schools do, there is less racial segregation within private schools.

—Private school curricula offer students a narrower range of educational options and are more focused on academic, as opposed to vocational, subjects.

—Students in private schools exhibit more self-esteem and "fate control" than students in public schools do.

Coleman and his colleagues concluded that parochial schools more closely approximate the "common school ideal" than public schools do in that they have more effectively reduced the performance gap between students of different racial and economic backgrounds. Anticipating the policy implications of his findings, Coleman further explained that the implementation of tuition vouchers or tax credits would benefit black and Hispanic students more than whites, since minorities were less capable of affording a private or parochial school education and more likely to be attending failing public schools. Once again Coleman would shake the foundations of the research community by forcing it to deal with questions that made it uncomfortable. Predictably, the reaction to "Coleman III" was swift, strong, and angry.[2]

A heated editorial in the *New York Times* commented that "sociologists invite trouble" when they seek "the stardom of advocacy based on fallible predictions."[3] The paper followed with a second editorial that accused Professor Coleman of being a hired gun for the Reagan administration, which favored tuition tax credits.[4] It was well known in education circles at the time that Catholic schools were suffering from severe enrollment declines and financial pressures, as white ethnic populations began to migrate from their large parishes in central cities to the suburbs. At their peak in 1966, Catholic schools accounted for 87 percent of the nonpublic school enrollment; by 1982 the share had dipped to 64 percent.[5] Church leaders were searching for new ways to finance their vast network of schools, which was a concern they passed on to the White House. However, to allege that Coleman's findings were conditioned by these concerns was groundless. If there was one quality that had defined Coleman's career as a researcher, it was independence.

Several social scientists criticized Coleman's methodology. They claimed that the size of the sample he had taken was inadequate to support his conclusions and that he had not properly controlled for the selection biases of students who attend private and parochial schools. They suggested that the higher performance of private school students might be driven by demographic variables.[6] It was an odd turn of events. This was the same Coleman who years earlier had concluded in a national survey of public education that schools do not matter very much in determining educational outcomes. Now that he had examined the distinct culture and curricula of private and parochial schools, he seemed to be reversing his position. But, in fact, his new conclusions were based on an entirely different body of data that allowed him to compare a broader range of schools. In 1987 Coleman completed a second analysis of the HS&B data that supported his first findings, this time imposing more rigorous controls for family background.[7] The new study also allowed him to take account of changing achievement scores. The results showed that Catholic schools were especially effective at raising the achievement of disadvantaged students.[8]

Although the public versus private school debate remains unresolved in the minds of many scholars, Coleman was professionally vindicated by his peers in 1988, when he received an award from the American Sociological Association's Section on Education. In accepting the award, he reminded those present of the raucous session that had taken place in 1976 when the president of the same organization made a motion to censor him for his study on white flight. He warned his colleagues against tolerating a set of professional norms that was increasingly endangering academic freedom and the free exchange of ideas on university campuses. Once again Coleman had made it more acceptable to discuss a topic that left people uneasy. This time his provocation gave birth to a robust literature on Catholic schools that would prove to have a great bearing on the question of educational equality.[9]

The Relevance of Catholic Schools

It is difficult to overstate the significance of Catholic schools in the context of the choice debate. First is their sheer number. Catholic schools are the nation's largest alternative school system. Approximately 51 percent of all private school students at the elementary and secondary level attend Catholic institutions.[10] While enrollment in these schools dropped by half between 1965 and 1990, the pattern began to reverse in the early 1990s.[11] Their mere existence significantly extends the range of choices available to parents whose children are not adequately served in public schools. Moreover, Catholic schools are available where they are needed most, in the inner city.

Catholic education has always been an urban phenomenon. Originally opening their doors to a wave of European immigrants who arrived in the large cities of the Northeast during the early nineteenth century, Catholic schools still cluster in urban settings.[12] As second and third generation Irish, Italian, Polish, and German families started to relocate to the suburbs, these same schools began to educate new arrivals to the city, most of whom were not of European ancestry and many of whom were not Catholic. Approximately 25 percent of the student population in parochial schools is now made up of racial minorities; 17 percent are not Catholic.[13] It should not be difficult to understand why inner-city minorities who have been denied access to high quality schools are attracted to Catholic institutions. If we are to believe Coleman's assertions, Catholic schools fill a gaping educational need: safe neighborhood schools that are capable of lowering the educational deficits stubbornly associated with race and class.

The academic debate goes on. Using different forms of statistical analysis, some scholars continue to claim that there is no significant difference in the achievement of public and private school students.[14] But the question to be answered here is more subtle than the comparison of public and private schools. The key issue to resolve in the quest for educational equality is the determination of which schools do a better job addressing the needs of students whose learning is negatively influenced by economic and social background. On this count Catholic schools excel; the evidence to support Coleman's conclusions has been mounting for nearly two decades. Andrew Greeley, a Roman Catholic priest and sociologist from the University of Chicago, was one of the first researchers to examine the social implications of Coleman's study. Greeley confirmed that minority students who attend Catholic schools do better than their public school peers, and he further discovered that minority students who were economically and educationally disadvantaged had the most to gain from the Catholic school experience.[15] Greeley's work, generated from the same HS&B data base as Coleman's, was subjected to similar methodological criticisms. His status as a Catholic priest led many academicians to dismiss the findings of his research out of hand. Subsequent research by other scholars, however, would also confirm a "Catholic school effect" that reduced the empirical connection between demographic variables and academic achievement.[16] Even as disagreement continues about test score results, there does seem to be an emerging consensus within the research community on several important points: disadvantaged minority students who attend Catholic high schools are more likely to graduate, go on to college, and earn a degree.[17] These points are conceded by even the most doubtful skeptics.[18] Given the profound effect that a diploma and a degree can have in determining the life plan of a young man or woman, it is difficult to overstate the significance of these points.

The most comprehensive study of Catholic education to appear since Coleman III was presented in a book by Bryk, Lee, and Holland, published in 1993.[19] As one reviewer commented, the book was a "social science tour de force," involving five thousand students in 84 Catholic high schools, fifty thousand students in 894 public high schools, and numerous site visits to Catholic institutions.[20] The effort added further credence to Coleman's claims of a "Catholic school effect," because neither of the study's two senior authors were advocates of choice, and both had rejected market explanations regarding the success of parochial schools. Bryk and his colleagues found Catholic schools to be an effective vehicle for educating the same minority populations that have not been well served by urban public schools. They agreed that Catholic schools do indeed more closely approximate the "common school ideal." But the real contribution of this book, the reason that it advanced the discussion in a significant way, was that it was able to explain in explicit detail why Catholic schools excel. Yes, Catholic school children are slightly more advantaged, but the institutions they attend are hardly elite academic institutions, as many independent private schools are. Contrary to popular belief, Catholic schools are not especially selective, nor do they readily expel students who do not meet exacting behavioral or academic standards.

What seemed to matter most, what distinguished Catholic institutions from their public counterparts, were the intangible qualities that define them as institutions: the spirit of community, the sense of caring, the assumption that all children are capable of learning at the highest level of comprehension. Catholic schools advance the democratic ideal envisioned by the Supreme Court in *Brown*. Their value system is premised on a belief in the fundamental equality of all children. Educationally, this translates into an operational policy that treats all students the same and expects all to attain similarly high academic outcomes. This means no tracking, no segregation, no exceptions to the rigorous academic curriculum.

While demographics explains some differences in performance between the advantaged and the disadvantaged, the gap is significantly reduced and educational equality is more closely approximated. As perceived by the authors, equality is at the core of an institutional ethos that is intended to transcend the school experience: "Fundamental to Catholic schools are beliefs about the dignity of each person and a shared responsibility for advancing a just and caring society."[21] These underlying ethical values have far-reaching political and social implications that will be discussed in a later chapter. Contrast this worldview with the assumptions that underlie many arguments against school choice: that poor parents are incapable of making intelligent decisions on behalf of their children, that they lack motivation, that they need public authorities to act on their behalf.

Perhaps personal testimony is the best way to cast light on the differing perspectives. Consider a recent volume by a distinguished group of black professionals who are the products of Catholic schools. Introducing essays by a dozen contributors, Janice E. Jackson identifies five themes that run through the book and that describe the features that set Catholic schools apart: high expectations for all students; a rigorous curriculum that signals a confidence in students to perform at a high level; a nurturing community; the development of a strong personal identity; and the cultivation of the spirit as well as the mind, or what some would call character development. She urges, "The lessons learned can be applied to the education of African American students in public schools, not just parochial schools."[22] This brings us to the final point about Catholic schools: how learning more about them can inform ongoing discussions related to school reform and choice.

As Bryk and his colleagues describe them, Catholic schools operate with a level of autonomy that would be the envy of most reform advocates. While typically part of a loosely coupled diocesan organization or attached to a particular religious order, principals and teachers are not encumbered by the large bureaucratic structure that typically burdens professionals who work in public schools. This structure of governance not only functions to allow a maximum degree of latitude at the school site, it also guarantees that a significantly larger proportion of resources are invested close to the classroom. On the whole, Catholic schools operate at approximately 60 percent of the per capita costs of public schools.[23] This is a powerful fact to keep in mind as we pour increasingly larger amounts of public money into failing inner-city school systems.

For many years the cost structure of Catholic schools was maintained by the availability of a voluntary work force of nuns, priests, and brothers associated with the religious orders that ran them. This has changed in recent years, as young people have become less inclined to enter religious life. The proportion of Catholic school teachers who belong to religious orders has plummeted from 58 percent in 1967 to 15 percent in 1990.[24] Because of their constrained resources, many of these inner-city institutions have become dependent on the good will and dedication of a core of professionals that works for relatively low wages and is committed to the educational mission. As such, Catholic schools are schools of choice—not only for parents and children, but also for the people who give their time and energy to make them the successful institutions that they are. What they lack in financial capital, they are able to make up for in human capital. These voluntary institutions benefit from a network of social relations that is characterized by mutuality and trust. To apply a term in common usage today, Catholic schools are enriched by a high level of "social capital"—a term, by the way, that was coined by James Coleman to describe the phenomenon he observed in these very same institutions.[25]

Politics of Choice

The book that catapulted school choice into the spotlight of national politics was Chubb and Moe's *Politics, Markets, and American Schools*.[26] It was the next of a long line of surveys to examine the HS&B data, supplemented by new information on the organization and administration of the schools involved. By now it was not especially noteworthy that these surveys found private and parochial schools to be more educationally effective than public schools. What distinguished this book were the policy implications the authors drew from their research and its unusually frank analysis of the political and institutional obstacles that prevented alternative policies from being implemented.

Chubb and Moe proposed a variation of Milton Friedman's market model. Instead of using the term "voucher," they introduced the term scholarship. Rather than advocating a fully privatized system of education, they proposed that private schools be allowed to compete with public schools for students and dollars. A year before the state of Minnesota passed the first charter school law, they recommended a model of governance that gave public schools operational autonomy from their local districts. They suggested that all private and parochial schools be allowed to participate in the scholarship program, but in deference to federal and state constitutional prohibitions that might arise, they agreed that each state should set its own policy regarding the eligibility of parochial schools. Although they would not limit the scholarship to students who were poor, they provided that scholarship amounts could vary to compensate students who could demonstrate special economic or educational needs.

Chubb and Moe's analysis of the institutional framework that determines education policy was standard fare within political science. Based on an interest group model of decisionmaking, it explained how the policymaking process that is ostensibly democratic becomes controlled by organized groups and institutions that do not represent the best interests of the public at large.[27] In analyzing politics at the state and local levels, the authors drew a conceptual distinction between constituents and customers—education professionals and the students themselves—that greatly resembled the dichotomy between constituent and client I had observed in writing about the New York City school system seven years earlier.[28] Their radical dissection of the body politic struck a raw nerve in the anatomy of the educational establishment. As they explained:

> When it comes to educational decision making, particularly at the state and local levels where effective authority resides, the most powerful political groups by far are those with vested interests in the current institutional system: teachers unions and myriad associations of principals, school boards, superintendents, administrators and professionals—not to mention education schools, book publishers, testing services, and many institutional beneficiaries of the institutional status quo.[29]

While their vivid portrait of the political process focused on the state and local environment, Chubb and Moe's book was instrumental in translating the concept of school choice into a national political issue. As their own analysis could have predicted, the nation was not yet ready for their far-reaching proposal. As with Coleman before them, Chubb and Moe's scholarship was resoundingly rejected by a large segment of the academic community, especially by many of those education researchers who had been the object of the authors' criticism.[30] Nevertheless, there are few books that have produced such a powerful momentum for discussing a major policy question. So far as education was concerned, this would prove to be the most important book of the decade.

Education reform had already erupted as a significant question in the 1988 presidential election. Throughout the early years of his administration, President George Bush took a cautious approach on the choice issue, focusing mostly on the merits of public experiments like those that had been instituted in Cambridge, East Harlem, and Minnesota. Then in 1992, a month before the New Hampshire primary where Bill Clinton launched his bid for the White House, Bush laid out his plan for a "G.I. Bill for Children." Adopting Chubb and Moe's terminology, he proposed that federal money be appropriated to states and local school districts to make two thousand scholarships available to poor and middle-income children. These $1,000 grants could be used at any accredited public, private, or parochial school. Up to half the scholarship could be used to pay for supplementary academic services and after-school programs. Given the minimal amount of the scholarship and the middle-income criterion set for eligibility, Bush's plan was as much targeted at middle-class constituents as at the poor. As if to remind him that he had moved too quickly, the year after George Bush was defeated for reelection, the voters of California dramatically rejected a voucher proposal that appeared on a statewide ballot. The referendum was turned down by a 7–3 margin after the California Teachers Association invested $12.6 million in a do-or-die political campaign to defeat the proposal.[31] Legislative proposals for vouchers had also been defeated in Oregon (1990) and Colorado (1992). But the issue would not die.

In 1996 Republican presidential candidate Bob Dole announced his own plan for school vouchers. He promised to spend $2.5 billion annually to provide low-income children support to attend private and parochial schools—up to $1,000 for elementary school, and $1,500 for high school.[32] Designed to penetrate a traditional Democratic stronghold for low-income parents, it failed to resonate among voters who could not afford to make up the difference between the scholarship and the cost of tuition. Once again the Republicans had flubbed it, unable to generate a concrete proposal to meet the needs of poor parents who could prove to be a natural constituency on the choice issue.

The paradoxical politics of choice would not come into full public view until Bill Clinton, a moderately liberal Democratic president, came face to face with a Republican-dominated Congress that refused to retreat on school choice. Bill Clinton had defined himself as a champion of the poor, a friend of racial minorities, and a supporter of public education. While a proponent of public school choice and charter schools as governor of Arkansas, he drew a very deep line in the sand when it came to vouchers. Throughout Clinton's first term in office, congressional Republicans circulated an assortment of voucher bills that would have created demonstration projects in poor communities. Things came to a head in the spring of 1997, at the beginning of Clinton's second term, when Republican majorities in both houses supported a bill that would have offered scholarships to two thousand economically disadvantaged children in the District of Columbia school system.[33] The bill was cosponsored by two Democrats—Representative Floyd Flake, a black minister from New York, and Senator Joseph Lieberman, a Jewish liberal from Connecticut. During the same session, Flake and Lieberman also cosponsored the American Community Renewal Act, in which school choice experiments would be piloted in 100 low-income areas as part of a larger developmental effort. But it was the District of Columbia proposal that rang so loudly with the irony behind the choice debate.

Under the latter proposal, a $3,000 scholarship would be made available on the basis of a lottery to any child in Washington, D.C., whose family income did not exceed 185 percent of the federal poverty level. The scholarship could be used at a public, private, or parochial school of the family's choice. The plan's provisions were clearly designed to help the poorest of the poor in one of the nation's most horrible urban school systems, and the size of the scholarship voucher was sufficient to pay for the full cost of tuition in many nonpublic schools in the area. The bill was strongly opposed by Americans United for the Separation of Church and State, which claimed that the bill violated the Establishment clause of the First Amendment. It was also opposed by the National Education Association, which ensured its defeat. The Clinton administration's position was signaled early, when Secretary of Education Richard Riley warned that vouchers would divert important support from the Washington, D.C., public schools. In his annual address on the state of American education, Riley also spoke ominously about those people who sought to destroy the public education system.[34]

Riley must not have been paying close attention to the condition of the Washington public schools. As far as the children in the nation's capital were concerned, public education was already in shambles, and the explanation had little to do with money. In fact, the Washington, D.C., public schools were a national disgrace, a dramatic example of many of the problems that plague urban education in America. The D.C. schools were a product of an aggressive school integration program that resulted in white flight: 96 percent of Washington's public school pupils are racial minorities; 88 percent are black. Between 1968 and 1998, enrollment dropped from a hundred and thirty thousand pupils to seventy-nine thousand. A report released by an independent financial control board at the end of 1996, entitled "Children in Crisis," drew a stark portrait of a dysfunctional bureaucratic system that had failed the capital's young people.[35] The District spends $7,655 per pupil, 26 percent above the national average. It spends more than twice as much on its central board of education and three times as much on its superintendent's office than comparable peer districts. Its ratio of administrative to teaching staff is nearly double that of its peers. Only 22 percent of the District's fourth-grade students scored at or above the basic achievement level in reading, and 53 percent of all students drop out after the tenth grade. It is no wonder that parochial school enrollment in the Washington area increased by 18 percent between 1993 and 1995. Those who left the public schools undoubtedly did so because they could afford the tuition. The voucher bill before Congress would have opened private school enrollment to many who could not have afforded it on their own.

Although a majority in both houses supported the choice measure, there were insufficient votes in the Senate to overcome either a presidential veto or a Democratic filibuster. The bill died, but not before treating the nation to a political spectacle that dramatized the paradox and irony behind the choice debate. A Republican House majority had drafted a law that was more consistent with the redistributive politics of liberal sociologist Christopher Jencks than with the market model of conservative economist Milton Friedman. It was defeated by a Democratic majority in the Senate at the behest of a Democratic president who had just enjoyed a resounding re-election victory with strong support from black voters. Clinton epitomized one of the great dilemmas of liberal Democratic politics: on the one hand, sympathetic to the plight of the disadvantaged, concerned with the tragic condition of public education in cities; on the other hand, deeply indebted to the education establishment and the powerful teachers unions. The National Education Association had fielded 405 delegates at the 1996 Democratic national convention— more than any state in the nation except California.[36] That same year the union invested $186 million to have its voice heard in national political contests.[37] The association and its sister organization, the American Federation of Teachers, had a well-defined position on school vouchers, and the president was well aware of it.

We had seen a similar balancing act played out before in Washington, when Lyndon Johnson took on the old Democratic party machines of the big cities in order to install his new vision of participatory politics. Since the election of Richard Nixon as president, the vitality of the Democratic party had been strung together on the strength of a delicate alliance between ambivalent partisans of the Old South, middle-class liberals of the East, the children and grandchildren of European immigrants who were moving to the suburbs, union members, and racial minorities who, to the consternation of the rest, had become inseparably identified with the controversial politics of the welfare state.[38] It was only the latter who had a direct stake in the voucher issue, and this time there was no Lyndon Johnson around to promote their cause.

By now the voucher issue had become largely associated with Republicans, conservatives, and the politics of the right. In reality, registered Democrats were more sympathetic to the idea than Republican voters. The Phi Delta Kappa/Gallup Poll that was released in 1998 showed that slightly more than half the nation's registered Democrats endorsed vouchers (51 percent for, 43 percent against), whereas Republicans were almost evenly split over the issue (48 percent for, 47 percent against).[39]

The irony of Clinton's staunch opposition to school vouchers for poor children in Washington, D.C., was not lost on its proponents. While openly professing his support for public education and enunciating the essential role of the public school in American society, Clinton and his wife—the Gores, and nearly every president in recent memory—sent their own child to a private school. As Bill Clinton vowed to reject the choice legislation proposed in Congress, his own daughter attended the elite Sidwell Friends School. An editorial published in the *Wall Street Journal* derided "Sidwell Liberals," who let economically deprived children remain trapped in inferior institutions that they would not allow their own children to attend.[40] The editorial cited a report published by the Heritage Foundation indicating that 34 percent of the members of the House of Representatives and 50 percent of the senators also had sent their children to nonpublic schools.[41] Only 14.1 percent of all American school children attend private schools; among blacks and Hispanics the figure is only 8 percent. An obvious swipe at the Washington political establishment, the Heritage Foundation report highlighted the class divisions that underlie the choice issue and its implications regarding equality. Clinton would continue to reject similar choice proposals put forward by Congress throughout his second term.

Nonetheless, 1997 was a pivotal year. With or without White House support, school choice would rise prominently in the public consciousness, as influential figures from all sides of the political spectrum came forward to declare their support. By then bruising political battles were well under way in Milwaukee and Cleveland, where black parents, frustrated with the condition of public schools, managed to get choice laws enacted and signed by their governors. In May Brent Staples wrote a signed editorial in the *New York Times* explaining how competition and choice in Milwaukee had begun to change the dismal public schools of that city for the better, much as Milton Friedman had predicted.[42] In June *Washington Post* columnist William Raspberry declared himself a "reluctant convert" and, for the sake of poor children in central cities, pleaded "Let's at least Experiment with School Choice."[43]

Six months earlier, William Galston and Diane Ravitch, two leading public policy scholars, published an op-ed piece in the *Washington Post* calling for a national demonstration program of means-tested scholarships.[44] Galston had served as a domestic policy adviser to President Bill Clinton; Ravitch was an independent-minded assistant secretary of education under President George Bush, who, to the chagrin of Washington Republicans, had refused to sign on to school choice while in office.[45] The political tide was rapidly turning, and school choice was on the verge of becoming a major battleground of redistributive politics.

Local Uprisings

As the Washington political establishment moved haltingly on the issue of school choice, an array of programs was being initiated at the local level by actors from a variety of sectors. Dozens of philanthropic efforts were initiated by business people and private foundations to provide poor children with an opportunity to escape the despair of failing public schools and to attend private institutions of choice. No two programs were exactly alike. Providing private school opportunities that would not otherwise have been available for poor children, these varied initiatives became laboratories for experimentation with an idea whose time had finally come.

Private Initiatives

The idea of raising private money to allow poor children to attend private or parochial schools is by no means novel. The Catholic Church has been particularly active in setting up scholarship funds for disadvantaged children in big cities like New York, Los Angeles, and Boston for many years. What is different about the new philanthropy is that beyond the noble mission of helping the poor, its contributors are also determined to advance a set of principles, most notably competition and choice. Since these ideas are being offered to change public policy, there is an unambiguous political dimension to the programs. Three of the original programs of this sort were initiated in the early 1990s: the Educational Choice Charitable Fund (ECCF) in Indianapolis (1991), Children's Educational Opportunity (CEO) in San Antonio (1992), and Partners Advancing Values in Education (PAVE) in Milwaukee (1992).[46] All were designed around a similar philosophy and plan: providing scholarships for poor children in urban settings that would reimburse parents for up to one-half the cost of tuition at a private or parochial school. The scholarships were made available on a first-come, first-served basis to low-income families; both public and private school children were eligible.

While the leaders of this philanthropic effort wanted to give poor families access to schools that had previously been out of their reach, they also stressed that parents should be expected to make a financial contribution to their children's education as a token of their commitment. Each program set a cap on the total amount of funding it would give per student. In Indianapolis it was $800; in San Antonio $750; in Milwaukee it was $1,000 at the elementary level and $1,500 for high school. The Indianapolis and San Antonio programs each awarded 1,000 scholarships a year. The PAVE program in Milwaukee has grown precipitously from 2,089 scholarships in 1992–93 to 4,201 in 1996–97. Much of this growth is attributable to PAVE's effort to fill a void created by litigation against the publicly supported program, where state aid was suddenly pulled from parents planning to enroll their children in parochial schools. We will return to that conflict later in the chapter.

Started by J. Patrick Rooney of the Golden Rule Insurance Company, Indianapolis's ECCF would become a prototype of foundations established by wealthy entrepreneurs throughout the nation. Such contributors were willing to invest their personal resources to promote the educational opportunities of poor children trapped in failing urban schools, while at the same time advancing an idea they had come to embrace. CEO America, begun by James Leininger in San Antonio, would develop into a nationwide organization designed to coordinate locally funded efforts.[47] This umbrella organization serves as a clearing house for information, financial assistance, and advocacy. By 1998 programs designed under its auspices existed in thirty locations, serving more than twelve thousand students.

Other models of philanthropy began to emerge around the country as the concept of choice caught on. New York City has spawned two innovative programs. The Student/Sponsor Partnership (SSP), founded in 1986, actually predated the Golden Rule effort by five years. Begun by Peter Flanigan, a managing director at Dillon Reed & Company, the idea was to link a student with a sponsor, who provides tuition assistance and serves as a mentor to a young man or woman. The overwhelming majority of participants are poor minority students who have not done well in public school. While there is no set income qualification for eligibility, all students who participate are either at risk of dropping out of school or have already done so. Under Flanigan's program, children receive full tuition to attend participating high schools, most of which are Catholic institutions. The SSP program is being replicated in Newark, the District of Colombia, Phoenix, Chicago, Fort Worth, and Bridgeport.

In 1997 a group of New York philanthropists set up the School Choice Scholarship Foundation, which gave 1,300 scholarships to low-income children in the amount of $1,400 each.[48] This effort became the model for similar programs set up a year later in Washington, D.C., and Dayton, Ohio.

In 1998 New York investment banker Ted Forstman teamed up with John Walton of Wal-Mart stores to establish the Children's Scholarship Fund (CSF), a national campaign designed to encourage local entrepreneurs to invest in privately funded scholarship programs to benefit poor children in cities across the nation. Beginning with a new program being launched in the District of Columbia, the CSF provides matching funds for local sponsors who are willing to set up scholarship programs in other urban areas. Their goal is to raise $200 million to promote fifty thousand partial scholarships to low-income children in thirty-eight cities over a period of four years.[49] Forstmann's initiative would represent both a new juncture in the choice debate and a widening of its political constituency beyond the usual array of Republican and conservative political stalwarts. The effort by Forstmann, a close friend of the Clinton administration, was openly endorsed by the White House. His bipartisan board of directors includes the names of Erskine Bowles, Barbara Bush, Joseph Califano, Henry Cisneros, Floyd Flake, Peter Flanigan, Martin Luther King III, Trent Lott, Daniel Patrick Moynihan, Colin Powell, Charles Rangel, and Andrew Young. Many of Forstmann's supporters, however—including the president—would continue to draw a distinction between choice that was privately funded and choice that was publicly funded, as would he.

By the spring of 1999, CSF had received 1,237,360 applications for 40,000 scholarships in the coming school year, following a well-organized publicity campaign that included public service announcements from baseball star Sammy Sosa and poet Maya Angelou.[50] At a ceremony held for lottery winners in New York, former Atlanta Mayor Andrew Young invoked the name of Rosa Parks as he addressed an audience of parents, business executives, politicians, and civil rights leaders:

In the words of the old Negro spiritual: Great Day! . . . I don't think when Rosa Parks sat down (on the bus) she knew what she was doing. I know the students who had the first sit-ins didn't know what they were doing. I don't think that John Walton and Ted Forstman knew what they were doing.[51]

John Walton was also the primary force behind another ambitious experiment that took form in the Edgewood School District of San Antonio. Launched under the sponsorship of CEO America, the new plan would raise $50 million over a period of ten years to pay the full cost of tuition for any student in the thirteen thousand-pupil district who wanted to attend a private or parochial school. As CEO president Fritz Steiger explained, the Horizon Program would give "every parent in that district a level playing field and an opportunity to make a choice."[52] Edgewood had been the scene of the landmark school finance case that was decided by the Supreme Court in 1973. Through this ruling, the Court rejected the notion that property-poor districts had a federal constitutional claim to fiscal parity with their suburban neighbors.[53] Now the small Hispanic district would become the scene of one of the most significant and informative experiments in American education.

Over the long term, the Edgewood experiment will provide a laboratory for answering many of the burning questions that surround the choice debate: How deep is the demand for choice among poor minorities? Who benefits from choice? Can choice really work to sever the connection between demographics and achievement? How will public schools respond to choice? How will private and parochial schools respond? Will competition function to improve public education? Will the availability of funds in the form of scholarships generate an increased supply of private options? All these questions will take time to answer. Years of experience will be required before the evidence will unfold. In the meantime, policymakers will have to rely on the scattered reports that emerge from less expansive endeavors in other cities.

One early assessment of private scholarship programs appeared in a book of essays edited by Terry Moe in 1995. It covered the programs in New York, Indianapolis, Milwaukee, and San Antonio.[54] In his introduction to the volume, Moe distinguished between the Student/Sponsor Scholarship Program in New York and the Golden Rule type of experiments found in the other cities. Summarizing data on the latter, he found higher levels of student performance and parental satisfaction among scholarship recipients as compared to their public school peers.[55] When asked why they chose to send their children to private schools, parents consistently noted the high academic quality of the institutions, their safer environments, and a general frustration with the public schools their children had formerly attended. Many parents who chose to opt out of public schools were also attracted by the religious aspect of the parochial school curricula. Similar parental attitudes have been expressed in private programs administered in Washington, D.C., and Dayton.[56]

Because of the income qualification, families participating in the program were, by definition, economically disadvantaged. They tended to be disproportionately black and Hispanic and were more likely than other public school families to have only one parent at home. The Indianapolis program attracted parents who were somewhat more likely to be white, to be married, and to have fewer children. The most distinguishing feature of parents in all three of the programs, however, was that even though they were poor, they were better educated and had higher educational aspirations for their children than other public school parents do.

Classifying the latter effect as skimming may be a bit of an exaggeration. Perhaps it is more reasonable to refer to these participants as the more fortunate among the disadvantaged. As Moe explains, some of this effect may be attributable to the design of the program itself. Requiring parents to pay half the tuition tends to exclude the poorest of the poor and to attract the most motivated parents who place a high value on education. The problem is exacerbated when the program distributes its rewards on a first-come, first-served basis and allows children already attending private and parochial schools to be eligible. Moe also points out that the sorting taking place among the poor in these programs is not any worse than the kind of stratification and segregation that usually occurs in public schools.

The observations recorded in the 1995 volume edited by Moe were generally confirmed in a series of studies edited by Paul Peterson and Bryan Hassel three years later, with some exceptions.[57] The later study of Indianapolis contained comparative performance data, which showed that, while transferring students lost some ground in the early grades (especially in math), they steadily improved throughout middle school to more closely approximate the achievement level of their new private school peers. Simultaneously, a broad population of public school students in Indianapolis began to experience a steady decline in the middle school years, a common occurrence in urban public schools. The cognitive advantage of private school attendance apparent in the Golden Rule data is consistent with the observations that contributors to the Peterson-Hassel volume made regarding San Antonio and Milwaukee.

Preliminary reports on the School Choice Scholarship Foundation (SCS) program begun in New York in 1997 indicated a similar profile of applicants interested in pursuing the private school option. Among the twenty-three thousand applicants for 1,300 slots appropriated by lottery, 47 percent were Hispanic, 44 percent black, 26 percent performed at grade level in reading, 18 percent were at grade level in math, average income was below $10,000, and 60 percent were on public assistance—once again predictable given the economic criteria set for eligibility (qualification for federally subsidized lunch). By and large, students who applied for the scholarship were more likely to be black, have lower incomes, and be on public assistance than their public school peers. For disadvantaged families, however, parental education was relatively high: some 10 percent of the parents had a college diploma and 41 percent of the mothers and 26 percent of the fathers reported "some college."[58] In New York, this high rate of college attendance is somewhat a function of a liberal open admissions policy at the City University of New York. When asked about the key factors they considered when selecting a school for their children, parents participating in the program listed three priorities: teacher quality (83 percent), safety (81 percent), and religion (83 percent).

After one year of operation, an evaluation of New York's SCS was conducted by Professor Paul Peterson in cooperation with Mathematica Policy Research. They found participating students performed better than a control group of peers by 2 percentile points in math and 2.2 percentile points in reading, with the largest differences occurring in the upper grades.[59] The modest but significant gain after just one year is only the first component of a four-year assessment that is planned. Because of the careful design of both the program and the assessment, this could prove to be the most scientifically rigorous study ever conducted on how choice affects student performance.

One of the most impressive experiences with private school choice is found in New York's Student/Sponsor Partnership program, also one of the oldest and most distinct of all scholarship initiatives. While SSP does not keep detailed demographic data on its students, a study prepared by Paul Hill for the Moe volume indicated that all 815 students participating in the program were either black or Hispanic, nearly 90 percent are from one-parent families, and, on average they begin the program two grade levels below the norm.[60] SSP gives attention to the academic progress of their students in a way that Moe describes as "nothing short of spectacular."[61] Some 70 percent of these high-risk students graduate from high school in four years, as compared to 39 percent of their public school peers and 29 percent of the students who live in the high-poverty areas from which program participants are drawn. Among the graduates, 90 percent go on to attend college. Perhaps the SSP experience in New York tells us as much about Catholic schools as it does about school choice, but the two are related. A blue ribbon panel report on Catholic schools completed in cooperation with the state department of education in New York indicated significantly higher performance levels in Catholic schools as compared to public schools, even when considering the relevant demographic characteristics that tend to complicate such comparisons.[62]

If there are any general conclusions that can be drawn from the array of private initiatives implemented thus far, it is to support Coleman's original 1981 claims. While data available and the controls used are limited, they continually suggest that children in urban settings tend to perform better academically when they attend private and parochial schools. Poor parents apparently appreciate that. When given the opportunity to make a choice, poor parents select nonpublic schools because of the schools' higher academic standards and the measure of safety and security they believe these schools provide. Some are also attracted by the religious content of the curriculum. These same parents also express higher levels of satisfaction with nonpublic schools after their children attend them. Whether such choice programs are capable of reaching the poorest of the poor, however, is largely a function of their design, that is, whether they are particularly targeted to poor and underperforming students, and whether parents are expected to pay a portion of the tuition costs. Such information is invaluable to policymakers who desire to improve the educational opportunities of the poor.

Milwaukee

Milwaukee is a classic case in urban education: an agonizing history of desegregation, followed by white flight, large amounts of spending, low achievement, and deep frustration on the part of minority parents. It is no wonder that the one-hundred-thousand-student district would become a national stage for testing the proposition that school choice could advance the unfulfilled quest for educational equality. Way back in 1976, Milwaukee adopted one of the first and most comprehensive programs for voluntary desegregation. Magnet schools were opened in the central city to attract white students from outside, and interdistrict busing plans were implemented so that inner-city blacks could attend decent schools in the suburbs.[63] The magnet programs were somewhat successful in promoting racial balance for city schools.[64] The brunt of the burden from busing, however, would fall on blacks. Many were not permitted to attend schools in their own neighborhoods because the schools were converted to "specialty schools" to attract white children.[65]

By 1990 five thousand minority students had been transported to forty suburban schools, whereas only thirteen hundred white suburban students had been brought to the city.[66] Beyond that, the problem remained that most students, especially black students, were not effectively being taught how to read, write, and compute. A comprehensive fifteen-month study completed in 1985 by an independent state commission appointed by Governor Tony Earl found an "unacceptable disparity in educational opportunity and achievement between poor and minority children and non-poor and white children." Yes, desegregation efforts had managed to achieve a better racial balance, but the learning gap continued to prevail. As Mikel Holt, a black activist and editor of the local *Community Journal* commented,

> They sold us desegregation as a panacea, a placebo. . . . It was supposed to be our Emancipation Proclamation, leading us out to educational equality. . . . For fifteen years, we've been on a bus ride to nowhere.[67]

One person touched by the abject failure of public schools in Milwaukee was Annette "Polly" Williams, a black, single mother, who had worked hard at a variety of jobs to support her four children before unemployment forced her to temporarily go on welfare. Williams decided to get involved in local politics after she refused to have her child bused to a school outside of her neighborhood. In 1980 she ran for and won a seat in the Wisconsin State Assembly. The new representative from the predominantly black Near North District of Milwaukee was destined to become a national spokesperson for school choice in America's failing urban school districts.

In 1988 Williams had become involved in a plan that would have set up a separate school district in the vicinity of North Division High School. Her chief ally in the campaign was Howard Fuller, a fellow North Division graduate who had once led the "Coalition to Save North Division." Williams and Fuller had sought to have their schools secede from the Milwaukee public school system and to establish elections for their own school board for the predominantly black district. While the term had not yet come into fashion, they wanted to set up their own charter school district—completely autonomous, allowing schools to operate on a site-based plan of governance. It was a far cry from the integrationist agenda advocated by groups like the NAACP. These were new times. As might be expected, the plan was opposed by the acting superintendent of schools, Hawthorne Faison. Although it was approved by the state assembly, it was defeated in the senate. Shortly thereafter Williams announced that she would campaign to have the legislature pass a bill to allow students to use publicly supported vouchers to attend private schools. As she explained it, "I came up with choice outside the public school system because I couldn't get choice inside it."[68]

After a new political coalition had taken charge of the city school board, Howard Fuller was chosen as superintendent of schools. In 1991, on the occasion of his new appointment, Fuller released data showing that only 23 percent of Milwaukee's black public school children read at or above grade level, just 22 percent performed at grade level in math, and a mere 32 percent graduated from high school—leading him to conclude that he had inherited "a failing system."[69] A report completed by the Wisconsin Policy Research Institute a year earlier had indicated that only 25.7 percent of every dollar spent on education in Milwaukee actually found its way to the classroom.[70] Fuller, a community activist with a background in social work, was an unorthodox candidate for the position of school superintendent. He was a leader who had little regard for the ways of the bureaucracy or for policies he thought were out of touch with the needs of students. A believer in vouchers, he had an understanding with the school board that he would neither support nor oppose them during his superintendency. His promise was to focus on improving the public schools and creating options for parents within the system.

Williams found significant political support for her voucher plan in Wisconsin Governor Tommy Thompson, a Republican, and Milwaukee Mayor John Norquist, a Democrat, who had run for office with little support from the teachers unions.[71] They were eventually joined by the Metropolitan Milwaukee Association of Commerce, whose members were finding it increasingly difficult to hire employees with basic skills, and Parents For School Choice, a group of low-income parents led by Zakiya Courtney.[72] It was an interesting political coalition, since Williams was a devoted Democrat, who had been very active in Jesse Jackson's 1988 bid for the presidential nomination. While always a loyal "Jesse-crat," she broke with him on the issue of school choice, as she would later with Bill

Clinton. Polly Williams was the personification of the growing tensions within the old Democratic coalition, which seemed to fester around the issue of choice. She explained, "I am not a Republican, I am not a conservative, I am not a backer of President Bush . . . but President Bush is right on parental choice, and Bill Clinton is wrong." Scolding both Jackson and Clinton on the issue, she exclaimed, "Look at him [Jackson] and Clinton sending their children to private school. He [Jackson] gets a piece of my mind on that, no question."[73]

But the local opposition to school choice was formidable. Weighing in against it were the Wisconsin Education Association Conference (an NEA affiliate), the Wisconsin Federation of Teachers (an AFT affiliate), the Wisconsin Association of School District Administrators, the Wisconsin Congress of Parents and Teachers, and State Superintendent of Public Instruction Herbert Grover, who declared that choice "could ruin public schools."[74] Grover had been elected in a statewide contest with strong support from the teachers union, as had most of the Democratically controlled legislature. Governor Thompson had circulated four different bills in support of choice beginning in 1987, all of which went down in defeat. Finally, with pressure exerted by black parents and their representatives, the legislature agreed to a watered down bill in 1990, which the governor signed. The costs exacted in the process of legislative bargaining were severe. The result was a weak law that imposed numerous limitations on parental choice.[75]

Scholarships were made available on the basis of a lottery to students with a family income that did not exceed 175 percent of the federally determined poverty level. The size of the program was limited to 1 percent (1.5 percent in 1994) of the city public school enrollment. There are approximately sixty-five thousand to seventy thousand students that meet the income requirements set by the law, but even in its expanded form, the program would award only fifteen thousand scholarships.[76] The amount of the scholarship was set at a level comparable to the per-pupil allocation of state aid ($2,500 in 1990, $3,000 in 1994), but the district was permitted to retain all of the locally generated funds for children who opted out. We have seen similar funding arrangements with public choice and charter plans reviewed earlier. The effect is to put choice students at a financial disadvantage and to reward the district that dissatisfied parents elected to leave. Parents whose children attended choice schools were not permitted to contribute anything above the amount of the voucher. Students already enrolled in a private school were ineligible to participate.

Ten days after Governor Thompson signed the choice bill, its opponents, urged on by Superintendent Grover and joined by the local chapter of the NAACP, filed papers in the Wisconsin Supreme Court to obtain a permanent injunction against the program, arguing that it involved an inappropriate use of public education dollars. Their request was turned down, but the quick ruling by Wisconsin's highest court marked only the beginning of a long and tortuous legal battle. A two-year contest ensued in the lower courts. While choice advocates prevailed in the first of several cases to be argued,[77] the litigation cast a dark cloud over the program and caused anxiety among parents who were considering moving their children out of public school.

Throughout its first two years of operation, the new program existed in a legal limbo. The program was only in its second year of operation, and the country in the midst of a heated presidential race between George Bush and Bill Clinton, when the Carnegie Foundation issued its highly publicized indictment against school choice. The report featured a critique of the Milwaukee program, which, it found, "failed to demonstrate that vouchers can, in and of themselves, spark school improvement."[78]

In 1993 the Landmark Legal Foundation brought a suit in federal court claiming that the exclusion of parochial schools from eligibility violated the Free Exercise clause of the First Amendment and the Equal Protection clause of the Fourteenth Amendment. A federal district court, focusing on a provision in the program that made tuition payments directly to the schools rather than reimbursing parents for their expenses, rejected the plea to extend participation to religious schools.[79] Shortly after the federal decision, Governor Thompson signed an amended version of the choice law.[80] It provided that the number of scholarships be increased, that vouchers be issued in the names of parents, and that religious schools be deemed eligible for participation.

The amendments led to another round of litigation in the state courts. This time choice opponents were joined in their challenge by the American Civil Liberties Union and People for the American Way, organizations with a long history of separationist leanings on the church-state issue. Here they were arguing their case on both federal and state constitutional grounds in order to exclude parochial schools from eligibility. We will deal with the legal issues surrounding the Milwaukee choice program more explicitly in later chapters.

In August 1995, the Wisconsin Supreme Court issued an order enjoining the state from implementing that part of the program allowing parents to use a voucher to send their children to religious schools.[81] This injunction stood in place for three years while the case worked its way up to the state supreme court, foreclosing any possibility that sectarian schools could participate in the program. The ruling was a severe blow to many black and Hispanic parents who had been planning to transfer their children to religious schools. As Joanne Curran, a divorced mother of four who had intended to send her daughter to All Saints Catholic Elementary School exclaimed:

> When I heard about the ruling last week I thought, "I'm not sending her to public school; I'd rather go to jail." . . . I don't think they're teaching the kids in the public schools. . . . I don't think there's enough discipline, and I want religion in the school. I want to stay here no matter what it takes.[82]

Ms. Curran had spoken for many poor parents who saw the church-state debate as a middle-class issue that was irrelevant to the concerns and problems of their community and that, in fact, further complicated their already difficult lives. Within a week after the fateful decision, the Lynde & Harry Bradley Foundation of Milwaukee announced that it would provide an $800,000 gift and $200,000 in matching money for a $1.4 million fund-raising drive to underwrite the costs for twenty-three hundred students who had intended to remain in religious schools while the case worked its way through the courts. Bradley and its president, Michael Joyce, had been major supporters of the PAVE program, the private initiative begun in Milwaukee in 1991. By this time, however, many religious schools had already begun to suffer from the exclusionary policy that had been in effect for several years.

Proponents of school reform suffered another setback in 1995, when the Milwaukee Teachers Education Association launched a major campaign to elect a new majority to the nine-person school board. Four out of five of the candidates the union supported were elected on an "antiprivatization" platform. Their target was Superintendent Howard Fuller, who was accused of selling out to downtown business interests in a plot to destroy the public schools. While Fuller had kept his promise to remain silent on vouchers, he had announced plans to close failing schools, to create charter schools that were outside the jurisdiction of the school district, and to engage private companies to run institutions under contract with the school district. As he explains it, the latter proposal "put the privatization word on my head in bright red letters."[83]

Fuller resigned, stating that he could not hope to bring about the transformation of the system while being uncertain about the depth of the support he had on the board.[84] His resignation allowed him to become a more
vocal advocate for vouchers, which he has done.

One of the first casualties of the restrictions against religious institutions was Juanita Virgil Academy, a school that focused on African and
African American cultures and that offered religious instruction as a part
of its curriculum. When the court order first came down, Juanita Virgil
decided to remove religion from its curriculum to qualify for eligibility,
causing many parents to transfer their children out. The school, which
had already been experiencing financial and enrollment difficulties, was
eventually forced to close its doors.

Another notable experience occurred at Messmer High School.[85]
Messmer had been part of the Catholic archdiocesan system of schools
until 1984, when the archdiocese decided that it could no longer afford to
keep the school open. The school was saved by a generous grant from the
DeRance Foundation, allowing Messmer to remain in operation as an
independent private school, no longer part of the archdiocesan network.
Its principal, Brother Bob Smith, was a former parole officer who had
distinguished Messmer as a school that worked successfully with at-risk
youths, most of whom were black and not Catholic. Brother Bob, a Capu-
chin monk, and two nuns who taught math were the only members of the
forty-four-member staff affiliated with religious orders.

Although Messmer continued to offer theology courses—from which
students could opt out—as part of its standard curriculum, Brother Bob
insisted that Messmer was "nonsectarian." After the principal submitted
an application to participate in the choice program, Superintendent Grover
launched an investigation to determine Messmer's eligibility. In an inquiry
that took place in a conference room at a local motel, one of Grover's depu-
ties pointedly queried Brother Bob concerning his accountability to the
authorities in Rome. In the end the committee had determined that Messmer
was too enmeshed with religion, and the school's application was denied.

Whether or not Messmer should have been allowed to participate in
the program based on the nonsectarian standards set by the state is debat-
able.[86] What remains absolutely sure is how the policy of excluding religious institutions from the program served to minimize choice for those
children who were looking for alternatives to the failing public schools of
Milwaukee. In 1995 more than a hundred nonpublic schools existed in
the city, ready to offer sixty-two hundred additional seats for participants

in the choice program. Nearly 90 percent of these private institutions were religious schools.

As a result of the court's restrictive injunction, only thirteen schools opened their doors to the choice students. In 1990, 84 percent of the pupils participating in the choice program were in four schools.[87] One was Juanita Virgil Academy, which eventually closed. The other three were Urban Day, Harambee, and Bruce Guadalupe. All focused on minority cultures and catered to poor communities. Grover had publicly derided these institutions as "souped up day care," even though several had been around for decades.[88] It was unreasonable to expect these schools to function with a lower ceiling of per capita funding than that given to public schools, especially since a disproportionate share of their clientele consisted of students who were not doing well in public schools.[89]

In 1990 Superintendent Grover appointed Professor John Witte, a political scientist at the University of Wisconsin, to conduct the state's official evaluation of the program. Witte's selection by one of the program's major opponents immediately cast a cloud of suspicion over the entire evaluation process. While both proponents and opponents of choice seemed, for different reasons, to gravitate toward his negative findings, Witte's overall assessment of the program was more positive than negative.[90] Witte found that the program provides alternative educational opportunities to families that would otherwise not be able to afford it. Witte found that, as configured, the program posed little harm to the Milwaukee public school system, either in terms of a substantial loss of students or the "creaming" of better students. Witte found higher levels of parental satisfaction within choice schools than in public schools. Witte found that choice schools provide opportunities for high levels of parental involvement in their children's education. However, on the bottom line question of student achievement, Witte found that choice students "perform approximately the same as MPS students."[91]

Even the last of Witte's conclusions is not particularly negative when one considers that choice schools operated with considerably less funding than public schools, a factor that Witte failed to note in his report. However, this final conclusion would become a source of raging discord within the research community, and many political opponents of choice zeroed in on it as evidence that choice does not work to improve the academic performance of poor children. Some of the controversy around Witte stemmed from the fact that he refused to make data available to other researchers when he performed his annual surveys. This allowed him to dominate the discussion on the most important experiment that had ever been conducted on the topic and to exclude the participation of other interested scholars for nearly four years. His first-year report provided a great deal of ammunition to the Carnegie Foundation when the prestigious organization issued its discouraging assessment of school choice.

One researcher who had unsuccessfully sought to acquire access to the data was Professor Paul Peterson of Harvard. It is difficult to recall any debate within the academic community that ever reached such a high level of personal animosity as the feud between Witte and Peterson.[92] When the dust settled, however, and Peterson eventually was able to reanalyze the data for himself, he raised a significant methodological point about the Witte reports that shifted the course of the discussion. Witte had compared students in choice schools to a randomly selected control group of students in the Milwaukee public schools. The available data had shown that these were different populations with regard to such crucial variables as race, income, family structure, and prior educational achievement. For example, 72 percent of the choice students were black, compared to 55 percent of the MPS control group; 20 percent of the choice students were Latino, compared to 10 percent of the MPS control group. In the first year of the program, only 23 percent of the choice students scored above the national average on reading and 31 percent in math, compared to 35 percent and 43 percent, respectively, in the MPS. Choice students reported family incomes of about half the average Milwaukee public school family. Only 24 percent of the choice students came from two-parent households, compared to 51 percent of the public school students; 57 percent were on public assistance, compared to 39 percent.[93]

Those parents who decided to enter the choice lottery were among the poorest of the poor whose children had been the most desperately ill prepared among students who attended public school in Milwaukee. To overcome the apples and oranges comparison that he discovered in Witte's report, Peterson compared the test scores of choice students with a control group of students who entered the lottery but who lost and had to stay in public schools. His results proved to be quite different. Peterson and his colleagues found that students who had participated in the program for four years scored 5 percentage points higher than their public school peers in reading, 12 percentage points higher in math.[94]

Declaring the Milwaukee experiment a success, Peterson soon became a target of choice opponents. His analysis and professional credibility were called into question by the National Education Association, the American

Federation of Teachers, and even U.S. Secretary of Education Richard Riley.[95]

In December 1996, Princeton economist Cecilia Rouse conducted a third analysis of the Milwaukee data to find that participation in the choice program had a significant positive effect on math achievement, but no benefit with regard to reading scores.[96] A month later, Witte wrote a paper in which he, as did Peterson and Rouse, compared choice students and "rejects" who did not get into the program. Here he also found that choice students did better in math after four years in the program but continued to insist that the comparison was "specious."[97] He and others have criticized Peterson's study for failing to account for attrition among choice students, which eliminated many of the lowest performers from the comparison.[98]

In June 1998, the Wisconsin Supreme Court overturned two lower court decisions and upheld the legality of the choice program that had stood in suspended animation for three years.[99] It ruled that providing tuition assistance for children to attend private and parochial schools is permissible under both the state and federal constitutions. The decision was immediately appealed to the U.S. Supreme Court, which refused to hear the case and let the decision stand. With the legal obstacles finally removed, that September sixty-two hundred students attended eighty-seven private schools—mostly religious—under the auspices of the Milwaukee choice plan. Choice had come a long way since 1990, when three hundred and fifty choice students attended seven nonsectarian private schools under the terms of the initial program.

The resolution of the legal question only set the stage for the next level of political and regulatory conflict to surround the controversial choice program. Opponents, including the state superintendent of public instruction, pledged to keep a close regulatory eye on its implementation, while supporters speculated that the power of the education bureaucracy would be used to burden and undermine its operation. A month after the U.S. Supreme Court denied certiorari, a coalition consisting of People for the American Way, the local NAACP, the ACLU, and the Milwaukee Teachers Union staged a rally where they announced an action plan designed to "stop the draining of funds from Milwaukee public schools" and to "toughen standards on voucher schools."[100] The rally's organizers pledged to ensure that private and religious schools participating in the choice program "are held to the same high standards of accountability and public reporting as the public schools."

The key speaker at the antichoice event was Congressman Jesse Jackson Jr., from Illinois, who told an audience of four hundred: "The crowd that lost the Civil War is now running the federal government, the government that they want to downsize, privatize, and shrink."[101] Carol Shields, president of People for the American Way, asserted that choice schools pick and choose children who are easiest to teach. The meeting ended with a plan to propose new regulations on nonpublic schools that were accepting choice scholarships.

On the other side of town, another rally was taking place at the same time. It was organized by supporters of school choice, attended mostly by parents whose children were enrolled in the controversial program. Its key speaker was Milwaukee's former superintendent of schools, Howard Fuller, who explained to the crowd of five hundred that the ability to exit public schools and take money with them has given parents a new-found power. He vowed, "We don't intend to move backward." A week after that, the University of Wisconsin at Milwaukee released the results of a poll indicating that 60 percent of those asked statewide said they favored the implementation of either a tax credit or voucher programs. It was an 11 percent increase over a similar poll that had been taken a year before.[102]

Cleveland

The Milwaukee story would be retold in slightly modified fashion in the city of Cleveland. In March 1998 U.S. District Court Judge George W. White put an end to a twenty-five-year legal battle over desegregation when he declared "the purposes of this desegregation litigation have been fully achieved."[103] The same court had terminated forced busing two years earlier, but the more recent decision let stand a prior agreement with plaintiffs that required the state to invest $40 million annually through the year 2000 for programs designed to overcome the harmful effects of racial segregation. If there were any question as to how minority students were doing in the troubled school district, it became clarified in another statement by Judge White, who explained that the persistent gap in performance between black and white students "is the result of socioeconomic status and factors directly related to it, not race."[104] That statement could provide the impression that all is well in the Cleveland public schools, if it were not for the effects of poverty that children brought into the classroom. The opinion of the court seemed to suggest that Cleveland's educational problems are a function of demographics that are resolvable, at least to some extent, by investing more money in the public schools. These impressions are not entirely supported by the facts.

There are 75,500 students in the Cleveland school district, of which 70 percent are black and 7 percent are Hispanic. The district spends $6,195 per student, 16 percent above the state average in Ohio. Its dropout rate is twice the state average; in 1994 only 9 percent of its ninth graders passed a state proficiency exam, compared to 55 percent in all of Ohio.[105] In 1995 a federal judge overseeing the desegregation case found the overall management of the district to be so inept that he ordered the state superintendent of education to take it over. It was during the same year that the Ohio legislature passed a law that would allow children in Cleveland to attend nonpublic schools at public expense.[106]

As in Milwaukee, the demand for school choice in Cleveland erupted in the black community, this time led by Fannie Lewis, a member of the Cleveland City Council, who represented the low-income community of Hough. Describing the despair that had overtaken her community, Lewis exclaimed, "The people in this neighborhood have been without hope for years. . . . This will give them hope."[107] Lewis was joined in her efforts by Akron industrialist David Brennan, a powerful advocate for school reform and a close political ally of the governor, who would invest his own money to open two new private schools in the central city. Lewis and Brennan found a willing ally and advocate in Republican Governor George Voinovich, a former Cleveland mayor who had originally proposed a choice bill to the legislature that would have set up programs in eight urban districts. The Cleveland bill that he signed in 1995 was a compromise.

Opponents of the law, led by the Ohio Federation of Teachers, argued that choice would divert much needed funding from the public schools, which at the time were suffering from a $90 million budget shortfall. Union president Ron Merec argued, "It allows [some of] them to escape the problem, but it doesn't solve the problem for 70,000 other kids."[108] There was also opposition from several black legislators, such as C. J. Prentice, who feared that the voucher plan would take the best students from the Cleveland public schools. But there was strong support for the plan from many parents. Parents, frustrated with the chronic failure of the public schools, no longer wanted to wait while the system tried to fix itself. As one parent explained, "I don't have time for the schools to get themselves together. I want my child to have the best opportunity, and it starts with education."[109] By 1996 eighteen hundred students would be given new opportunities in the form of tuition scholarships. Enrollment expanded to three thousand in the second year of the program.

Under the Cleveland plan, scholarships were awarded by lottery. However, the drawing was set up to favor low-income families. Of the 6,244 students who applied, 58 percent reported incomes below the poverty line.[110] Students who did not participate in the choice program were eligible for a special tutorial grant that was made available to low-performing students in the city school district. The amount of the scholarship made available to choice students varied by income. Students whose family income was at or below 200 percent of the federal poverty level could receive funding for 90 percent of tuition costs up to $2,250. Students with family incomes above that amount were eligible to receive $1,875, or 75 percent, of the total tuition costs, whichever was less. Even at the higher level, the amount of the scholarship was equivalent to about one-third of the per capita total spent on public school students in Cleveland.

From the outset of the program, students were permitted to use their scholarships to attend either a nonsectarian or religious school located within the city boundaries. All participating institutions had to meet state minimum standards for chartered nonpublic schools that had been put into effect in 1992. Students could also use their scholarships to attend public schools in adjacent suburban school districts that volunteered to participate in the program; however, none of these neighboring districts wanted any involvement. Approximately fifty-five private and parochial schools in the city did express interest and welcomed the two thousand scholarship winners into their classrooms.

Before the choice program even got off the ground, the Ohio Federation of Teachers and the American Civil Liberties Union initiated a lawsuit in state court claiming that the participation of religious schools violated both the federal and state constitutions. While in July 1996 a trial court upheld the program's legality,[111] a subsequent ruling handed down by a unanimous appellate court the following May found that the participation of sectarian schools violated both federal and state standards.[112] As choice supporters began proceedings to appeal the decision to the state's highest court, the state attorney general granted a stay that allowed the program to continue until a final decision was handed down. We will return to these judicial contests in a subsequent chapter. Here we will focus on the persistent question of how students who took advantage of the program performed in the new schools.

The evaluation of the Cleveland program was not without controversy, but it never reached the high level of personal acrimony that accompanied the Milwaukee assessment. Once again a key figure in the research was Professor Paul Peterson of Harvard. Initially, Peterson and his team undertook two kinds of reviews. First, they conducted parental interviews: a total of 1,014 with scholarship winners and 1,006 with applicants who applied for but did not win scholarships.[113] This accounted for 32.4 percent of all applicants. The two populations were demographically similar. Although the average family income of scholarship recipients from public schools was less than that of nonrecipients from public schools, they did not differ measurably in race, their mother's education or employment status, family size, family structure, or religious affiliation. Scholarship recipients were somewhat less likely to have been previously involved in either special education or gifted programs.

The survey showed that among the scholarship recipients from public schools, 79 percent of the parents were "very satisfied" with the educational experience that their children had in private schools; only 25 percent of the nonrecipients whose children remained in public schools expressed that they were "very satisfied" with their children's educational experience. On the issue of school safety, 60 percent of the recipients were satisfied, compared to 25 percent of the nonrecipients. When scholarship recipients were asked why they had applied to the program, the two leading reasons given were improving the academic quality of their child's education (85 percent) and greater safety (79 percent). A significant number of participants (37 percent) also were attracted to the religious component of the curricula in parochial schools. Once again, poor people participating in a choice program gave substantive explanations for why they exercised the exit option, showing themselves to be intelligent shoppers when it came to accommodating their educational priorities.

Peterson and his colleagues also conducted an in-depth investigation of student achievement in two new private schools that had been created to accommodate students in the choice program.[114] Hope Academy and Hope Ohio City were the brainchild of philanthropist David Brennan. The new nonprofit, nonsectarian private institutions served 15 percent of all students participating in the program, as well as 25 percent of those coming from public schools in grades one through three. During the 1996–97 school year, the program's first year of operation, students tested on the nationally normed examination gained an average of 5 percentile points in reading and 15 percentile points in math. These improvements were recorded in all grades. Scores declined by 5 percentile points in language skills. The latter was a function of a 19-point drop among first graders, with second and third graders improving by 3 points and 13 points, respectively.

Shortly after Peterson's team completed its work, another study was performed by Professor Kim Metcalf from the School of Education at Indiana University, who had been retained by the Ohio Department of Education to evaluate the program.[115] Comparing test scores of ninety-four third graders from choice schools with a sample from public schools, the Indiana researcher and his graduate students found no improvements among the scholarship students. Peterson and his colleagues responded to the Indiana study with a methodological critique.[116] They criticized the report for focusing on just a single grade and claimed that baseline data from the second grade lacked plausibility, that the assessment had not properly controlled for demographic variables, and that the comparison group of public school students was not representative of the public school population. They pointed out that the Indiana University evaluation did not include any students who attended the two new Hope Schools, which served 25 percent of all the scholarship students.

When Peterson and his team reanalyzed the data from the Indiana study, they found that scholarship students scored 4.1 points higher in language, 4.5 points higher in science, 2.5 points higher in reading, 2.5 points higher in social studies, and 0.6 point higher in math.[117] The Indiana group retorted that the Peterson study was flawed and insisted that no definitive conclusions could be reached regarding student outcomes after only one year of the program.

In November 1998 the Indiana team released the results of a second evaluation study.[118] This one, drawing on a second year of experience, showed mixed results. It found that students who used vouchers to attend established private schools in Cleveland performed slightly better than their public school peers in language skills and science, but did about the same in reading, math, and social studies. The more startling discovery in the report concerned the two Hope academies. Metcalf's team found that students attending these two schools performed worse in all subject areas tested than either the Cleveland public school students or choice students attending other, more established private schools.

It is difficult to put much stock in either Peterson's or Metcalf's achievement studies. Neither worked with a scientifically selected control group. Moreover, the two-year experience on which their studies were based is too limited to lead to any compelling conclusions on student performance. Peterson's data on parental attitudes are more persuasive as a true barometer of client assessment, and they fall very much in line with parental opinions on other choice programs that have been examined.

Lessons to Be Learned

What can policymakers learn from the various private and public experiments that have been implemented thus far in cities throughout the country? Several lessons seem to be very clear. The first, foretold by public opinion polls cited in the first chapter, is that poor people want alternatives to the usual array of public schools that are made available to their children in urban areas. When provided with new options in the form of private and religious schools, they oversubscribe in a magnitude that far exceeds the number of openings that are made available to them. Overall, these parents are attracted to the superior academic programs and safer environments that they believe these schools offer; and after their children attend these schools, they are generally pleased with the experience their children have had. These results parallel the findings on charter schools recounted in the last chapter. Parents whose children have been given the opportunity to attend religious schools as a result of private or public choice programs have identified an additional benefit. They find the religious aspect of the curriculum and the values fostered by these institutions to be a positive aspect of their child's education that cannot be obtained in public schools.

Another lesson derived from these experiments—although on somewhat more ambiguous evidence—is that, as a group, minority and poor children who do not perform well in public schools do better academically when they have an opportunity to attend private and parochial schools. This finding confirms the conclusions reached by Coleman and others more than a decade before choice programs began to appear across the broad landscape of American education. Whether choice functions to the benefit of the most disadvantaged depends on a variety of factors, not the least of which is the very design of the programs that policymakers conceive. A key consideration is whether programs are specifically structured to target poor families, which can be done by setting income criteria for eligibility, by providing adequate funding to pay for the entire cost of private school tuition, by offering a sufficient number of scholarships to accommodate every poor child whose family wants one, and by allowing parents who desire it to select a sectarian school that reflects their individual values. The last point may not be so apparent as the others from the evidence that has been presented thus far, but it will be fully explicated in the next chapter.

Those poor parents who take advantage of choice programs tend to be better educated than those who do not. However, whether providing greater educational opportunities to poor people who find themselves in a more preferable social position than the most disadvantaged members of society can be reasonably classified as "skimming," is highly contestable from a number of perspectives. The term itself is distasteful because it connotes that some people or their children are inherently inferior to others. Anyone who begins the discussion with that premise cannot be expected to either fully comprehend the complexity of human equality or address the devastating problem of educational inequality. Notwithstanding the economic and social disadvantages that may afflict inner-city populations, the problem of educational opportunity has more to do with the quality of schooling that is made available to poor people than with the personal attributes of the people themselves. This should be evident by now from the research conducted by Coleman, Greeley, Bryk, Lee, and Holland; Chubb and Moe; and, more recently, Peterson. While social scientists debate the validity of those studies, poor parents who are allowed to exercise choice consistently tell us that their children are better off for it. Policymakers, however, armed with the skepticism offered by researchers, continue to withhold choice as if they were protecting some public good.

The perceived danger that critics of choice describe as a "skimming" problem rests on an assumption that many poor people will remain left behind in failing public schools when others are allowed to choose. Even if that assumption were true, it would mean that more children had an opportunity to receive a decent education than is currently the case. It remains, however, a gravely cynical assumption. It accepts the premise that under a system of choice, failing institutions would be allowed to persist much as they do now. Proponents of choice, those who have confidence in the power of the market, would argue that if real competition were present, failing institutions would be forced to close, and even children of the most unmotivated and uninformed parents would not find themselves in a failing school. Further, they would argue, the empowerment of poor people to vote with their feet would actually result in the growth and expansion of new educational institutions designed to meet their specific needs. As of yet we have no firm data to either confirm or reject these assertions. There is some encouraging evidence on the effect of competition from the interdistrict choice program in Minnesota, as well as from the extensive networks of charter schools in Arizona and California. But it is inconclusive. Economists such as Carolyn Hoxby have developed econometric models that support the Friedman thesis: that the competition engendered by choice would provide incentives for the improvement of public education and the expansion of educational opportunities.[119] But these models, as sophisticated and persuasive as they might be, are based on theoretical assumptions that are grounded in a limited range of experience. I say this not to be critical of the work done by these economists but to comment on the current state of experimental research in the area of school choice.

What must be kept in mind when assessing the wide array of programs that have been implemented thus far is that they are yet mere experiments operated under an artificial set of circumstances, most often under severe constraints. While the generosity that has accompanied private initiatives is indeed commendable, it cannot make up for the lack of government funding that might allow these programs to flourish if students attending failing public schools were given a full scholarship. Although public support for school choice appears to be growing among Americans, the present political climate remains prohibitive. Even when the political process concedes some ground on the issue, it does so begrudgingly so that innovative programs are set up to fail. The circumstances that prevail are part of the political bargain that has been struck as the price for allowing experimentation.

One reason it is difficult to assess the full effect of competition is that public policy has been designed to ensure that true competition does not actually occur. Not only are traditional public schools held financially harmless under choice schemes, but the number of nontraditional alternatives made available to parents is too minuscule to function as a mechanism for real competition. We have witnessed this phenomenon with charter schools, where opponents have guaranteed that relatively few of these innovative institutions are allowed to enter the educational marketplace; and the situation with private school choice is even more constrained. Is it fair to expect the Hope Academy in Cleveland to compete with the public school down the block that receives three times the per capita allocation of funds from government? Can thirteen small private institutions in Milwaukee be expected to exert competitive pressure on the public schools in a district where such a large portion of the one-hundred thousand students are inadequately served? Are we likely to see many new private institutions open their doors if they are provided with just a fraction of the financial support given to regular public schools? Yes, we have implemented some interesting experiments around the concept of school choice, but be reminded: Americans have not yet fully tried it. This will change, at least in an experimental sense, when the program envisioned by CEO America for the Edgewood School District in San Antonio is finally implemented.

Even if the Edgewood program demonstrates beyond a reasonable doubt that choice can improve the quality of public education and enhance educational opportunity for the least advantaged members of society—as might be expected from the econometric models that Hoxby and others have developed—it remains to be seen how the political system will respond.[120] Another enduring obstacle that has complicated the implementation of school choice programs in places like Wisconsin and Ohio is legal in nature.

Opponents of school choice continue to argue that, notwithstanding its merits as a vehicle for fulfilling the promise of educational equality articulated in *Brown*, the expenditure of public funds for students to attend religious schools violates federal and state constitutional law. If this were true, it would significantly limit the range of choices available to parents; it would foreclose the participation of a large number of institutions that have a demonstrated capacity to reduce the influence of social deprivation on academic achievement. Even though the legal arguments may not be legitimate, they have been used successfully to confound and impede choice as we await the final determination of these questions by the federal and state courts.

CHAPTER FIVE

Equality as Religious Freedom

IT IS NOT INCIDENTAL to the choice debate that many poor parents are attracted to parochial schools by the religious content of their curricula. Up until this point in the book we have viewed educational opportunity in a minimalist way, measured in terms of safe, decent schools that effectively deliver instruction in basic skills such as reading, writing, and math. Because public schools have failed to provide most low-income children with even this morsel of opportunity, the idea of factoring value-based considerations into the calculus of educational equality may appear lofty. But if the societal objective is to give all parents an opportunity to choose a school that is most appropriate for their child, then such considerations are germane to the discussion. Middle-class parents make value-driven choices as a matter of course. Families with strong religious convictions select sectarian schools when they want their children educated in an instructional environment that reinforces values taught in the home. Why shouldn't poor parents enjoy the same prerogative?

The quick and easy answer to this question is that poor people do have a right to send their children to religious schools. They just cannot expect the state to pay for the costs, because to do so would violate constitutional principles that require the separation of church and state. But, in fact, the First Amendment does not require complete "separation." A literal reading of the text indicates that the Constitution imposes two requirements: first, it prohibits the government from setting up a state-established church;

second, it assures that every individual has the right to practice religion freely without interference from public authority.[1] The language of separation is something constitutional scholars commonly attribute to the writing of Thomas Jefferson, who happened to be out of the country when the Bill of Rights was drafted. His famous metaphor has acquired such a hallowed place in constitutional discourse, that one could be led to believe that the words erupted from the document itself. Unfortunately, the phrase has been a source of enormous confusion, and it has so distorted the choice debate that it requires a good deal of explaining.

First Principles

Our Constitution is a living document, a plan for governing a free people that has been adapted to changing circumstances for more than two centuries. But if the Constitution is to serve as a "text for civic instruction" on how to resolve contemporary political quarrels, it must be understood as a source of enduring universal principals. With hope of acquiring that understanding, scholars and judges have habitually returned to the writings of the Founders, only to find that the original architects of our democratic experiment were not entirely in accord.

Jefferson's Metaphor

The phrase "wall of separation" is attributed first to Roger Williams, who fled Congregationalist Massachusetts in 1636 to set up Providence as a place that would allow complete freedom of worship. Williams's new settlement was one of the few in colonial America that did not have an established church supported by public taxes. The primary motivation behind his separationist admonitions was to protect the church against the taint of civil authority, or, as Mark DeWolfe Howe explains, to insulate the "garden" of the church from the "wilderness" of worldly corruption.[2] Jefferson's agenda was notably different when, as president, he wrote his celebrated letter to the Danbury Baptist Association refusing to honor a tradition begun by George Washington and John Adams that declared a national day of fasting and thanksgiving. A close reading of the document is instructive not only as an exposition of Jefferson's commitment to religious freedom but also for his understanding of its limits, or more specifically, the proper balance between public and ecclesiastic authority.[3] Here lies the difference between Williams's wall and Jefferson's. As two distinguished historians of the period explain:

Williams was libertarian because he condemned the world, and he wanted to separate church and state so that the church would not be contaminated by the state. Thomas Jefferson loved the world and was dubious about the spirit, and he sought to separate church and state so that the state would not be contaminated by the church.[4]

The state envisioned by Jefferson would protect religious beliefs, professions, and arguments, but individual conduct would be subject to public authority.[5] Jefferson's perspective was very much aligned with the political writings that had emerged from the European Enlightenment. He, as most political thinkers in America at the time, was profoundly influenced by the English philosopher John Locke.[6] The essence of Locke's approach to religion was an appreciation of two contending universes, a City of God and a City of Man, each entitled their due. In one world, individuals were motivated by conscience and a belief system that was the consequence of divine inspiration; in the other, norms for behavior were established through the rational application of human intelligence in the governmental process. Owing to the diversity of faiths in a free society, conscience was deemed a potentially divisive force, if not saved by the authority of government enforcing civil order. Locke's liberalism, therefore, entitled individuals to freedom of thought and conscience, but government would set the boundaries of permissible action.[7] Many of Locke's contemporaries during the Enlightenment—such as Montesquieu, Blackstone, Hume, and Adam Smith—supported the establishment of Henry VIII's church because they believed that the secular influence of public authority would moderate the dogmatism of the clergy.[8] Under the guise of religious freedom, the government could tolerate the existence of Catholics and more fervent Protestant sects, while putting them at a political disadvantage to the one true Anglican church.

Jefferson was more separationist than Locke. Locke had supported the idea of an established church in England; Jefferson opposed any form of establishment, singular or multiple, even though the latter type of arrangement was common in eighteenth-century America. Jefferson insisted on a public domain that was decidedly secular. The citizen might be a churchgoer in private life but was expected to leave those beliefs at the door when entering the halls of government. A true son of the Enlightenment, Jefferson was enamored with the power of the human intellect, which he believed could liberate men from religious tradition and the power of the church to cultivate a more rational civic life.[9] For Jefferson, requiring that religious conviction be separated from political deliberation was what made liberal democracy possible.[10] Whether one could forsake deep-seated theological convictions when considering important political and moral issues is highly contestable from an ethical perspective, but Mr. Jefferson would require it.

I do not mean to suggest that the prolific statesman was entirely consistent in his thinking on religion. Between 1776 and 1786, he had drafted a number of bills for the Virginia legislature that were far more accommodationist than his other writing would lead one to expect.[11] Ambivalent about his own faith, at various times he referred to himself as a deist, a theist, a Unitarian, and a rational Christian.[12] This is the same Mr. Jefferson, you will recall, who summoned the deity as a witness to human equality when drafting the Declaration of Independence. As explained earlier, Jefferson's notion of political equality proved to be circumscribed when considered in a larger social context. So, too, would be his ideal of religious freedom. As with his egalitarianism, the limitations imposed by Jefferson's notion of religious liberty become more apparent when we apply it to contemporary issues. The choice debate is an exquisite case in point.

Just as providing a poor person with the same political rights as a wealthy person in no way assures the former that he will enjoy the same political influence as the latter, telling a poor mother that she may choose to send her child to a private or religious school on her own accord does not give her a real choice at all if she does not have the means to support it. On a practical level, those families who are economically disadvantaged do not enjoy the prerogative to have their children educated in a way that supports their particular view of the world. When confronted with a situation where the public school their child is forced to attend conveys values that are insensitive or hostile to their moral or religious convictions, the poor parent's dilemma is even graver.

I am reminded of a situation in New York City several years ago when the board of education decided that, as part of its sex education program, every student in public school should be taught how to use a condom, even though the practice violated the religious beliefs of several groups, including Catholics, Orthodox Jews, and Muslims. For a period of time, families who were offended by the practice were not given a chance to opt out of the program. These parents had but two choices: either allow their children to participate in a program that undermined deep-seated religious convictions, or, if they were fortunate enough to be able to afford it, leave the public school to attend a private or religious institution where the curriculum was more compatible with their own values. If the parents could not afford to pay for tuition, then they had no choice at all. These parents, of course, were free to entertain any religious beliefs that they had; but in the end their free exercise rights, their ability to follow the dictates of conscience, was burdened by public policymakers who felt that their political and social agenda must take precedence over the concerns of a religious minority.

I do not question the merit of a practice that was designed to curb disease and unwanted pregnancies among young people. I am troubled by the actions of policymakers who would impose their practices on religious believers in so insensitive a way when alternative measures were available, especially when such actions begin to raise serious constitutional concern for those affected.

One is led to wonder in situations such as the episode in New York whether the principle of separation was, as Roger Williams insisted, designed to protect individuals from the state or, as Jefferson might intimate, the wall was built to preserve the prerogatives of the polity. Certainly the former interpretation is more consistent with the concept of constitutionalism and its common usage in political and legal theory.[13] The architects of liberal democratic systems write constitutions to limit the authority of government and to protect individuals from the excessive use of public power. The latter interpretation becomes conceivable, nevertheless, when one appreciates the suspicion with which religious beliefs are treated within the liberal tradition—as irrational, as otherworldly, as a form of superstition, as a divisive force within society that could compromise a citizen's loyalty to the state.[14]

European liberalism played an important role in the crafting of American democracy. The American constitutional tradition must be perceived, however, in a larger context; and there is no better medium for that broader understanding than the writing of another gentleman from Virginia, James Madison.

Madison's Political Pluralism

Sometimes it appeared as though Madison was of two minds on the church-state issue. Years after leaving the presidency he wrote the often quoted "Detached Memoranda."[15] In it he criticized the payment of military chaplains with public funds and the celebration of Thanksgiving at the White House as practices that fed the erroneous implication of a national religion. When he was the nation's chief executive, Madison approved payment for the same chaplains, and it was he who reinstituted the Thanksgiving Day proclamation that had been temporarily interrupted by his predecessor, Thomas Jefferson. Much earlier in his career, as a member of the Virginia General Assembly, Madison endorsed religious celebrations for Thanksgiving, and he is said even to have supported a bill that would have punished Sabbath breakers.[16] Perhaps there was a philosophical difference between the elder Madison and the younger man who served as the principal author of the American Constitution and whose writings in the *Federalist Papers* have furnished us with the most illuminating insights on our philosophical and legal heritage.

A closer reading of the *Memoranda*, however, reveals its fidelity to an important theme that was evident throughout Madison's earlier work. Madison was concerned that a majoritarian consensus built around a certain notion of Christianity would serve to undermine the equality of lesser sects and that the power of the state might be used to coerce individuals from following the commands of their own conscience. His warning is worth quoting at length, for it is so central to the principles that undergird American political theory: its striving for equality, its concern for the protection of minorities:

> The establishment of the chaplainship to Congress is a palpable violation of equal rights. . . . The tenets of the chaplains elected (by majority) shut the door of worship against the members whose creeds and consciences forbid participation in that of the majority. To say nothing with other sects, this is the case with that of Roman Catholics and Quakers who have always had members in one or both of the Legislative branches. Could a Catholic clergyman ever hope to be appointed a Chaplain? To say that his religious principles are obnoxious or that his sect is small, is to lift the veil at once and exhibit in its naked deformity the doctrine that religious truth is to be tested by numbers, or that the major sects have a right to govern the minor.

Madison's later reservations about the practices he had endorsed as an officeholder were inspired by a keen awareness of a tendency on the part of his fellow countrymen to favor one faith over another. The same political activists who rebelled against the Church of England during the revolution were often known to hold a narrow view of religious propriety, and this worried Madison. His preoccupation with equality of treatment for minority sects is evident in much of his early writing.

Strict separationists and opponents of school choice are often drawn to the words Madison wrote in his famous "Memorial and Remonstrance."[17] Drafted in opposition to a bill before the Virginia legislature in 1785 that would have allocated state funds to support "Teachers of the Christian Religion," the document is rightly interpreted as a tract against religious establishment and an early appeal for religious equality.

The proposed bill had been put forward by a coalition that included Patrick Henry, George Washington, and John Marshall. This eminent group of patriots was concerned that the disestablishment of the Anglican Church had led to a declining public morality that might weaken the foundation of government. Madison, joined by Thomas Jefferson and George Mason, led the opposition to the bill because he saw it as an attempt to set up a new, loosely assembled form of Christian establishment. Madison argued that each individual must have "equal title to the free exercise of religion according to the dictates of conscience," that public support for religion "violates equality by subjecting some to peculiar burdens," and that "we cannot deny an equal freedom to those whose minds have not yielded to the evidence that has convinced us." Thus we find Madison not only anxious about the treatment of individuals belonging to smaller religious sects, but also appealing for equality between believers and nonbelievers.

As Roger Williams before him, Madison was persuaded that a close institutional connection between government and the church would demean the latter. Madison was also aware of the potential conflict between public authority and individual religious morality. Unlike Jefferson and Locke, who would subordinate the latter to the former, Madison comes out strongly on the side of religious freedom in both thought and action. In the same "Memorial and Remonstrance," he urges:

> Before any man can be considered a member of Civil Society, he must be considered as a subject of the Governor of the Universe: And if a member of Civil Society, who enters into any subordinate Association, must always do it with a reservation of his duty to the general authority; much more must every man who becomes a member of any particular Civil Society, do it with a saving of his allegiance to the Universal Sovereign.[18]

What may first appear as ambivalence in the mind of Madison is more properly understood as signs of a grueling intellectual struggle to reconcile the philosophical leanings of two compatible but distinct intellectual traditions that informed the writing of the Constitution. He too owed a great intellectual debt to the European liberalism of John Locke, but Madison's great achievement was to reconcile the philosophical liberalism of the Enlightenment with the republican tradition of another age. Each tradition had inspired the thinking of those individuals who had attended the Philadelphia Convention, and their respective approaches to organized religion revealed a tension that only the brilliance of a Madison could resolve for distilling an operable theory of government.

Scholars emphasizing the republican strains of early American political thought point to an emphasis by Publius and others of the need for a virtuous citizenry to sustain a democratic government.[19] The virtuous citizen is one who puts the common interest before his or her own. This conception of citizenship has an obvious connection to classical political theory in which public affairs was considered the highest calling, where, among the ancients, religious life was intricately connected to civic life. Unlike the liberals of the Enlightenment, who feared the divisive effect that religion could have on the polity, republicans believed that within the religious congregation, people could develop values such as self-restraint, public-mindedness, deliberation, and consensus—all of which function to bolster good government. It was with this civic goal in mind that Washington and others urged their fellow Virginians to appropriate public funds for the teaching of Christianity. Their objective was governmental, not ecclesiastic. While recognizing the danger that an established religion posed for religious minorities and nonbelievers, Madison was also sympathetic to the republican idea that religion could serve as a positive political and social force. His response to the difficult dilemma presented when religious fervor of the majority might compromise the religious freedom of minorities was not less religion, but more. Madison saw a robust religious pluralism as a sound foundation for the democratic government that he played so paramount a role in constructing.

By now Madison's *Federalist Paper No. 10* has become an axiom of American political theory. The solution to the tyranny of the majority, in the eyes of the Constitution's principal author, is an extended republic that is composed of numerous and diverse factions.[20] A pluralistic political culture composed of many different groups and interests would make it difficult for any one group or interest to dominate. So too with religion. Notwithstanding Madison's famous prescription, less attention has been given to his understanding that religious groups were among the most significant political factions in America, whose proliferation and diversity were needed to promote the political pluralism he envisioned. This insight is apparent in *Federalist Paper No. 52*, where Madison explains:

> In a free government the security of civil rights must be the same for that of religious rights. It consists in one case in the multiplicity of interests, and in the other the multiplicity of sects. The degree of security in both cases will depend on the number of interests and sects.

It was an astute observation for a commentator on America in the eighteenth century. It would prove prophetic as the nation approached a new millennium two hundred years later. When transposed from a political context to the ethical, Madison's pluralism and his passion for equality would be invigorated by the core values of mutual respect, toleration, and liberty.[21] Government was expected to play a neutral role in dealing with people of different persuasions; but religion, in its many forms, would remain at the center of public life. Commenting on Madison's role in the drafting of the Bill of Rights, Harvard theologian and political philosopher Ronald Thiemann explains:

> Madison's argument for the free exercise of religion provides a fundamental justification for a pluralistic society. Madison begins by asserting that human freedom is a gift of a benevolent Creator. Having been created by God, human beings have an obligation to return to the Creator the "homage due him." . . . Because human beings are free, the forms and patterns of worship will inevitably differ; nevertheless even in their differences they stand equal before God. Genuine freedom implies diversity; diversity before God entails equality; and equality demands the toleration of the various forms of human worship.[22]

How might these important principles of government be applied to a contemporary social setting? In what manner does Madison's Constitution require us to balance the power of public authority with individual expectations for religious freedom? Does his formula assist us in resolving ongoing debates about school choice and other issues that divide us regarding the First Amendment? How might his governmental formula be made to operate in a society that has grown increasingly diverse in its religious orientations and yet decidedly more secular in its cultural attitudes?

First of all, a reading of Madison demands that no priority should be given to one religion over another. That requirement is explicit, clear, and straightforward. A more implicit demand that emerges from Madison's writing requires that religion should not be given priority over nonreligion (although this position was not universal among the framers). One should be as free to practice no religion as she is free to practice any religion. Both rules support the egalitarianism inherent in Madisonian political theory. They are quite relevant to our ongoing constitutional quandaries, and their continuing relevance marks the genius of the man who was the chief architect of our government.

But not even Madison could have anticipated the turn that constitutional discourse would take by the end of the twentieth century. He could never have foreseen arguments proposed by modern scholars purporting that nonreligion must be given priority over religion as a way of protecting religious freedom. The argument is a paradox, yet it looms boldly in First Amendment dialogue, especially as it relates to the choice debate. Madison could never have predicted the day when the United States Supreme Court would rule that religious institutions or those individuals who associate with them could not participate in public benefits that are provided by the government on a universal basis. But the High Court has done so on several occasions, and its actions have provided legal precedent for those who would use the Constitution as a tool for restricting religious freedom.

Neither Madison nor the other framers of the Bill of Rights could have imagined a form of legal argument that would juxtapose the Establishment clause against the Free Exercise clause as if the two were not designed to protect the same religious liberty so paramount in their thinking. But such arguments have been treated seriously by the legal establishment, and the consequences have been profound. Nor would the members of the first Congress have anticipated the day when schools supported by the state would apply public authority to alienate children from the religious beliefs of their parents; but these are the compelling issues of our time. Let us now consider how and why we have come so far from our lustrous starting point.

Constitutional Tensions

It is difficult to conceive that anyone familiar with the early history of the American republic could presume that the authors of the Bill of Rights were motivated by the kind of separationist sentiment opponents of school choice commonly associate with the First Amendment. Such sentiment would have been inconsistent with the political culture of eighteenth-century society and was not in any way reflected in the thrust of public policy that emerged from the new government. On the same day that the first Congress of the United States adopted the Bill of Rights, it sent a delegation to President George Washington requesting that he issue a proclamation of public Thanksgiving and prayer to "acknowledge the many signal favors of Almighty God."[23] Washington responded enthusiastically, declaring "It is the duty of all nations to acknowledge the providence of Almighty God, to obey His will, to be grateful for His benefits and humbly to implore His protection and favor."[24]

Washington's Thanksgiving proclamation was in keeping with the general disposition he displayed toward religion as a national political leader. When Washington was commander of the Continental Army, it was he who had petitioned Congress to authorize the appointment of military chaplains, and General Washington actually required church attendance by his soldiers. In 1777, at Washington's urging, Congress approved the purchase of twenty thousand Bibles for use among military personnel.[25] Washington himself was not a particularly religious man, nor, as president, was he intent on promoting a new establishment in America. The "father of our country" was thoroughly persuaded, however, by the republican notion of the religious congregation as an incubator for civic virtue that could serve as a foundation for democratic government. Washington's Farewell Address to the nation at the end of his second term is probably one of the strongest statements to appear in American history to make that very point:

> Of all the dispositions and habits which lead to political prosperity, religion and morality are indispensable supports. . . . Whatever may be conceded to the influence of fine education on minds of peculiar stature, reason and experience both forbid us to expect that national morality can prevail in exclusion of religious principle.[26]

Religion played a vital part in every aspect of American society at the Founding, and for this reason must be understood as a key element of the civic culture that produced our system of government.[27] Family life itself was inseparable from both the religious congregation and the political community, which in most cases were one. Births, marriages, and deaths were all recorded in the family Bible; nuptial and divorce laws were derived from church or canon law. When education was not administered in the home, it was ordinarily given over to the local pastor, whose instructional and ministerial services were paid for with local taxes.[28] As late as 1833, Tocqueville would observe that in America, "almost all education is entrusted to the clergy."[29] Before independence, the various colonies had developed several forms of establishment arrangements.[30] These ranged from a rigid emulation of the English model through local option and multiple establishment schemes. The distinct compromises reached were a product of each colony's unique historical circumstances. Separation from the Crown brought a strong reaction against the Anglican Church in those states such as Virginia where it had enjoyed a privileged position as an official religion. For these former colonies, disestablishment was closely tied to the struggle for political independence.

By the time the framers sat down to draft the Bill of Rights, a clear pattern of religious toleration had begun to appear. Every state, except Connecticut, had adopted a constitutional provision protecting religious freedom, but what exactly this meant varied by state. The common element of disestablishment found among the former colonies was a decided aversion to setting up a single official church at the state level; and this instinct, pursued most aggressively against the Anglican Church, was at least in part inspired by a hatred of the British. Public support for organized religion remained common, however, with a majority of the states following some form of locally determined system of choice. Yes, the Anglican establishment had been expelled by the revolution, but civil authority could still be brought to bear against someone who violated the religious mores of the community. One could be severely punished for failing to observe the Sabbath or committing the sin of blasphemy.

The spirit of civic republicanism evident in Washington's Farewell Address affected every aspect of public life in the young nation. The same first Congress that wrote the Bill of Rights also voted to adopt the Northwest Ordinance that was originally passed under the Articles of Confederation. It was approved without alteration. As the document read, "Religion, morality and knowledge being necessary for good government . . . schools and the means of education shall forever be encouraged."[31] The language was taken from the Massachusetts Constitution of 1780, drafted by John Adams, and was later copied into the New Hampshire Constitution of 1784.[32] Later, the Ohio Company was given a land grant with the specification that a substantial portion of it be used "for the support of religion" among the Indian population. In a treaty with the Kaskaskia Indians that was signed by President Thomas Jefferson, the federal government agreed to provide money for the upkeep of a priest,

the building of a school, and the erection of a church.[33] The constitutionality of the action was upheld by the United States Supreme Court in an
opinion drafted by Chief Justice John Marshall.[34]

Early Decisions

I do not cite the events that inspired the writing of the First Amendment to argue for government support of religion or direct aid to parochial schools. My objective is to debunk the myth that our Constitution
was crafted by individuals determined to achieve a complete separation of
church and state, or that the same authors feared any connection between
the two estates would compromise the health of the democratic system
they designed. The idea of imposing public authority to interfere with
familial control over education was so contrary to the thinking behind the
Constitution that no discussion along those lines appears in the record. As
originally drafted, the First Amendment was intended to outlaw the establishment of a national church and to prevent the federal government from
acting in a way that inhibited religious freedom. Its authors had no desire
to tamper with the role that religion played within the various states, for
that would have been viewed as a serious infringement on state authority.
It was not until 1940 that the United States Supreme Court incorporated
the Free Exercise clause under the protections of the Fourteenth Amendment for application to the states when, in *Cantwell v. Connecticut*, it
overturned the conviction of a Jehovah's Witness in Connecticut who failed
to acquire a license for religious solicitation.[35] It was seven years after
that, in the landmark *Everson* decision, when the Court incorporated the
Establishment clause.[36]

By the early part of the twentieth century, however, a federal jurisprudence had begun to unfold that would begin to provide some guidance on
the appropriate relationship between church and state and its bearing on
education. The approach taken by the High Court was more
accommodationist than it was separationist.[37] It set down principles governing parental rights and aid to students in religious schools that are
relevant to contemporary debates on school choice. An examination of
this jurisprudence and of its evolution through the twentieth century demonstrates that, practically speaking, the idea of strict separation is of recent
vintage and, so far as the Supreme Court is concerned, was short lived.

One of the most significant decisions handed down in the first quarter
of the present century concerned an Oregon statute that required all children between the ages of eight and sixteen to attend public schools, effec-

tively making private schools unlawful. The circumstances surrounding the *Pierce* case of 1925 point to one of the darkest periods in the history of the First Amendment, and we will return to the subject in the next chapter. For now, we will focus on the legal case itself. Two years earlier, in *Meyer v. State of Nebraska,* the High Court had struck down a Nebraska law that made it a criminal offense to teach in a language other than English in a public or private school.[38] *Meyer* had been argued from the perspective of the due process rights of a convicted teacher; but then the case was decided in concert with another case in which a parent claimed that the law in question violated his liberty, free exercise, and equal protection rights.[39]

Taken together, the *Meyer* and the *Pierce* rulings would serve to establish the fundamental right of parents to have their children educated in schools that reflected their own values. But it was the language of the latter ruling that would echo for generations to come, at once affirming the right of parents to control the upbringing of their children and the commensurate permissibility of private and parochial schools to exist as viable alternatives available to parents. A unanimous Court proclaimed:

> The fundamental theory upon which all governments in this Union repose excludes any general power of the state to standardize its children by forcing them to accept instruction from public teachers only. The child is not the mere creature of the state; those who nurture him and direct his destiny have the right coupled with the high duty to recognize and prepare him for additional obligations.[40]

Since the Court had not yet incorporated the protections of the First Amendment for enforcement against the states, it based the *Pierce* ruling on the Fourteenth Amendment, emphasizing the liberty rights of parents and the property rights of private school operators who "attacked the pernicious policy of state monopoly in education." As important a victory as *Pierce* was for parents, it was only a limited one. So long as public funding available for education was restricted to public schools, parents who chose to have their children attend private or parochial schools would bear an extra burden—paying taxes to support government-run institutions, while absorbing the full cost of tuition for nonpublic schools. For those parents who could not afford the tuition, there remained no real choice at all. As explained earlier, this situation creates a severe dilemma for deeply religious parents or parents whose values are not in concert with those taught in the public schools. The issues are indeed complex, for even at the threshold of the twentieth century, providing aid to religious schools would have raised a serious constitutional question with regard to the Establishment clause.

In 1930, five years after *Pierce*, the Supreme Court handed down another landmark decision in *Cochran v. Board of Education*. This case involved a Louisiana statute that set aside tax funds for supplying textbooks to children in public, private, and parochial schools. Again preceding incorporation, this law had been challenged on the basis of the Fourteenth Amendment. Petitioners, challenging the law, claimed that it was a taking of private property for a private purpose without due process. The Court disagreed:

> The appropriations were made for the specific purpose of purchasing school books for the use of the school children of the state, free of cost to them. It was for their benefit and the resulting benefit to the state that the appropriations were made. True, these children attend some school, public or private, the latter sectarian or nonsectarian, and that the books are to be furnished them for their use, free of cost, whichever they attend. The schools, however, are not the beneficiaries of these appropriations. . . . The school children and the state alone are the beneficiaries.[41]

The Court seemed to grant in *Cochran* that education is indeed a legitimate public purpose and one that could be fulfilled through either public, private, or parochial institutions. Children, moreover, do not automatically forfeit claims for public support by choosing to attend nonpublic schools. This was the first time the High Court expounded upon the "child benefit" concept, which draws an important legal distinction between aid provided to institutions and aid given to the children who attend those institutions. While the case did not address the issue of student tuition, the child benefit concept it proclaimed would serve as an important legal guideline for protecting the free exercise rights of parents without compromising the Establishment clause.

Seventeen years after the *Cochran* case, the Supreme Court reviewed a New Jersey law involving the reimbursement of transportation costs to the parents of parochial school children. It was here, in *Everson* in 1947, that the Court specifically incorporated the Establishment clause protections of the First Amendment and simultaneously invoked the famous Jeffersonian metaphor of separation. As Justice Hugo Black wrote in his oft-quoted opinion:

The "establishment of religion" clause of the First Amendment means at least this: Neither a state or the Federal government can set up a church: Neither can pass laws which aid one religion, aid all religions, or prefer one religion over the other. . . . No tax in any amount, large or small, can be levied to support any religious activities or institutions, whatever they may be called, or whatever form they may adopt to teach or practice religion. . . . In the words of Jefferson, the clause against establishment of religion by law was intended to erect a wall of separation between church and state."[42]

It is no wonder that opponents of school choice are attracted to these famous words, not only for the dramatic use of Jeffersonian logic and imagery, but in hope that this decision would ensure a wall of separation would govern the relationship between religious bodies and the states as well as the federal government. What many of the same legal scholars and advocates fail to emphasize about the landmark decision is that it upheld the constitutionality of the statute in question. Perhaps their reading of the decision is influenced by their reluctance to recognize that the same court already had incorporated the free exercise protections of the First Amendment and had adopted a child benefit principle that would serve to reconcile the two. The *Everson* court unambiguously applied the reasoning articulated in *Cochran* to hold that attendance at a sectarian school is a form of religious exercise protected by the First Amendment that could not be encumbered by the state. The same Justice Black wrote:

New Jersey cannot consistently with the "establishment of religion" clause of the First Amendment contribute tax funds to the support of an institution which teaches the tenets of faith of any church. On the other hand, other language in the amendment commands that New Jersey cannot hamper its citizens in the free exercise of their own religion. Consequently it cannot exclude Catholics, Lutherans, Mohammedans, Baptists, Jews, Methodists, Non-believers, Presbyterians, or other members of any other faith, or lack of it, from receiving benefits of public welfare legislation.[43]

The *Everson* decision elevated the constitutional protection covering benefits to parochial school children to a new height, incorporating it under the shelter of the First Amendment and balancing the requirements of the Establishment and Free Exercise clauses in favor of the latter. If, as Jefferson urged, the First Amendment was to proscribe privileges on the basis of religious affiliation, so to, as Madison would have it, was the Constitution to ensure that one's entitlements are not abridged by that same affiliation. To deny parochial school children the opportunity to participate in a program made available to others is a form of religious discrimination that compromises the egalitarian principle on which our pluralistic system of government rests.

An Opaque Boundary

While *Everson* effectively linked the child benefit concept to the First Amendment, it also set the federal judiciary on a futile search to define a standard of permissible interaction between religion and public education. Its exact target—a clear line of demarcation to determine legality—proved to be elusive. In 1948 the Supreme Court invalidated a released time program in Champaign, Illinois, that allowed public school children to take religious instruction on the premises of a public school.[44] Even though the program was voluntary, administered by outside personnel, and paid for with private funding, the eight-person majority grounded its ruling on the fact that religious instruction was being given in a tax-supported public building.

Four years later the Court affirmed the constitutionality of a similar released time program in New York, emphasizing that the latter was not administered on the grounds of the public school.[45] Of particular note in *Zorach* v. *Clauson* was the far-reaching accommodationist language employed by Justice Douglas, who at the time commented, "We are a religious people whose institutions presuppose a Supreme Being." He went on to explain in tones reminiscent of Washington's farewell, "When the state encourages religious instruction or cooperates with religious authorities . . . it follows the best of our traditions."

Through the stewardship of Chief Justice Earl Warren, the Court maintained a sympathetic view toward religion and went to great lengths to ensure that governmental power—including its own—was not used to burden the free exercise rights of individuals. In 1961 the Warren Court handed down four decisions upholding Sunday closing laws. While recognizing that the original purpose of these laws was to encourage church attendance, the chief justice found that their contemporary objective is more secular—"to set aside a day of rest and recreation."[46] In 1972 the Court sided with a group of Amish parents in Wisconsin, who, for religious reasons, refused to abide by a state compulsory education law that required children to attend school beyond the eighth grade. Noting that Amish society exemplifies the cultural diversity that Americans supposedly "admire and encourage," the Court ruled in the famous *Wisconsin* v. *Yoder* decision: "This case involves the fundamental interest of parents, as contrasted with the state, to guide the religious future and education of their children . . . now established beyond doubt as an enduring American tradition."[47]

In the area of education, the Warren Court continued to abide by the child benefit principle on aid to parochial schools but strove vigilantly to keep religious activity out of the public schools. It invalidated the recitation of a Regent's Prayer in New York[48] and the Lord's Prayer in Pennsylvania[49] as violations of the Establishment clause. It was in the latter *Abington School District* v. *Schempp* case that the Court set down "purpose and effect" criteria in determining neutrality, that is, whether the law in question advances a secular purpose and has a primary effect that either advances or inhibits religion. Petitioners would later use the *Schempp* test to challenge a textbook loan program in New York that was made available to all school children in the state whether they attended public, private, or parochial institutions. Citing *Cochran* and *Everson*, the Supreme Court upheld the "child benefit" in question and found that the challengers had failed to demonstrate that the "process of secular and religious training in religious schools are so intertwined that secular textbooks furnished to students by the public are in fact instrumental in teaching religion."[50]

In ruling against the petitioners in the latter *Board of Education* v. *Allen* case, the Court put forward a rather dubious standard for review of state aid to religious schools. On the one hand, it affirmed the rights of parents to choose a religious education for their children without penalty; on the other hand, it registered a concern over the integration of religious and secular themes at these schools, suggesting that if a meshing could be demonstrated, the Court would deny assistance to the children and their parents. This reasoning sidestepped the fact that religious values are fully infused within the entire culture of a sectarian school. These values are what defines religious schools and are a major reason why parents choose them. To impose such a standard as a criteria to determine eligibility for aid is to deny these institutions their purpose and identity.

If the Court was worried about excessive entanglement between church and state, this concern seemed to have taken a respite in 1970, when it reviewed the practice of providing tax exemptions for religious institutions. In this first major decision handed down by the Burger Court, the

chief justice rejected the idea of complete separation in favor of a "be-
nevolent neutrality."[51] In a concurring opinion, Justice Harlan prescribed
"an equal protection mode of analysis"[52] that assured religious organizations that they were entitled to the same privileges as other political, social,
and charitable institutions. In another concurring opinion, Justice Brennan
echoed Madison in supporting the exemption, stating that "government
grants exemptions to religious organizations because they uniquely contribute to the pluralism of American society by their religious activities."[53]

A reading of the latter *Walz* v. *Tax Commission* decision might very
well create the impression that the Burger majority was about to inaugu-
rate an era of Supreme Court jurisprudence characterized by clear standards of interpretation and a philosophical leaning that was at least as
accommodationist as the preceding Warren Court. This impression would
prove incorrect. The Burger Court ushered in a ten-year period of judicial decisionmaking that was confused and incoherent in its thinking. If
there was any rhyme or reason to the Burger Court's First Amendment
jurisprudence, it coalesced around a separationist philosophy that was
insensitive to the interests of religious believers and out of touch with a
tradition of toleration that dates back to the first Congress of the United
States. This disturbing decade of Supreme Court history has provided
opponents of school choice with an arsenal of legal precedent on which
to rest their case.

A High Wall of Intolerance

The constitutional argument against school choice rests on a three-legged
stool of cases that are commonly cited by legal scholars and litigating
attorneys. The first, already discussed, was the *Everson* decision. While
rich with imagery, the Jeffersonian wall of separation referred to in Justice
Black's opinion was overshadowed by the ruling itself. Guided more by
the imperatives of the Free Exercise clause than by a restrictive reading of
the Establishment clause, in the end the *Everson* Court proved unswervingly
sympathetic to the rights and interests of children who attended parochial
schools. The second leg of the strict separationist argument is the *Lemon*
v. *Kurzman* decision of 1971.[54] *Lemon* borrowed from the "purpose and
effect" reasoning used in the *Schempp* case and enshrined it on a pedestal
of judicial review that was both imprecise and restrictive. The three-part
"*Lemon* test" prohibits government action that (1) has no "secular purpose," (2) has a "primary effect" of advancing religion, (3) fosters "excessive entanglement" between church and state.[55] In this particular case the

Court held that giving salary supplements to parochial school teachers who taught secular subjects is unconstitutional because it would require such a high level of oversight by the state that it would lead to "excessive entanglement."[56] In a spirited dissent Justice White reminded his colleagues, "The Establishment Clause . . . coexists in the First Amendment with the Free Exercise Clause" and went on to explain that the latter, "counsel[s] against refusing support for students attending parochial schools simply because in that setting they are also being instructed in the tenets of the faith they are constitutionally free to practice."[57]

Lemon marked the beginning of an interlude in judicial decisionmaking during which religious organizations and practices were treated with deep suspicion, as if they represented a potential threat to the health and welfare of the republic. Any governmental action that even incidentally benefited a religious institution could be deemed to have a "primary effect" of advancing religion. And it became increasingly difficult for the Court to find a legally acceptable secular purpose in any policy that minimally benefited religion no matter what its social merit. The *Lemon* opinion itself was both convoluted and inconsistent in its thinking. At one point in it Chief Justice Burger is quoted admitting, "Our prior holdings do not call for a total separation between church and state; total separation is not possible in such an absolute sense. Some relationship between government and religious organizations is inevitable."[58] The chief justice also referred liberally to the *Walz* decision and its warning against "sponsorship, financial support, and active involvement of the sovereign in religious activity."[59]

Taken together, the two decisions, written a year apart and linked together by the same Court, are a bold exercise in judicial contrivance. If forgiving an organization of its tax burdens does not constitute a form of sponsorship or support, then it is difficult to imagine what does. Certainly the exemption would advance the interests of the organizations in question, albeit in an indirect, pluralist, and nonpreferential way. Why should the processing of a salary supplement to teachers who provide instruction in secular subjects be treated with a higher level of suspicion? Did not the efforts made by these teachers contribute to a worthwhile public objective?

The confusion of mixed messages that emerged from the bench permitted the judges to act with only a hint of philosophical order to guide their First Amendment decisions. In 1973 the Supreme Court handed down the *Nyquist* decision, the third leg of the three-legged stool on which it would mount its high but permeable wall of separation. *Nyquist* struck down a complicated New York statute that provided maintenance and repair grants to nonpublic schools, offered tuition allotments to the poor, and extended tax relief to parents whose children attended private and parochial institutions. Given the case history, it was not surprising that the *Nyquist* Court rejected direct aid to parochial schools. More curious was its response to the last provision of the law that provided tax relief to parents. Writing for the majority, Justice Powell opined:

> Special tax benefits . . . cannot be squared with the principle of neutrality established by the decisions of this Court. To the contrary, insofar as such benefits render assistance to parents who send their children to sectarian schools, their purpose and inevitable affect are to aid and advance those religious institutions.[60]

By focusing on the second prong of the *Lemon* test, the Court let its preoccupation with the law's secondary effect on religious institutions dull its appreciation of the primary benefit that it might have on children and parents. It seemed to be abandoning the child benefit principle that prevailed earlier in *Cochran* and *Everson* and the significance of the important legal distinction between direct and indirect aid. As incoherent as they might be, *Lemon* and *Nyquist* would serve to anchor a number of decisions rendered during 1973 that would obstruct any form of aid that could be traced to a religious institution. In one case it ruled that Pennsylvania's partial tuition reimbursement for the parents of children attending nonpublic schools had "an impermissible effect of advancing religion" because it furnished "an incentive for parents to send their children to private schools."[61] Here Justice Powell, writing for the Court, ventured to conclude that the "intended consequence is to preserve and support religion-oriented institutions."[62]

The *Sloan* v. *Lemon* decision was astounding on a number of counts. Now the Court was saying that any sign of a secondary benefit derived by a religious institution could be construed as evidence that such a benefit was the primary motivation of the policy in question. Whether the policy benefited children or parents or society as a whole seemed to be a less significant consideration so far as the majority was concerned. The Court also construed assistance to the parents of parochial school children as a form of public incentive for families to choose these schools. It is difficult to believe that parents who are not so inclined would send their children to a religious school so long as they continued to enjoy access to public schools. In reality, the system of public incentives that exists in American education works in exactly the opposite way. Since government-operated

schools are the only means through which parents can acquire a free education, the system of financial incentives functions to discourage families
from attending religious schools, and in fact burdens parents who actually
make the choice to have their children do so.

The Supreme Court found in *Levitt* v. *Committee for Public Education
and Religious Liberty* that it is an "impermissible aid to religion" when a
state reimburses parochial schools for expenses incurred performing functions mandated by the state, including the administration, grading, and
reporting of standardized tests.[63] In this decision and others rendered during the 1973 session, the Court seemed to be moving toward a new standard of review that would deny parochial schools and the children who
attend them the same benefits that are made available to the general population.[64] This is the kind of unequal treatment that the Free Exercise clause
was designed to prevent; now the Court was using the Establishment clause
as a justification to undermine that very objective. In just one year the
Court had moved an enormous distance from the accommodationist principles it had espoused for nearly a half-century. The disturbing message of
the new jurisprudence was that if parents wanted to educate their children
in accord with their own religious values, they would be required to forego
certain supports made available to all others.

It would be misleading to suggest that, even though the High Court
was moving in a particular direction on the church-state issue, it was in
the process of articulating clear criteria for constitutional review. The fine-
line distinctions drawn by the Burger Court defied reason.[65] Textbook
loans to parochial school students were deemed a benefit "to parents and
children, not to schools," but loaning instructional materials and equip-
ment "has the unconstitutional primary effect of advancing religion because of the predominantly religious character of the schools benefiting
from the act."[66] Although the Court deemed it permissible to provide transportation to parochial schools, it imposed no obligation on the states to
provide this service to private and parochial school students.[67] And for
some reason a bus ride from school to a park or museum was declared to
be in violation of the Constitution, while a ride from home to school was
not.[68] Tax relief to parents, of course, was viewed with disfavor—at least
temporarily.[69]

Toward Equality of Treatment

The high wall of separation constructed by the Burger Court began to
fall in 1980, when the Court upheld a New York law that appropriated

funds to private and parochial schools for the administration of state examinations and the collection of school enrollment and attendance data.[70] The major breakthrough occurred, however, in 1983, when the Court in *Meuller* v. *Allen* approved a Minnesota provision granting a tax deduction to parents for tuition, textbooks, and transportation. Unlike the law reviewed in the previous *Nyquist* case, which benefited only private and parochial school children, the Minnesota assistance was made available to both public and nonpublic school populations, a fact the Court found to be significant in its determination.

Meuller would prove to be a landmark ruling for several reasons. Not only did it validate tuition relief for parochial school parents, but in drawing the distinction between direct aid and indirect aid, it reinforced the notion of parental choice and revitalized the child benefit concept. Justice Rehnquist wrote for the majority that, whereas "aid to parochial schools is only a result of decisions of individual parents, no 'imprimatur of state approval' can be deemed to have been conferred on any particular religion, or on religion generally."[71] Recognizing that most parents who had taken advantage of the Minnesota law had children in Catholic schools, Rehnquist observed, "There is a strong public interest in assuring the continued financial health of private schools both sectarian and nonsectarian." He elaborated:

> Parochial schools, quite apart from their sectarian purpose, have provided an educational alternative for millions of young Americans; they often afford wholesome competition with our public schools; and in some states they relieve substantially the tax burden incident to the operation of public schools.

As a presage of things to come, the future chief justice suggested that it was now time to relax the "primary effect" prong of *Lemon*. While admitting that judicial inquiries in this area have been "guided . . . by the three-part test," he declared that it is no more than "a helpful signpost in dealing with Establishment Clause challenges."[72] Justice Rehnquist sent another strong message of disapproval pertaining to *Lemon* in a dissenting opinion he wrote in the *Wallace* v. *Jaffree* case. Taking umbrage with the majority for striking down Alabama's moment of silence, meditation, and prayer, he assumed the role of legal historian when he explained, "There is simply no historical foundation for the proposition that the Framers intended to build the 'wall of separation' that was constitutionalized in *Everson*."[73] Furthermore, he explained, the *Lemon* test merely repeats the historical error, promoting a body of case law that "has no basis in the history of the amendment it seeks to interpret, is difficult to apply, and yields unprincipled results."[74] While voting in the minority in this 1985 case, Rehnquist would soon lead a new majority on the Court that would extend the principles articulated in *Meuller* and adopt a more permissive attitude toward financial assistance to students attending religious schools.[75]

In 1986 a unanimous Supreme Court held in *Witters* v. *Washington Department of Social Services* that the First Amendment was not offended when a blind student used a public scholarship to attend a Bible college. The reasoning in *Witters* focused on the fact that, unlike the circumstances in *Nyquist* and *Sloan*, the financial aid given here was made available to all students, not just those in sectarian schools. Justice Marshall, writing for the majority, indicated that while some of this aid would find its way to religious schools, the benefit is "only the result of the genuinely independent private choices of aid recipients."[76] In a concurring opinion, Justice Powell, who had written for the majority in *Nyquist*, outlined three factors that, until this day, set the standard for reviewing aid to religious schools and their students. To pass constitutional muster a program must meet the following criteria: (1) the program is neutral on its face regarding religion, (2) funds are equally available to public and private school students, (3) any aid to sectarian institutions is the result of private choices by individuals.[77]

In 1993 the Court, in *Zobrest* v. *Catalina Foothills School District*, reversed a Ninth Circuit decision and upheld the right of a Catholic high school student to receive the service of a sign language interpreter under the provisions of the Individuals with Disabilities Act. Attorneys for the losing side would have denied this handicapped student the same services that were available to public school children because his parents had chosen to send him to a religious school. Citing *Meuller* and *Witters*, Chief Justice Rehnquist and a majority of the Court disagreed, declaring:

> When the government offers a neutral service on the premises of a sectarian school as part of a general program that "is in no way skewed toward religion" . . . it follows under our prior decisions that provision of that service does not offend the Establishment Clause.[78]

Several philosophical directions would begin to define the First Amendment jurisprudence of the emerging Rehnquist majority. The first was a more positive attitude toward religion and its role in society, most evident in the Court's reluctance to equate disestablishment with the demand for a complete separation of church and state. Beyond this was a greater caution not to misinterpret the Establishment clause so that it might be applied to burden or curtail the free exercise rights of religious believers, although its position was not entirely consistent over time.[79] The contribution of the Rehnquist Court with regard to school funding would be fully realized by integrating its commitment to religious liberty with the Equal Protection guarantees of the Fourteenth Amendment to ensure that individuals and organizations would not be placed at a legal disadvantage because of their religious affiliation or orientation. The hallmark of the Rehnquist Court would be to guarantee equality of treatment before the law for believers and nonbelievers alike. This thinking comes through in a variety of decisions that go beyond the aid issue and even schooling.

In 1988 the Supreme Court ruled that federal funds appropriated under the Adolescent Family Life Act could be given to Catholic organizations that discouraged teen sexual activity and abortion.[80] In 1991 the Supreme Court, in *Mergens*, upheld the constitutionality of the Equal Access Act when it ruled that public schools must permit student religious clubs to meet on campus under the same terms as other noncurricular organizations. To do otherwise, the Court reasoned, would violate freedom of association and free exercise rights as well as the Fourteenth Amendment and would "demonstrate not neutrality but hostility toward religion."[81] Three years later, the High Court determined that free speech is violated when a public school denies the use of its facilities to a church wishing to show a film with a religious viewpoint.[82]

The funding and free speech issues were joined in the *Rosenberger* v. *Rectors of the University of Virginia* decision of 1995, when the University of Virginia refused to allow a student organization to use student activity fees to publish a newspaper with a Christian message. The Supreme Court rejected the action by the university administration. In an opinion drafted by Justice Kennedy, the majority distinguished "between government speech endorsing religion, which the Establishment Clause forbids, and private speech endorsing religion, which the Free Speech and Free Exercise Clauses protect."[83] Since the funding sought by the religious organization was made available to a wide array of student organizations, the program was deemed to be religiously neutral. To deny the aid "would risk fostering a pervasive bias or hostility to religion."[84]

In a concurring opinion, Justice Thomas took advantage of the opportunity to launch a more extended critique of past "Establishment Clause jurisprudence," which he described as being "in hopeless disarray." He pointed to the great irony inherent in the *Walz* decision, which allows tax exemptions for religious institutions while the Court agonizes over aid to the same organizations.[85] The underlying message of Justice Thomas's opinion struck a note that would amplify the distinction between the Rehnquist Court's interpretation of the Establishment clause and that of the Burger Court: "The Clause does not compel the exclusion of religious groups from government benefit programs that are generally available to a broad class of participants."[86]

If there was any doubt left that the Supreme Court was involved in a deliberate rethinking of the principles that guided its decisionmaking during the 1970s, the question was resolved in *Agostini* v. *Felton* in 1997. *Agostini* reversed *Aguilar*, a 1985 decision that had prevented public school teachers from providing federally supported remedial services to poor children on the premises of parochial schools. Once again the Court affirmed the principle of neutrality toward religious and nonreligious institutions[87] and emphasized that "*Aguilar* . . . [is] no longer good law."[88] Citing *Witters* and *Zobrest*, it further explained that "more recent cases have undermined the assumptions upon which . . . *Aguilar* rests."[89]

By no means was Justice O'Connor's carefully crafted opinion for the narrow 5-4 majority in *Agostini* conceived as a rejection of the three-point *Lemon* standard that guided earlier jurisprudence. To the contrary, she emphasized, "we continue to ask whether the government acted with the purpose of advancing or inhibiting religion." What changed was the willingness of the Court to accept certain assumptions that shaped previous decisions, specifically: that a public employee who works on the premises of a religious school is presumed to inculcate religion; that the presence of that employee creates a symbolic union between church and state; and, most significantly, that public aid that directly aids the educational function of a religious school impermissibly supports religious indoctrination. The Court affirmed the neutrality of the Title I services that are granted in a manner that "neither favors nor disfavors religion," because they are available to all eligible students "no matter what their religious beliefs or where they go to school."

By specifying that the program in question was supplementary in nature, Justice O'Connor may have left the door open for a challenge to more generalized aid to religious schools. *Agostini*, nonetheless, represented a deliberate confirmation of the Court's changing jurisprudence. The Court's subsequent refusal to hear an appeal of the Wisconsin Supreme Court's voucher decision adds further credence to the claim of an important philosophical shift—especially since the Wisconsin opinion was so clearly focused on the recent federal case law.

Still, A Limited Freedom

In this chapter the equality discussion was extended to include religious liberty. We found in the jurisprudence of the Rehnquist Court an interpretation of the Constitution involving the First and Fourteenth Amendments, requiring that nonreligious and religious people be treated alike before the law. This interpretation is consistent with the pluralist political tradition on which our governmental system is based, the sense of religious freedom that motivated the authors of the Bill of Rights, and the case law of the Supreme Court that helped shape church-state relations throughout most of the twentieth century. The Rehnquist Court's reading of the Constitution has served to reverse a pattern of judicial decisionmaking that confuses disestablishment with separation and forces government institutions to deny religious organizations and their members the public benefits to which all people are entitled.

The Rehnquist Court has promulgated a set of legal principles that make it possible for the government to provide tuition assistance to parents of children who attend religious schools so long as such aid is administered in a neutral fashion and students attend such schools as a matter of parental choice. Furthermore, any government action that specifically excludes religious institutions from participation in a publicly sponsored choice program open to nonreligious private schools is likely to raise questions of discrimination before the Court. On the whole, the series of decisions handed down by the High Court over the last two decades has improved the prospects for parents who want to send their children to schools that reflect their own values. This was the promise of the *Pierce* decision of 1925. Like *Brown*, however, *Pierce* remains a hollow promise, conditioned to a large degree by the economic position of parents.

While states may not be able to discriminate against religious schools in developing choice programs involving other private institutions, there is nothing in the case law to suggest that states have a constitutional obligation to develop choice programs that involve nonpublic schools. Such matters of public policy are left to the discretion of legislative bodies whose political agendas are shaped by majoritarian politics or powerful groups that control particular areas of public policy. In the realm of education, policy is strongly influenced by organized interests that have a stake in ensuring that there are few practical alternatives to public education. As Madison had foreseen, these legislative bodies—creatures of majoritarian politics that they are—have been historically insensitive and even hostile to the interests of religious minorities.[90] Many states have provisions within their constitutions that set strict separationist standards and prohibit direct or indirect aid to religious institutions. Opponents of school choice commonly portray these prohibitions as measures designed to enhance religious liberty. An examination of their history paints a very different picture and reveals a troubling connection between their requirements and the evolution of the American common school that illustrates the kind of threat Madison had in mind when he wrote the *Federalist Papers*.

CHAPTER SIX

Religion and the Common School

I T IS SOMEWHAT inappropriate to speak of an American constitutional tradition. American federalism is a synthesis of many
legal traditions: an overarching set of principles outlined in the national
Constitution and fifty distinct constitutional arrangements that govern
the states. Since schooling has always been considered a state and local
function in this country, educational policymaking remains highly decentralized.[1] Within the framework of certain constitutional standards set by
the federal courts, the role of religion in education remains very much a
product of legal norms that have evolved in the various states over time,
each defined by a distinct history and culture. While the architects of the
American Constitution were mindful of crafting a government that would
temper majority rule with a respect for minority rights, constitution making at the state level is largely a product of majoritarian politics.

There is no episode in the American chronicle that better illustrates the
inherent dangers of majority rule that so preoccupied Madison than the
history of the common school. It is a story that continues to unfold. The
tensions between religion and public education that characterize contemporary struggles over school choice have always been a subplot in the
developing drama.

145

From Pluralism to Patrimony

There was an intimacy between religion, education, and government in the early American experience that would be viewed with alarm today. Yet because of the distinct origin of each colony, there was a reigning pluralism within the political culture of the early republic that was eventually quashed with the common school movement, precipitating problems of another order. The end result was a system of education that was oppressive in its own right, and that was detached from the ethos of political pluralism that animated the writing of the Constitution.

If the founding of the American republic was to grow into one of the greatest experiments in democracy known to modern civilization, it was in large part made possible by the unique way that each of the original colonies sought to define religious freedom.[2] In New England, for example, with its strong disposition toward localism, each town would choose its own minister and enact taxes to support its church. Because the populations of the towns were dominated by Congregationalists, so were the churches of Massachusetts, Connecticut, and New Hampshire.

New York had a unique form of establishment among the colonies. When the English conquered New Amsterdam in 1664, the Dutch Reformed Church had been recognized as the official creed. The English replaced this with a system of multiple establishments, requiring each town to select a Protestant church and minister that it would support with local taxes. Because the population of New York was so diverse even then, the outcome of local decisionmaking, though favorable toward Anglicans, was more pluralistic than in New England. Virginia, Maryland, and the Carolinas favored the Anglican establishment before the revolution, as did Georgia; but unlike the other southern colonies, Georgia, excepting its discrimination against Catholics, displayed a certain tolerance toward other Christians and even Jews.

Four colonies had no form of religious establishment at all. In New Jersey the idea of a single established church would have been impractical because of its heterogeneous population. Rhode Island was founded by Roger Williams as a safe haven for religious dissenters from Massachusetts, and William Penn set up Pennsylvania and Delaware for the Quakers; none of the three was well disposed toward the idea of an established church.

After independence was achieved, Connecticut, with its strong Congregationalist tradition, was the only state in New England to retain a preferred church. Although Congregationalists still dominated Massachusetts, they now shared tax moneys with Baptists, Quakers, Episcopalians, Methodists, and Unitarians. New Hampshire permitted its towns to select a church to support with local taxes, but did not require it. Vermont, which became the fourteenth state to join the union in 1791, had already adopted a system of local discretion, as was customary in the region. Though all citizens in Vermont were expected to select a church that they would attend and support, nobody was forced to support an official church if they preferred to worship elsewhere. As might be expected, every one of the five southern states broke the monopoly held by the Anglican Church after separation from the Crown. North Carolina was the first among them to completely end the practice of supporting religion through public taxes. Virginia, Maryland, South Carolina, and Georgia adopted a practice of nonpreferential aid that taxed people to support the church of their choice.

Well into the middle of the nineteenth century, it was not unusual for religious schools in New York, New Jersey, Connecticut, Massachusetts, and Wisconsin to be supported with public funds.[3] In many cases it was difficult to distinguish between public and private institutions, since they were often housed in the same building. Frequently, the lines were purposely blurred by Democratic party politicians in cities to appease their Catholic constituents. In 1835 Lowell, Massachusetts, initiated an experiment that incorporated the Catholic schools into the public school system.[4] Between 1850 and 1855 the California legislature found it expedient to let religious bodies control a large part of the school budget because the public schools were unable to accommodate the large immigrant populations that demanded educational services. This changed when a strong anti-Catholic lobby in California passed a law to end public funding of religious schools.[5]

By the middle of the nineteenth century, the idea of a common school system began to capture the imagination of educators across the nation. At the time, a wave of immigration from southern Europe had brought many people to our cities that were unschooled and unaccustomed to the American way of life. Ideally, the common school would provide a decent education to all regardless of their social standing.[6] Education, an integral part of the American dream, would be the great social leveler. But the process of cultural assimilation would come at a severe price. In exchange for the acceptance into the American fold that common schooling was to smooth, the immigrant population was expected to sublimate a certain sense of self—ethnic identity, the mores of the old world, and, yes, religious tradition.[7] The one-size-fits-all approach to education that to this day defies American pluralism was conceived by the originators of the common school. By the end of the nineteenth century, a new profession of education administrators would appear, touting their expertise as justification for the development of a rigid hierarchical system that left little room for shared decisionmaking—by either the armies of women who staffed the classrooms or the parents of the children who were in their charge.[8]

Horace Mann's Religious Neutrality

Nobody so personified the essence of the common school as did Horace Mann, the secretary to the board of the nation's first public school system, in Massachusetts. With his strict Calvinist upbringing, Mann appreciated the role that religion could play in cultivating morality and civic virtue among the immigrant masses. As a public official, he pledged strict religious neutrality in the schools and called for the "entire exclusion of religious teaching."[9] In truth, Mann's claim of neutrality was a veneer to cover a political agenda that used the public school classroom to promote the teachings of mainstream Protestantism, which he believed would rescue the souls of his subjects as well as the fortunes of the republic.[10] In his words, "It may be easy to make a republic, but it is laborious to make republicans."[11]

To suggest that Mann wanted to erect a new form of religious establishment would be an exaggeration. His objective was more subtle. Mann's inclination was to allow the Yankee culture handed down over generations, along with its religious traditions, to define what it meant to be an American. And what better institution to convey these values than the public school? On a practical level, this meant that some forms of worship would be favored over others, and that certain creeds—most notably Catholicism—would be deemed anathema to the civic order. The joining of public authority and religion created a political environment that became hostile to newcomers who were devoted to their own faith. Mann's schools required the daily reading of the King James version of the Bible, the recital of prayers, and the singing of hymns. These were practices imposed on all children, Jewish and Catholic, Baptist and Quaker alike. Mann was convinced that if students were to read the Bible without commentary from their instructors, it was a neutral act that permitted them to reach the truth on their own. His intentions, nonetheless, were unambiguous.

On the occasion of his final report to the board of education in 1848, he explained:

> Our system earnestly inculcates all Christian morals; it founds its morals on the basis of religion; it welcomes the religion of the Bible; and in receiving the Bible it allows it to do what it is allowed to do in no other system, to speak for itself.[12]

If Mann's religious chauvinism was offensive to minorities, it was also indicative of the thinking prevalent among the ruling elite of nineteenth-century American government, once described by Mark DeWolfe Howe as a "de facto Protestant establishment."[13] In 1852 the Massachusetts legislature enacted the nation's first compulsory school attendance law. The bill had been advocated by the nativist Know-Nothing party in response to Catholic protests against the requirement of Bible reading in the Cambridge public schools. On the occasion of the law's passage, an editorial appeared in the *Common School Journal* that read:

> The English Bible, in some way or another, has, ever since the settlement of Cambridge, been read in its public schools, by children of every denomination; but in the year 1851, the ignorant immigrants who have found food and shelter in this land of freedom and plenty, made free and plentiful through the influence of these very Scriptures, presume to dictate to us, and refuse to let their children read as ours do, and always have done, the Word of Life. The arrogance, not to say the impudence, of this conduct, must startle every native citizen, and we can not but hope that they will immediately take measures to teach these deluded aliens that their poverty and ignorance in their own country arose mainly from their ignorance of the Bible.[14]

One cannot reasonably separate the founding of the American common school from the obtrusive nativism that had its origins at the Protestant pulpit during the early nineteenth century. By the time Horace Mann opened the doors to his first school in 1837, a network of Protestant newspapers was in circulation, delivering a distinctly anti-Catholic message, since Catholics—emboldened by their numbers and devoted to papal authority—appeared to represent the greatest threat to the old order. It was under the influence of Reverend Lyman Beecher's inflammatory sermons that an angry Boston mob burned down the Ursuline convent in 1834 because Catholics had dared to protest Bible reading and prayer recitals in the public schools.[15]

This ugly experience in Massachusetts signaled an erupting national mood.[16] While Massachusetts was the only state in the union to pass a law mandating Bible reading in the public schools during the nineteenth century, between 75 and 80 percent of the schools in the country followed the practice.[17] When a group of Catholics in Maine challenged the expulsion of fifteen-year-old Bridget Donahue for refusing to read the Protestant Bible in class, the state's highest court ruled in 1854 that being required to read the King James version of the Bible is not an infringement on religious freedom.[18] This was the first of twenty-five similar suits (fifteen by Catholics) brought in nineteen states through 1925, only five of which resulted in favorable rulings for the plaintiffs.[19] Pleas by Catholics to eliminate the King James Bible from the curriculum were joined increasingly by Jews and Protestants who were offended by the custom, but only Catholics had the political clout to act on their outrage.[20]

Most judges at the time refused to recognize the Bible as a sectarian book, even though only one version was put to use in the classroom. Protestantism had been so ingrained in the American conscience that it was difficult for the average person to understand the dismay of religious minorities. The common school was meant to function as an instrument for the acculturation of immigrants, making them good, productive citizens in the image of the governing majority. The Bible, the Protestant Bible, was a sacred implement to their noble cause. One detailed examination of the McGuffey Readers, which were distributed widely in public schools at the time, described the Readers as more resembling theology texts than school books.[21] As historian David Tyack and his coauthors explain so cogently:

> Protestant ministers and lay people were in the forefront of the public school crusade and took a proprietary interest in the institution they had helped to build. They assumed a congruence of purpose between the common school and the Protestant churches. They had trouble conceiving of moral education not grounded in religion. The argument ran thus: "To survive the republic must be composed of moral citizens. Morality is rooted in religion. Religion is based upon the Bible. The public school is the chief instrument for forming moral citizens. Therefore pupils must read the Bible in school.[22]

The history of the common school movement is a telling story of the risks involved when a political majority is allowed to establish a monopoly over education and impose its values on other people's children. The movement itself is a lasting testimony to the prescience of Madison. As one anguished nineteenth-century observer commented, "We have made a sort of God out of our common school system. It is treason to speak a word against it."[23] Under such conditions there is no room for dissent. The rights and concerns of minorities become easily dismissed, ignored, or trampled on—often unknowingly, sometimes intentionally, but always with injury to the democratic ideal. Without meaningful alternatives offered for the education of their children, minorities are forced to accept the majority's world view.

By the middle of the nineteenth century the Catholic population in many big cities had increased in sufficient numbers to demand an education alternative. Church leaders in Chicago, Philadelphia, Boston, Cincinnati, Baltimore, San Francisco, and St. Paul all began to lobby their state legislatures for public funds to create their own school systems.[24] One of the most dramatic of these battles occurred in New York. When Bishop Hughes entered the fray in 1842, his residence was destroyed by a mob, and militia had to be called out to protect St. Patrick's Cathedral.[25] When Catholics in Michigan proposed a bill for the support of Catholic schools, opponents portrayed their plan as a nationwide plot hatched by the Jesuits to destroy public education. Parochial school advocates in Minnesota were accused of subverting basic American principles. When the Know-Nothing party gained control of the Massachusetts legislature in 1854, it drafted one of the first state laws to prohibit aid to sectarian schools. The legislature simultaneously instituted a Nunnery Investigating Committee, which conducted surprise inspections of convents to check whether young girls were being held against their will. This same Massachusetts body, counting twenty-four Protestant clergymen among its members, also tried to pass legislation that would limit the franchise and the right to hold office to native-born citizens. In the same year the anti-Catholic Know-Nothing party elected seventy-five members to Congress, a distressing sign of the times.[26]

The Blaine Amendment

In 1872 local school boards in Cincinnati, Chicago, and New York, moved by Catholic protests, voted to prohibit Bible reading and religious exercises in the public schools. The political ascent of the growing "Catholic menace" in urban areas spurred many Protestant churches to align with newly formed nativist groups to launch a two-pronged campaign to preserve Bible study in the public schools and deny government support to parochial schools.[27] Increasingly, the content of the common school curriculum evolved from its open embrace of mainstream Protestantism to a blatant anti-Catholicism. In her survey of more than a thousand of the most commonly used elementary school textbooks in nineteenth-century public schools, Ruth Miller Elson found two themes that were prevalent: one was the cultivation of an American cultural tradition defined in terms of patriotism, capitalism, and Protestantism; the other was a fierce anti-Catholicism in which the church was portrayed as a national threat, loyal to a foreign power in Rome.[28] As legal historian Douglas Laycock has explained, aid to religious schools did not become a controversial subject in America until the Catholics started to demand the same support for themselves.[29] The refusal of public authorities to grant such aid did not arise from any well-established constitutional doctrine or from a high-minded desire to protect religious freedom, but rather from a raw hatred of Catholics, especially the Irish.

In 1875 President Ulysses S. Grant, acquiescing to mounting political pressure, made a highly publicized speech in Washington promising to "encourage free schools, and resolve that not one dollar be apportioned to support any sectarian schools."[30] Grant followed his pledge with a message to Congress, in which he proposed a constitutional amendment that would deny public support to religious institutions. This move by the president would plant the national Republican party firmly in the camp of the anti-Catholic wing of the public school lobby, delineating the contours of a bitter partisan struggle that was to follow.[31] In order for Grant's proposed amendment to be passed, it would need a congressional sponsor. That role was enthusiastically filled by Representative James G. Blaine of Maine. Blaine sought to obtain the Republican nomination to succeed Grant in the White House. He fully understood the wide political appeal of the nativist and anti-Catholic rhetoric that accompanied the president's agenda and intended to take full advantage of it. In an open letter to the *New York Times*, the Maine congressman claimed to be correcting a "constitutional defect."[32] At the time it was widely understood that there was no constitutional prohibition against aid to religious schools, and Blaine publicly grieved that "states were left free to do as they pleased."

Blaine's transparent political gesture against the Catholic Church provoked considerable press commentary. A resentful editorial in *Catholic World* issued a condemnation of "politicians who hope to ride into power by awakening the spirit of fanaticism and religious bigotry among us."[33] The *St. Louis Republican* observed, "The signs of the times all indicate an intention on the part of the managers of the Republican party to institute a general war against the Catholic church." Even the *Nation*, which was generally sympathetic to Blaine's legal position, conceded:

> Mr. Blaine did indeed bring forward a . . . Constitutional amendment directed against the Catholics, but the anti-Catholic excitement was, as everyone knows now a mere flurry; and all that Mr. Blaine means to do or can do with his amendment is, not to pass it but to use it in the campaign to catch anti-Catholic votes.[34]

Blaine's amendment got strong backing in both houses of Congress, but it fell four votes short of the required two-thirds majority in the Senate to pass. The movement it propelled, however, would prove to be largely successful. Its principles were incorporated into the Republican party platform, a solid plank in the campaign against "rum, Romanism, and rebellion." Although Blaine never won the presidency or secured passage of his controversial amendment, his name would live in perpetuity as a symbol of the irony and hypocrisy that characterized much future debate over aid to religious schools: employing constitutional language, invoking patriotic images, appealing to claims of individual rights. All these ploys would serve to disguise the real business that was at hand: undermining the viability of schools run by religious minorities to prop up and perpetuate a publicly supported monopoly of government-run schools.

Blaine's political campaign would prove to have a profound and lasting effect. Although Republicans could not muster the super-majority of votes to pass a constitutional amendment, they commanded a sufficient congressional majority to affect policy in other ways. Legislation was passed requiring that any state admitted to the union after 1876 set up a system of public schools free from sectarian control. The enabling legislation of 1889 that divided the Dakotas into two territories and admitted them with Montana and Washington into the union required that each state would include Blaine-like provisions in its constitution.[35] New Mexico was admitted on the condition that it adopt a similar provision in its constitution.[36]

Following the Civil War, Reconstruction era Republicans seized the opportunity to influence the development of education in the South to match their own political priorities.[37] Congressional leaders had also come to understand that federal aid could be used as a wedge for manipulating policy in the states. Most states west of the Mississippi were receiving more than 10 percent of their education revenues from federal grants and in return were submitting to expanding federal guidance.[38] These measures, however, were not rude thrusts of congressional power imposed on the states. Republican domination of Washington was symptomatic of a national consensus built around the mentality of the Blaine amendment. This was also a period of busy activity in the state capitols. Many legislatures were in the process of reconsidering their own charters, and the spirit of Blaine seemed to have been present throughout their deliberations. By 1876 fourteen states had enacted legislation prohibiting the use of public funds for religious schools; by 1890 twenty-nine states had incorporated such provisions in their state constitutions.[39]

New York is a conspicuous case in point. It neither had been part of the old Confederacy nor a new territory seeking statehood. It had, however, been a place where nativist-Catholic tensions reached a fierce level of political combat. As early as 1844 its legislature passed a law prohibiting aid to religious schools. In 1894 the ban was etched into the state constitution, which forbade both direct and indirect aid to parochial schools.[40] That same year the Reverend John Wilson delivered a sermon at the Eighth Street Methodist Church that was printed in the *New York Herald Tribune*, in which he denounced the Catholic Church as "everywhere and always an enemy of civil liberty."[41] When New York elected William Grace its first Catholic mayor in 1880, the *New York Times* speculated with considerable angst that the public schools might now become "Romanized."[42] To this day opponents of school choice in New York point to the "Blaine amendment" in the state constitution as a legal defense for their argument. As recently as 1967 the "Blaine amendment" emerged as the major issue of contention at a state constitutional convention, when its opponents launched a failed attempt to have it abolished.[43]

The "unholy" alliance between the public school lobby and nativist political forces would carry over well into the twentieth century. There is no episode in the nation's history that better illustrates the terrible progeny of that marriage than what occurred in Oregon in 1922.[44] In that year the voters of the state approved an initiative requiring all children between the ages of eight and sixteen to attend public schools, effectively making it unlawful to attend private schools. The initiative was cooked up in a campaign organized by the Ku Klux Klan and the Scottish Rite Masons. The Masons contended that compulsory public education would ensure the "growth and higher efficiency of our public schools" and accused the Roman Catholic hierarchy of wanting to abolish public schools.[45]

For some odd reason, the Klan—whose members believed in the superiority of white Protestants and the inferiority of blacks, Jews, Catholics, and immigrants—had come to the conclusion that forcing all these groups to attend school together under the supervision of public authority would fortify American democracy. Private schools encouraged private ideas, which was considered dangerous. Compulsory education in state-run schools could avert the risks created by social pluralism. The expansion of religious schools would lead to the destruction of public schools: the foundation of a free society, the sacred "temples of liberty" in America. As King Kleagle, Pacific Domain of the Knights of the Ku Klux Klan explained:

> To defend the common school is the settled policy of the Ku Klux Klan and with its white-robed sentinels keeping eternal watch, it shall for all time, with the blazing torches as signal fires, stand guard on the outer walls of the temple of liberty, cry out the warning when danger appears and take its place in the front rank of defenders of the public schools.[46]

The new law was opposed on several fronts: by blacks and Jews, who feared what would occur when bigots controlled a school board; by Catholics, Lutherans, and Seventh-Day Adventists, who wanted to educate their children in their own schools; and by Presbyterian, Unitarian, and Congregational ministers, who simply believed that the restriction was unconstitutional. No major denominational body endorsed the effort to pass the referendum, nor were public school leaders at the forefront. But many Protestant ministers and school board members supported it.

The Oregon measure was eventually challenged by the Sisters of the Holy Names of Jesus and Mary, who ran a number of parochial schools, and the directors of the Hill Military Academy, a nonsectarian private school. They succeeded in obtaining an injunction in federal court to prevent the state from enforcing the law. Subsequently, the attorney general for the state of Oregon appealed the decision to the United States Supreme Court. Two years earlier, the High Court had heard an appeal from a Lutheran school teacher in Nebraska who had been criminally convicted for conducting a class in German. Nebraska was one of twenty-one states with statutes that made it illegal to teach in any language other than English, either in a public or private school.[47] All such laws were enacted with the same purpose in mind: to harry sectarian schools, which often provided instruction to immigrant populations in their native language.

With the *Meyer* and *Pierce* decisions—discussed explicitly in the previous chapter—the United States Supreme Court had affirmed the natural and constitutional right of parents to control the education of their own children as well as the collateral right of religious schools to thrive alongside government-operated institutions. But these entitlements could not yet be taken for granted. The assault on parental prerogatives in education had just begun to move at full throttle, and the campaign against religion in education was far from over.

From Separation to Secularization

By the turn of the century, a new revolution was stirring in American cities. This time change would be carried forward under the flag of Progressive reform. The same Democratic party that was so accommodating to the needs of immigrant populations had also been responsible for converting municipal government into a sinkhole of patronage and corruption. As a cure for the incompetence that ailed city government, reformers sought to institute a professionalized civil service of expert managers.[48] Organizationally, this meant the decentralized ward-based system of governance that was the foundation of machine politics would be replaced by a hierarchic form of organization that permitted little managerial discretion by street-level service providers who worked directly with the populace. The first decade of the twentieth century brought a growing fascination with the creed of scientific management. Conceived in the industrialized world of the American factory and proselytized by Frederick Taylor, scientific management introduced a new paradigm of government administration. As Taylor saw it, the techniques of observation, analysis, and experimentation that were typically applied in the laboratory could be adapted to the workplace to improve efficiency.[49] Placing decisionmaking in the hands of specially trained managers at the top of the organizational hierarchy would reduce the risk of error (and corruption) by those unthinking functionaries at the tail end of the assembly line.

There were several subtexts to the crusade against wrongdoing and ineptitude undertaken by the Progressives. At least at the outset, reformers perceived the move to professionalize government as part of a moralistic Protestant campaign that would allow America to reach its destiny as the leader of the free capitalist world. As one writer from the period proclaimed, "We will never realize fully either the visions of Christianity or the dreams of democracy until the principles of scientific management have permeated every nook and cranny of the working world."[50] It was

President Grant himself who had appointed the first Civil Service Commission in 1871 to eradicate the Jacksonian system of spoils. Behind the veil of reform raged a bitter partisan struggle between the old Republican Protestant establishment and the urban-based Democratic party of ethnic and religious minorities. The prize was to determine who would control big-city politics.[51]

The entire conflict and its outcome had a special significance in education. Transferring the factory model of organization from business and government over to education was particularly appealing to education administrators, whose newly formed profession was just beginning to come into its own. Removing education policymaking from the hands of corrupt politicians was a convenient rationale for turning it over to career administrators. It was these "schoolmen," now prepared in esteemed schools of education, who had an exclusive claim to expertise when it came to running the schools. Nobody had the political, managerial, or moral authority to challenge them. School teachers who worked in the system were expected to do what they were told. Parents of urban schoolchildren, most of whom were barely literate themselves, had no basis on which to question policies handed down from on high.

The most damaging effect of factory model management, as envisioned by its fathers (women were excluded from any serious decisionmaking role), is that it effectively removed the function of public education from direct democratic control. Bureaucracy would replace politics. Even the popularly elected school board was perceived by Progressive reformers as a sacred trust rather than a representative body.[52] In the minds of school leaders the abuses of the political machine had exposed the limitations of democratic government, and only they could offer salvation. Their hold has persevered for more than a century, never seriously challenged until the community control movement of the 1960s led to demands for parental participation in decisionmaking.

John Dewey, Philosopher Pragmatist

John Dewey was this century's intellectual heir to European liberalism and its most influential thinker in the field of education. Like Horace Mann, he believed that the public school had a major role to play as an incubator of public values that would strengthen American democracy.[53] But here the resemblance between the two men ended abruptly. Although Dewey's writings, especially in his early years, are generously seasoned with the pious language of the pulpit that reflected his New England Congregationalist upbringing, by the age of thirty Dewey was ready to abandon his church membership and dismiss all organized religion as otherworldly.[54] Reflecting on the undue influence of religious teaching in American society, Dewey held that there is "nothing left worth preserving in the notions of unseen powers, controlling human destiny to which obedience, reverence and worship are due."[55] He referred to sectarian doctrines as "the most savage and degraded beliefs."

In the spirit of the Enlightenment, Dewey was an empiricist, who was convinced that science would liberate humankind from the "servile acceptance of imposed dogma" at the hands of the clergy. Similar to the way Newtonian physics and its vision of a great mechanical world had freed seventeenth-century thinkers from the idea of a divinely structured universe, Dewey's science of education, which integrated philosophy, psychology, and the social sciences, would ground the next generation of schoolchildren in a method of learning that was informed by hard evidence.

According to Dewey, education is "art based on scientific knowledge";[56] the public school teacher "is the prophet of the true God."[57] For this self-proclaimed pragmatist, the revelation of truth could only come about through the experimental process. The laboratory was his sanctuary, the schoolhouse his temple. As he preached in an essay that appeared in the *New Republic* in 1922, "If we have any ground to be religious about anything, we may take education religiously."[58] Of course, Dewey's reference to religion in the context of education was as satiric as it was metaphoric. By the latter part of his career, Dewey's attitude toward religion was nothing less than contemptuous. While he shared Horace Mann's conviction that the common school could help foster an American civic culture, he was uncompromisingly determined to remove all religion from the classroom. Dewey understood that the science of education and the science of democracy would evolve in tandem. Under the guidance of a liberal education, each child would cultivate critical thinking skills that would prepare her to question all forms of illegitimate authority, whether its source be governmental or ecclesiastic.

If Mann's religious neutrality was marred by an arrogant favoritism toward one particular religious tradition over others, Dewey's error was to favor irreligion over religion. His aggressive secularism would become a creed in itself that was no less offensive to the principle of religious pluralism than was Mann's patronizing Protestantism. According to the tenets of Dewey's philosophical pragmatism, the separation of church and state required a subordination of the church to the state in the service of a common good. Religious schools were politically and socially divisive. As he enunciated in explicit detail:

> The alternative plan of parceling out pupils among religious teachers drawn from their respective churches and denominations brings us up against exactly the matter which has done most to discredit the churches, and to discredit the cause, not perhaps of religion, but of organized and institutional religion: the multiplication of rival and competing religious bodies, each with its private inspiration and outlook. Our schools in bringing together those of different nationalities, languages, traditions and creeds, in assimilating them together upon a basis of what is common and public in endeavor and achievement, are performing an infinitely significant religious work.[59]

Dewey's lasting effect on American education was to give credence to the attitude that organized religion was damaging not only to rigorous teaching and learning but also to democracy itself. His animosity toward the Catholic Church was legendary, and the sentiment was returned.[60] He was an ardent opponent of government aid to religious schools and even became embroiled in a public debate against giving public school children in New York City released time for religious instruction. Like Horace Mann before him, John Dewey was incapable of comprehending the oppressive nature of his own self-righteous approach to education. He did not understand the negative effect his philosophy could have on groups that did not share his faith in science or that were guided by strong religious views. Nor could he appreciate the threat that his thinking, when sanctioned by public authority, might pose to the democratic values that he claimed to hold so dear.

Dewey really believed that the public school would serve as an engine for social change. At heart, he was an egalitarian who thought that each child deserved a decent education. But his idea of a decent education was ensconced in a system of subjective values that belied his claims of scientific objectivity. In 1918 the U.S. Bureau of Education distributed a report on the purposes of secondary education that was drafted under the auspices of the National Education Association. What became known as the "Seven Cardinal Principles" would be read and memorized by anyone seeking a teaching license for several decades to come. Much of its content was based on Dewey's *Democracy and Education*,[61] which had been published two years earlier. Declaring that the aims of education should be determined by the "needs of society to be served, the character of the individuals to be educated, and the knowledge of education theory and practice available,"[62] only one of the principles outlined had anything at all to do with academic subject matter. And that vaguely worded principle—command of fundamental processes—only appeared in a late draft of the document.[63]

In later years Dewey would come to reject much of the confused pedagogy that was being formulated under the umbrella of Progressive education, especially its focus on vocational education.[64] Dewey, nevertheless, helped cast the die that would shape the character of public schooling in America throughout the remainder of the twentieth century: its pretentious claim of authority, its readiness to compromise academic studies in pursuit of a broad social agenda, its use of the public school as an instrument for conveying political values, its obstinate secularism. In its modern form, American education would remove religious doctrine from the classroom and replace it with a devotion to secular humanism. The new ethos of public education was no less value laden than the Protestantism of Horace Mann and at times was equally repugnant to those minorities who wanted to educate their children according to their own religious traditions.

By the middle of the twentieth century, professional educators had become enraptured by a campaign for instruction in "life adjustment." Its arrival on the education scene was marked by the appointment of a National Commission on Life Adjustment for Youth in 1947 and the creation of a second panel in 1950 that promoted the concept until 1954. The new creed drew from many of the themes stressed under the Seven Cardinal Principles, giving primacy to the nonacademic needs of the child such as "physical, mental and emotional health . . . preparation for future living . . . the importance of personal satisfactions and achievements."[65] The agenda was widely supported by the education establishment, endorsed by such organizations as the U.S. Office of Education, the National Education Association, the American Association of School Administrators, and the National Council of State School Officers. The emerging consensus within the profession also provided a convenient target of criticism from outside that would sound the death knell for Progressive education and its several ideological offspring. The Progressive Education Association itself went out of business in 1955.[66] Long before that, its members and their influence were becoming identified with all that was perceived to be wrong with education: its anti-intellectualism, its fostering of particularistic values, its moral relativism, and, in the end, its irrelevance to the quest for a higher social order.

While the blanket of criticism directed at the Progressives was not cut in a consistent pattern, each switch contained a thread of truth—not only about the condition of education in its current form, but of what the future held for the last half of the century. Starting in the 1930s, respected educators such as William Bagley had begun to attack Progressivism as being devoid of substantive content.[67] Dewey himself warned against an unstructured approach to learning that was based on whim or impulse.[68] In 1943 Professor I. M. Kendel, of Teachers College, took his colleagues to task for promoting a pedagogical approach that was superficial and detached from any intellectual tradition that might be rooted in the past.[69] Robert Hutchins described the profession as philosophically bankrupt.[70] And Arthur Bestor, in an influential book entitled *Educational Wasteland*, assailed educators for failing to develop the most essential of skills needed to nourish a healthy democracy, the ability of students to think.[71]

All other criticisms aside, religion would emerge as one of the most conspicuous and indisputable casualties of the modern public school curriculum. In 1949 Bernard Iddings Bell observed that the school had taken over domestic and developmental functions that properly belonged to parents, and did so to the total exclusion of religion.[72] Several years later, in a book called *Quackery in Education*, Albert Lynd lamented that professional educators had established a monopoly over schooling and had taken control out of the hands of the public whom it was supposed to serve. He identified the public school as "one of the neatest bureaucratic machines ever created by any professional group in any country anywhere."[73] In the name of value neutrality, it became fashionable for educators to assert that it is not appropriate for schools to attempt teaching the difference between right and wrong. One widely adopted educational handbook published in the 1970s advised teachers to cast themselves in the role of a moderator rather than an instructor when it comes to the subject of values clarification.[74] But beneath the moral nihilism rested a clearly formulated set of standards that had a profound effect on teaching and learning.

Freedom from Religion

When Pulitzer Prize-winning author Francis Fitzgerald completed her landmark study of American history textbooks, she concluded that by the end of the nineteenth century, religion had virtually disappeared as a subject of importance.[75] Before then, most schoolbooks had been written by ministers or teachers in religious schools. By the 1890s public schools had grown more common; teachers had been made employees of the state;

and the subject matter of history, now devoid of religious content, increasingly had become the affairs of government. Paul Vitz found a similar pattern of neglect in his comprehensive study of elementary school texts through the early 1980s.[76] These findings have been corroborated by the work of other scholars. In fact, there is a disturbing consensus, among some researchers at least, that the place of religion in American culture has been so purposely understated in public school texts that the literature has distorted the historical record.[77] Publishers and their authors, so afraid of provoking controversy or offending the educational administrators who select texts, prefer to sacrifice historical accuracy rather than lose sales. When religion makes for bad business, secularism carries the day.

Just the mere mention of God or religion in a public school setting is liable to bring a severe reprimand from school officials. I'm not referring to the teaching of religion under the guise of neutrality, as did Horace Mann, nor even the introduction of a "nondenominational" prayer by school authorities, which I believe is likely to offend some students or at least create an uncomfortable environment for them. What I am referring to here is an intolerance toward any manifestation of one's faith on the grounds of a public school. Take, for example, the case of a fifth-grade teacher who was told that she could not read a Bible during her class's silent reading period. Or consider the ninth-grade student who received an F for a paper she wrote on Jesus Christ because she had violated a rule against taking up religious issues in the classroom. Think about the high school valedictorian who was removed from a graduation program when she refused to delete references to her religious upbringing from the talk she had prepared. All of these incidences took place in public schools since 1990, and the reprimands meted out by school authorities were upheld by federal courts.[78]

Nat Hentoff relates the story of six-year-old Zachary Hood, a first grader at Haines Public School in Medford, New Jersey. He had been given an opportunity to demonstrate his reading proficiency by reading a story of his choosing to his class. When he selected a story from the Book of Genesis out of the Beginner's Bible, he was told that it was not allowed because it is religious. After a humiliated and teary-eyed Zachary returned home, his parents complained to the school and were rebuffed. When they subsequently sued, their pleas were rejected by both a federal district court and an appellate court.

Hentoff cites an *amicus* brief submitted to the Third Circuit Court of Appeals by the Americans United for Separation of Church and State, the

Anti-Defamation League, and the American Jewish Congress in support of the school, charging "Zachary Hood alleges a deprivation of . . . a constitutional right to proselytize his classmates in class regardless of the teacher's considered judgment that the selection was educationally inappropriate." The incident led Hentoff, a journalist with a long history of civil rights advocacy to comment,

> There are times, and this is one of them, that certain institutions zealously intent on keeping schools religion-free become mirror images of Pat Robertson's insistence that this is a Christian nation.[79]

It is tempting to suggest that secularism has become a part of a contemporary public philosophy, but the claim does not stand up well to evidence showing that most Americans consider themselves religious people. In a national poll taken in 1996, six out of ten Americans said that religion is a very important part of their lives, and three-quarters admitted that they are absolutely certain about their belief in God.[80] The constraints that secularism imposes in the modern liberal state are more subtle and complex. Religion is tolerated so long as it does not intrude on public life. As Stephen Carter has poignantly explained, the American political system treats religion as a trivial endeavor.[81] Most public officials will defend to the end the abstract notion of freedom of conscience, but they recoil when an individual or group attempts to act on their religious convictions in the public arena.

People of faith, such as Richard Neuhaus, rue that public life has become inhospitable to religion.[82] In a manner of speaking, the situation is far worse than even Father Neuhaus might imagine. The reason why the liberal notion of separation has prevailed in defining church-state relations is that many, if not most, Americans subscribe to it—even the great majority who claim to be religious. Take note of a recent book by Alan Wolfe. While 84 percent of the people he interviewed said they believe in God, the same group also felt that religion should be removed from politics.[83] Wolfe celebrates the "quiet faith" of middle America, which allows it to keep religion a private matter. While obviously struck by what he found, Wolfe might not have fully appreciated it for what it tells us about ourselves. What Wolfe really discovered in his research was the depth (or lack of it) of religious conviction held by most of the people he surveyed.

Many Americans who value religion for its ritualistic and communal rewards do not allow it to govern the way they lead their lives. The majority accepts the secularization of public life because it does not interfere with their private existence, nor does it encumber the watered-down version of religious practice they espouse. This view of religion enables people to disconnect teaching or dogma from behavior. It is compatible with the Enlightenment liberalism of Locke and Jefferson and Dewey, which protects one's right to believe what one will but readily subjects religiously motivated action to the authority of the state. It is a more limited view of religious freedom than Madison and the framers had in mind when they wrote the First Amendment.

The liberal approach assumes that individuals can marginalize religious convictions, keep conscience in its place, and live around it rather than through it. This is a reasonable expectation for the great majority of people who, in Carter's words, "treat religion as a hobby"; but it is insensitive to the small minority of devout believers whose relationship with their church and their God requires them to live their lives according to the dictates of their faith. At times the obligations imposed on these minorities through public policy enacted in the name of the majority are outright hostile to their beliefs.

To the average Catholic parents, a school curriculum that prescribes the use of birth control may not constitute an affront to personal standards of morality, even though the practice is opposed by their church. Chances are that they practice birth control themselves, and they probably did so before they were married. To the religious Catholic who equates birth control with the suppression of life, the curriculum creates a serious dilemma. It is an anxiety that most people have trouble comprehending. It appears to be driven more by faith than by hard evidence of a life-threatening situation. It, nevertheless, is a genuine and legitimate point of view of the devout believer.

There is a tendency on the part of many liberal social analysts to dismiss opinions that are faith based. Religious viewpoints are not especially persuasive for nonbelievers. They do not hold up to empirical scrutiny, and at times they appear to be downright foolhardy. To reject the veracity of faith-based claims is a reasonable response for the nonbeliever; to treat them with disdain is another matter.

We do not need to return to the eighteenth-century writings of the Enlightenment or Dewey to confront such negative attitudes toward religion. Consider the work of Yale law professor Bruce Ackerman. In a widely read book entitled *Social Justice in the Liberal State*, Ackerman advocates removing religious considerations from public discussions of policy, which he refers to as "some conversation with the spirit world."[84] Ackerman obviously perceives divinely inspired arguments as patently ridiculous, which he is certainly entitled to do. He may even be correct in the eyes of most reasonable people. But his facile dismissal of religiously motivated thought and action points to a fatal flaw in liberal social theory. Assessing the credibility of religious thought by empirical standards, even the crude tools commonly applied by social scientists, is like using a stopwatch to measure the temperature of oil in a frying pan. As Locke understood (and Augustine before him), the "City of God" and the "City of Man" are philosophically derived from separate universes.

The calculus of religious liberty in a free society is determined by the measure of religiously motivated thought and action that is insulated from public authority. Madison and his fellow authors of the First Amendment were clear on that. Their conception of religious freedom was designed to protect all forms of religion regardless of how absurd they might appear to the average citizen. The framers had not intended to define the scope of religious freedom in the arena of majoritarian politics. To the contrary, they constructed the First Amendment, and the entire Bill of Rights, as a barrier of protection from majoritarian politics.

The liberal idea of religious freedom is a limited guarantor of civil rights. It works best for those who do not take religion seriously, that great majority of people whose connection to sectarian institutions is more ceremonial than conscientious. It fails the small minority of devout believers who live their lives through their faith, the very segment of society that the First Amendment was designed to shelter.

One reason why some liberal social theorists are so ready to negate the concerns of people with strong religious convictions is that they don't like them very much. Many religious zealots are associated with the political right, the powerful Christian Coalition. The coalition's position on such issues as social welfare, feminism, and homosexuality is revolting to the liberal agenda. They offend the liberal conscience. These are all issues that need to be debated vigorously in the political arena. Constitutional principles, however, should not be sacrificed on the altar of political debate, no matter how significant the issues. When the left adopts a political strategy that has the effect of eliminating religion from the face of civil society, it runs the danger of trampling on the constitutional rights of all those who take their faith seriously, including many who support a large part of their political agenda. To do so violates the basic rule of political etiquette that applies in a democratic society.[85]

It is no secret that public schools have become a battleground of the culture wars being fought between the right and the left.[86] It is an egregious occupation, especially when political activists use the public authority of the school board to pursue goals that are either insensitive or hostile to the religious traditions of certain groups. These transgressions have been perpetrated from all sides of the political spectrum and serve to reinforce the fact that schools are indeed political institutions. In 1997, for example, a group of Jewish parents had to resort to litigation when an Alabama school board required their children to remove their yarmulkes and bow their heads during the recital of a Christian prayer.[87] Stephen Bates tells the story of the trials and tribulations of a fundamentalist mother in Tennessee whose child was required to read literature that offended her religious beliefs.[88] Rosemary Salomone has written a case study about the plight of two women in the wealthy hamlet of Bedford, New York, who opposed aspects of a "New World" curriculum that was taught in their children's public school.[89]

History unfortunately does repeat itself. The attempt by an Alabama school board to impose Christianity on Jewish children reads like a page out of the book of Horace Mann. But the lesson to be drawn from the common school experience is not the threat one group or another poses to individual rights, whether the attack is launched from either the left or the right. History's lesson speaks more directly to the concept of the common school itself, existing as the sole institution through which parents may attain a free education for their children. If there is anything to be learned from a century and a half of school wars waged around the confrontation between the public values of a ruling majority and the private values of political minorities, it is the inherent danger of giving the larger group absolute authority over the education of the smaller group without providing the latter with meaningful alternatives that reflect their own moral standards. As Steven Arons, one of the first scholars to comment on the preposterous nature of the public school culture, warned:

> The history of conflict over school orthodoxy changed profoundly with the advent of compulsory attendance laws. Once the audience became virtually captive and the control became majoritarian, it was necessary for a variety of social groups to contest with each other over whose values and world view would be adopted by the local public school. Parents were to be viewed by educators as presumptively incompetent; and schooling became less an issue of individual

development and family aspiration and more an issue of social needs and group values.[90]

The majoritarian persuasion grew more imposing as it became so openly antireligious. The objective now was not only to remove religion from the public schools, but also to eradicate its influence in the upbringing of children so that they could be cleansed of the hidebound traditions heaped on them by their unenlightened parents. Again, references to the contemporary scene suffice to make the point. In a widely read book published under the title *Democratic Education*, Princeton political theorist Amy Gutman presumes that education must function as a mechanism to "convert children away from the intensely held [religious] beliefs of their parents."[91] Educator John Goodlad agrees that "[s]chools should liberate students from the ways of thinking imposed by religions and other traditions of thought."[92]

Liberal academics and intellectuals have fallen into an easy alliance with the public school lobby led by the teachers unions. The spontaneous attraction between the two forces was so compelling: one carried intellectual weight, the other raw political power. One could adorn politics with the language of freedom, the other could ensure victory. For liberals there was this sentimental connection to the unions with a long history of advocacy for the downtrodden. The advance of the religious right exposed a common terror to ultimately drive the two together in one cause. It was a strange bed for liberal intellectuals to make nonetheless. It is a view toward religion that is difficult to reconcile with the redistributive social agenda that so many of the same liberal intellectuals espouse.

The liberal position on school choice is an affront to egalitarianism and is out of touch with the needs and sentiments of the poor. As we have seen, poor people are among the most ardent supporters of school choice. They have supported the idea because they place a high value on religion, because they perceive choice as a mechanism for improving educational opportunity, and because they understand that the policy arrangement prevalent in most jurisdictions offers real educational options only to those with the personal means to afford it. The opposition to religion is so vehement in some circles that it has overshadowed concerns for educational equality. The same social theorists who claim to be advocates for the political and social equality of the poor disregard the pleas of the poor when it comes to the issue of school choice. They mount their assault on the principle of separation, as if religion were inherently inimical to a free society, as if they were protecting a venerable constitutional mandate passed down by the framers of the Bill of Rights.

State Constitutional Law

In the last chapter I reviewed a body of case law promulgated by the Rehnquist Court that suggests there is nothing in the United States Constitution prohibiting the expenditure of public funds to pay tuition for children to attend private and religious schools. This jurisprudence served to overturn a series of rulings handed down by the Burger Court during the 1970s, which imposed standards of separation that had questionable grounding in the First Amendment or its interpretation by the Supreme Court through most of the twentieth century. Beginning with the *Meuller* decision of 1983, followed by *Witters* (1986) and *Zobrest* (1993), the Court reasoned that tuition aid is permissible provided that it is administered on a religiously neutral basis and assistance is appropriated to parents rather than schools. In a related set of opinions *Bowen* v. *Kendrik*(1988), *Mergens* (1990), *Lamb's Chapel* (1993), and *Rosenberger* (1995)—the Court declared that to deny religious institutions or those who attend them the same benefits that are provided others on a universal basis runs afoul of both the First Amendment and the Equal Protection clause of the Fourteenth Amendment. For anyone who was unclear about the change in thinking that had occurred on the High Court, a majority affirmed more recently in *Agostini* (1997) that the strict separationist interpretation that prevailed on the Burger Court is no longer considered good law.

The Court's return to the more accommodationist standards of the past has prompted opponents of school choice to focus their political and legal strategies at the state level, where they are more likely to get a sympathetic hearing. As a legacy of nineteenth-century politics, many states have separationist provisions within their own constitutions that are more restrictive than federal requirements. Moreover, state judges, the preponderance of whom are chosen through a majoritarian process of political elections, are vulnerable to the pressures of local interest groups that do not want private and parochial schools to compete for public education dollars.[93] Notwithstanding the last two decades of federal jurisprudence, many local judges are inclined to be persuaded by the limiting interpretations of a prior era—notably, *Lemon* (1971), *Nyquist* (1973), and their progeny—when dealing with the First Amendment. When that fails to meet their political objectives, they have their own state constitutions to draw on and a local body of case law that remains in incredible disarray.

Diverse Standards

If there is one characteristic that defines church-state jurisprudence at the state level, it is the enormous range of diversity that reigns among the fifty distinct jurisdictions. In a recent survey of state constitutional provisions and judicial rulings, Kemerer found that the states divided into three categories on the basis of accommodation: seventeen are restrictive, fourteen are permissive, and nineteen are uncertain.[94] Of the seventeen in the restrictive category, fourteen are in the West, where new states were admitted to the union following the proposal of the Blaine amendment in Congress and the imposition of added restrictions on entering territories. According to Kemerer, five state constitutions explicitly prohibit direct or indirect aid to private schools, and twelve impose more general restrictions on aid. Thirteen of these same jurisdictions have set constitutional restrictions limiting the use of public funds exclusively to public schools. As recently as 1970, Michigan passed a referendum that proscribed giving vouchers or tax benefits to anyone who attends a private or parochial school.

If religious liberty in America appears to be in a chaotic condition, the situation is at least in part a function of the fact that in any one of fifty jurisdictions, the legal boundary of separation is determined by a dynamic interaction between federal and state standards set by constitutional law, statutory requirements, and judicial interpretation. This discord among the states and between the levels of government is in keeping with the American model of federalism.[95] It is entirely permissible for states, when they choose, to define the legal boundary of protection for civil rights more broadly than the federal government does. Some have done so rather aggressively over the past twenty-five years.[96]

The problem arises when state authorities act to abridge federally defined rights, which is impermissible under the Constitution. First Amendment jurisprudence is ripe for such transgressions for a number of reasons. To begin with, it is sometimes difficult for even the best intentioned jurist to recognize when a strict enforcement of the Establishment clause carries one over the permissible line of separation to infringe on the Free Exercise rights of others. The task has been made more challenging by the inconsistent criteria set by the Supreme Court over time. Beyond these analytic problems, some state judiciaries are more inclined than others to follow the lead of the federal courts in interpreting the First Amendment; and there are those state judges, animated by their own legal philosophy, local constitutional traditions, or plain, ordinary politics, that openly flout guidelines set by the Supreme Court.

While the empirical research available on state jurisprudence is somewhat limited, it nevertheless reveals a high level of tension between state and federal judicial standards. One survey found that courts in nearly half the states have indicated they do not consider Supreme Court rulings on the First Amendment binding in interpreting their own constitutions.[97] Through prior judicial decisions, twelve states have indicated they have stricter standards of separation. Several have openly rejected the "child benefit" concept, claiming that it promotes form over substance. Some states have struck down programs that provide transportation and textbooks to parochial students, even in the face of federal decisions permitting such benefits.

Consider the state of Washington, which, at Congress's bequest, modeled its state constitution after the Blaine amendment. In 1949, two years after the Supreme Court upheld a similar program in New Jersey, a Washington court struck down a busing program that benefited parochial school children, explaining:

> Although the decisions of the United States Supreme Court are entitled to the highest consideration . . . we must, in light of our state constitution and our decisions thereunder, respectively disagree with those portions of the *Everson* majority opinion which might be construed, in the abstract, as stating that transportation, furnished at public expense, to children attending religious schools, is not *in support* of such schools.[98]

Although the Washington judiciary has been among the most contentious in its attitude toward the Supreme Court, it is not the only state that has drawn on its own constitution to scuttle federal guidelines. In 1987 the Massachusetts Supreme Judicial Court issued an advisory opinion on a proposed bill that would give a tax deduction to parents of parochial school children. The bill was similar to the Minnesota statute that the Supreme Court had approved in the landmark *Mueller* case of 1983. Rejecting the "child benefit" argument, the Massachusetts panel ruled "if aid has been channeled to the student rather than the private school, the focus is still on the effect of the aid, not on the recipient."[99] In 1992 the Supreme Court of New Hampshire wrote an advisory opinion to the state legislature regarding a proposal that would partially reimburse private and parochial school families for tuition expenses. It found that the plan violates the state constitution, which prohibits appropriations "toward the support of schools of any sect or denomination."[100]

The relationship between the federal and state courts has not been entirely characterized by discord. On occasion some states—notably Wisconsin, New Jersey, and New York—have actually revised their constitutions to align them with evolving federal standards.[101] Nor is it uncommon for parochial school students to receive some form of state aid. Another survey shows that forty-two states offer some form of assistance, usually in the form of transportation, textbooks, educational materials, health services, or meal plans.[102]

In 1999, citing federal case law, the Arizona Supreme Court approved a state tax credit for contributions made to private scholarship programs that benefited religious and independent school students. The opinion went to great lengths in tracing the origin of "Blaine amendment" provisions in state constitutions to a period of "religious bigotry," rejecting the suggestion that such a provision had any bearing in Arizona.[103]

Recent and Ongoing Litigation

Four major school choice cases have been wending their way through state courts over the past several years: the two original suits in Wisconsin and Ohio, plus contests of a slightly different nature in Vermont and Maine. (And litigation has now been initiated against the Florida statute enacted earlier in 1999.) None of the first four are states with fervent separationist legal traditions, nor have their judiciaries displayed a disposition to use their own constitutions to undermine federal standards.[104] But these were high-profile politicized cases, where the stakes were high. While each suit emerged in response to specific local developments, some of the key parties remained constant throughout all the proceedings, serving as a constant reminder that these battles would be played out in a national theater.

On one side stood the American Civil Liberties Union, the key strategist for the anti-choice forces, occasionally joined by such groups as People for the American Way, Americans United for the Separation of Church and State, and the National Association for the Advancement of Colored People. A local affiliate of either the National Education Association or the American Federation of Teachers would serve as a litigating party in every case. On the other side stood the Washington-based Institute for Justice. The organization's two principal legal strategists, Clint Bolick and

William Mellor, describe it as a "libertarian public interest law firm."[105] They have been associated with a number of conservative causes, such as opposition to racial gerrymandering in elections and racial quotas in hiring, but they have also represented minority and disadvantaged clients in an assortment of cases ranging from commuter van drivers in New York to African American hair braiders in Columbus, Ohio (both regarding regulatory issues).

By the time the challenge to Milwaukee's choice program reached Wisconsin's highest court, it had been rejected at both the trial and appellate levels. Even though the state supreme court eventually approved the law that allowed poor children to attend private and parochial schools through publicly supported vouchers, and the U.S. Supreme Court let the decision stand, choice opponents had achieved a tactical victory. Through litigation they succeeded in delaying the full implementation of the program for three years. Although the lower courts had studiously avoided federal constitutional issues in reaching their decisions, the state supreme court dealt with the First Amendment issues head on. Following precedents set down by the Rehnquist Court, a 4–2 majority (with one judge recusing herself) ruled in June 1998 that the First Amendment was not violated in Milwaukee because (1) the program is neutral regarding the religious and secular options that were made available, (2) the funds were appropriated to parents and children rather than schools, (3) funds were directed to parochial schools only as a result of individual choices made by parents. Responding to claims that religious schools were the primary beneficiaries of the choice program, the court found that the primary beneficiaries were parents and children, holding, "The purpose of the program is to provide low-income parents with an opportunity to have their children educated outside the embattled Milwaukee public school system."[106]

The Wisconsin Supreme Court also rejected challenges made on the basis of state constitutional law. With regard to the state's public purpose doctrine, it explained, "Education ranks at the apex of a state's function." The decision continued, "This court has long recognized that equal educational opportunities are a fundamental right . . . and that the state had broad discretion to determine how best to ensure such opportunities." Citing *Pierce* and *Meyer*, as well as state precedents, the court affirmed, "Wisconsin has traditionally accorded parents with the primary role in decisions regarding the education and upbringing of their children." It then quoted at length from an 1899 decision of its own that went to the heart of the choice question, recognizing that:

Parents as the natural guardians of their children [are] the persons under natural conditions having the most effective motives and inclinations and being in the best position and under the strongest obligations to give to such children proper nurture, education and training.[107]

The majority's reasoning was so at odds with the thinking that shaped the lower court decisions that one would think they were based on entirely distinct legal traditions. The opinion of the lower courts are worthy of attention, however, because they are indicative of the kinds of arguments that are sure to resonate in future litigation. The trial court decision was handed down by Judge Paul B. Higginbotham in January of 1997. Judge Higginbotham proceeded on the basis of the "independent and more prohibitive basis for review" required by the Wisconsin constitution as compared to federal jurisprudence.[108] Though limiting his findings to state law, he did not hesitate to register his disagreement with the jurisprudence that had come to dominate the United States Supreme Court. His strongly worded opinion protested, "It can hardly be said that this does not constitute direct aid to sectarian schools. Although the U.S. Supreme Court has chosen to turn its head and ignore the real impact of such aid, this court refuses to accept the myth."[109]

Judge Higginbotham conceded that offering alternatives to poor children in Milwaukee's failing public school system was "sound public policy" that could benefit students who participated. But he was more concerned about the benefits that might accrue to religious institutions and the incentives that the aid would provide for students to attend these schools. He ignored the structure of economic incentives that applies when government-run schools enjoy a monopoly over public support. He focused on the fact that government checks for tuition reimbursement were made out jointly in the name of families and the schools they had selected, which he cited as evidence of direct assistance. This argument was rejected by the state supreme court. It viewed the check cashing policy as an administrative procedure designed to prevent abuse, which at the same time did not compromise the parental prerogative to exercise choice.

Insisting that the "authors of the Wisconsin Constitution intended to much more specifically curtail what the State may do in its interactions with religion than did the drafters of the Bill of Rights," the Wisconsin appellate court upheld Judge Higginbotham's findings in a 2–1 decision rendered in August 1997.[110] When the state supreme court reversed that decision, state Superintendent of Instruction John Benson publicly called for "a moment of silence for the loss of religious liberty" and suggested that the door was now open for people like the Oklahoma City bomber Timothy McVeigh to start his own religious school in Milwaukee.[111]

The Ohio court battle was also enveloped by political controversy, much of it sensationalist in character. What stood out in this 1997 case, however, was the remarkable legal reasoning by the appellate court that unanimously overturned Judge Lisa Sadler's trial decision. Judge Sadler had upheld the legality of the choice program in Cleveland on both federal and state constitutional grounds. The Ohio constitution contains some of the most accommodationist language of any in the union. It is derived directly from the Northwest Ordinance, adopted by the first Congress to govern the territory from which the state was carved. The same article of the state constitution that forbids the government to compel anyone to support a particular form of worship or to favor one religion over another goes on to read:

> Religion, morality and knowledge, however, being essential to good government, it shall be the duty of the general assembly to pass suitable laws to protect every religious denomination in the peaceable enjoyment of its own mode of worship, and to encourage schools and the means of instruction.[112]

The appellate panel cited a significant body of state case law to suggest that its own constitutional provisions are "coextensive" with First Amendment protections, but then went on to say that the state's own "protections" were "at least as great as that provided by the Establishment clause."[113] It conducted a significant review of federal case law, covering both the separationist opinions of the Burger years and the more recent holdings of the Rehnquist Court. But it drew its own opinion from the former. The appellate court then focused on the concept of neutrality and cited two pieces of evidence it believed indicated that the Cleveland program had failed such a test. First, it found fault with the nonparticipation of suburban schools. This was quite astonishing, since these public schools had been given the opportunity to participate in the scholarship program, and all turned the money down and refused to partake. The court expressed dismay that districts on the outer ring of the city were not compelled to open their doors to the Cleveland students. Its majority seemed to believe that it would be better for the poor students to commute to suburban schools where they were shunned than to attend private and parochial schools in their own communities where they were welcome.

Under the terms of the program, economically disadvantaged children who remained in the Cleveland public schools were eligible to obtain special tutorial grants. But this did not satisfy the judicial panel, raising the second point that spoke to the neutrality question. Here the court explained:

> Given the well-documented failure of the Cleveland School District, which is the Pilot program's *raison d'être*, it can not be seriously argued that sending a child to a private sectarian school at state expense, and providing a child attending a Cleveland City School District school with tutoring at state expense are even remotely equivalent benefits.
>
> Because the scholarship program offers vastly greater benefits to parents who send their children to private, mostly sectarian schools, . . . the Pilot Program creates an impermissible incentive for parents to send their children to sectarian schools.[114]

For choice proponents, however, this was the whole point. The purpose of the program was to avail poor parents of an opportunity that they did not previously enjoy. Of course, this would motivate some parents to transfer their children to private or parochial schools, especially if these children previously attended public schools they found unsatisfactory. Why else do this if not to give parents something that would be expected to benefit their children?

Perhaps if the parochial schools of Cleveland were as bad as the court believed the public schools to be, the judges would have allowed parents to choose the latter for their children. In the meantime, better for them to stay in the failing public schools.

When the Ohio Supreme Court handed down its decision in May 1999, it found that the choice plan did not violate either the Establishment Clause of the First Amendment or the religion clause of the Ohio constitution. While acknowledging that most of the program's beneficiaries attend sectarian schools, the majority emphasized that "no money flows directly from the state to a sectarian school and no money can reach a sectarian school based solely on its own efforts or the efforts of the state." It further explained that "sectarian schools receive money . . . only as the result of independent decisions of parents and students," rejecting claims that the statute did not have a secular purpose but primarily had the effect of advancing religion or entangled government with religion.[115] In the end, the court struck down the law on the basis of the Ohio constitution's "one subject rule" when the law was passed as a rider to an appropriates bill.

In order to avoid immediately disrupting the lives of the 3,700 students attending nonpublic schools under the choice program, the court allowed the program to continue for several weeks, until the end of the school year. In the meantime, choice advocates pledged to re-enact the law so that it met the technical criteria that had been raised, while opponents promised that they would challenge any new provision right up to the U.S. Supreme Court.

The choice program in Vermont was not conceived as an initiative to help poor people specifically. It is universal. The oldest choice law in the nation, it was passed by the legislature in 1869 to allow students who do not have public schools in their own towns to attend a public or private school elsewhere at state expense. As of 1997 ninety-one school districts were participating in the program. Over the years, students in the program had attended public, private, or parochial schools in other Vermont districts as well as in other states—Maine, New Hampshire, Connecticut, even as far as Pennsylvania, Illinois, and Michigan. Vermont has a strong accommodationist political and legal culture that dates back to 1783, when its Ministerial Act created taxing authority for towns to set up houses of worship. Its hundred-year-old constitution is notable today for its open embrace of religious institutions.[116] As recently as 1994 the state supreme court in *Campbell* v. *Manchester Board of School Directors* allowed the town of Manchester to reimburse a family for tuition paid at an Episcopalian school.[117]

In 1995 the state commissioner of education issued a statement to local school boards declaring that the reimbursement for tuition at sectarian schools is not permitted under either the Vermont constitution or the Establishment clause of the First Amendment. He also announced a new policy requiring that all payments for private school tuition must be made directly to the institution rather than indirectly through parents. This was the first time in the 126-year history of the tuitioning program that any public body had offered an opinion on the manner of payment. Its significance was unmistakable: direct payment to the schools would make the program more vulnerable to judicial scrutiny even under the terms of the child benefit concept.

The commissioner's legal opinion, which carried an endorsement by the state attorney general, was challenged by the Chittenden school board after it had approved funds for fifteen students to attend a local Catholic high school. At the trial level, Rutland County Judge Alden Bryan, concentrating on the direct payment issue, upheld the commissioner's policy of excluding religious institutions. He refused to consider their being singled out as a form of discrimination. Reminding the aggrieved families that "all Vermont parents have the right to send their children to parochial schools," he was unwilling to recognize the financial disincentives against doing so under the commissioner's new regulations.[118]

The most interesting part of Judge Bryan's 1997 decision concerned larger issues of public policy. Anticipating the consequences of a full choice program, he warned that "new sectarian schools of all kinds, perhaps on the fringe of the religious mainstream, seeing the potential for financial support, would open their doors." He woefully predicted that controversies over education spending "will intensify and divide over religious lines."[119] This was an astounding commentary from the bench. The choice debate had crossed a new threshold: political and religious pluralism were now shown as the culprits in the school wars over vouchers, best remedied by limiting public support to government-run schools.

Judge Bryan's ruling was upheld in part by a unanimous decision of the Vermont Supreme Court in June 1999. Sidestepping First Amendment issues, the court found that the Chittenden school district had violated the state constitution by not adequately ensuring that public funds were not used for "religious worship" in sectarian schools. While the ruling theoretically allowed for corrective action, it is hard to imagine how or why sectarian schools would undermine the core religious values that give meaning to their educational mission.

The choice law in Maine is similar to that of its New England neighbor. Its roots can be traced back two hundred years to a time when no public secondary schools existed and Maine towns paid tuition for students to attend private schools.[120] The framers of the Maine constitution deemed these institutions to be of such crucial importance that they mandated the state to support and encourage them.[121] Until 1981 it was customary for students to attend both independent and religious schools under the plan. Then the legislature passed a law excluding religious schools. The 1981 statute was prompted by an opinion letter from the Maine attorney general, which declared that the inclusion of religious schools violated the Establishment clause of the First Amendment.

In July 1997 five families from the town of Raymond initiated a suit in state court challenging the exclusion of sectarian institutions as a violation of their free exercise and the equal protection rights under both the federal and the state constitutions. A separate group of Maine taxpayers joined the suit as intervenors on behalf of state defendants represented by attorneys for the state teachers union and the Maine Civil Liberties Union. Nine months later a trial court issued a cursory four-page opinion upholding the exclusion on both counts. Citing *Lemon* and *Nyquist*, it further explained that to provide tuition payments for sectarian schools violates the Establishment clause because it would "subsidize and advance religion."[122]

The latter ruling was upheld in a 6-1 decision handed down by the Maine Supreme Court in the spring of 1999. The majority rejected the idea that excluding religious schools from the tuitioning program violated the free exercise and equal protection rights of the appellants and found that tuition support for parochial school children was prohibited by the Establishment clause of the First Amendment. Although the higher court conceded that changes had occurred in Establishment clause jurisprudence since *Lemon* and *Nyquist*, it was clearly the earlier federal rulings from which it drew its conclusions. Acknowledging that Maine had permitted religious schools to participate in the tuitioning program until 1981, the majority reasoned that the restrictive action taken by the state legislature that year, and the accompanying opinion by the state attorney general, were "a direct response to developments in Establishment Clause jurisprudence during the 1970s."[123] It was as though more than fifteen years of federal case law from the U.S. Supreme Court had been deemed irrelevant to the Maine proceedings.

Politics and Law

The escalating debate over the proper place of religion in American politics serves to underscore the meaning of constitutionalism in a free society, defining immutable public values that are sheltered from the ordinary passions of politics. A constitution is a higher form of law, meant to protect individuals from legislation or other kinds of governmental action that infringe on individual rights.[124] The ability to follow the dictates of one's conscience, the freedom to practice one's religion, are among the most cherished entitlements within the American constitutional tradition. Because the propensity of some to indulge these liberties to the fullest is somewhat misaligned with the mainstream of contemporary American culture, matters of conscience are also among the most vulnerable of the rights outlined in the Constitution. They are easily dismissed by most citizens, who conceive of religion very differently from the way it is treated by devout observers.

American federalism provides a gaping window of opportunity for those who would use the political and legal process in ways that undermine certain aspects of religious belief and practice. Education has persistently been at the center of our constitutional traumas because Americans habitually have used their schools as institutional vehicles for inculcating important political and social values. In this sense the common school experience has been incurably preposterous, at one time serving as the pulpit for religious doctrinaires, at another telegraphing an open disdain for communities of faith. If one were not familiar with the politics that drives education policymaking in government, the contours of the entire debate would seem rather incredible: how little imagination has been applied to resolve the religious issue in schools; how, when educators finally decided to adopt a secularist curriculum in public schools, they did not bother to work out fair and serious options for those families who do not lead secular lives.[125]

The recent state supreme court decisions enacted in Wisconsin, Ohio, Vermont, and Maine leave unresolved the two central questions that must be addressed at the federal level: whether it is permissible for a state to pay for the costs of a parochial school education when parents prefer it to public school, and whether a state can discriminate against parochial schools in a publicly supported program open to other private schools. There is no doubt that as more cases percolate up through state judiciaries around the nation, the Supreme Court will be required to speak directly on the voucher issue. My own reading of the case law amassed by the Rehnquist Court suggests that, when the time comes, the Court will rule that it is constitutionally permissible to reimburse parents for tuition in a neutral fashion, and that it will strike down laws that specifically exclude religious schools or their students from benefits provided on a universal basis. This interpretation of the First Amendment is consistent with the pluralistic and egalitarian values that shaped its writing.

In the end, however, the relief that advocates of school choice can expect to derive from the High Court will prove to be circumscribed and unsatisfying. No state is currently under any constitutional requirement to provide publicly supported choice outside of the public school system. Whether state legislators and other elected officials expand the range of educational options given to parents remains largely a function of politics. For this reason, the monopoly that government-operated institutions enjoy over public funding remains secure. And it was for this reason that I earlier described religious liberty in America as a limited freedom.

CHAPTER SEVEN

Education, Choice, and Civil Society

EDUCATION IS the most reliable predictor of participation in public life. The probability that Citizen Jones will vote in elections, give money to political candidates, petition government for favors, or join voluntary associations in his community is strongly related to his level of educational achievement. Of course, the connection between education and civic involvement is complicated. Education can also be an indication of other social attributes—wealth, occupation, and skill—that affect Jones's propensity to get involved. These same individual characteristics enable Jones to achieve his political or social objectives when he decides to act, and his own sense of personal efficacy provides him with an incentive for further involvement. Without a decent education, nevertheless, it is less likely that Jones will emerge as a participant in the affairs of the city or town where he lives.

The central role that education plays in promoting an active civil society has been demonstrated and reinforced by five decades of research in political science.[1] We now know with great certitude that a well-educated citizenry is among the most critical factors for ensuring the stability of a democracy.[2] In a recent empirical study on political participation in America, Norman Nie and his colleagues distinguished between two dimensions of democratic citizenship, both of which are correlated with education: "political engagement" refers to the capability of citizens to pursue their interests through governmental channels; "democratic enlightenment" pertains to an understanding of and commitment to democratic norms.[3] One prepares citizens to be effective competitors in the political process, the other predisposes them toward accepting the outcome of the process even when their own priorities are not met. In the former, education functions as a sorter between winners and losers. In the latter, it serves as an agent for political acculturation and legitimacy. Jones becomes an effective participant in government through the acquisition of information, knowledge, understanding, and skills that pertain to the political process; he becomes a good citizen of democracy by developing values such as tolerance, deliberation, and the willingness to compromise.[4]

In a large way it can be said that the mound of research evidence that has accumulated over the years validates the underlying principles of the common school. Public education indeed serves as a foundation for American democracy as we know it. It has succeeded in socializing generations of immigrants to become loyal and engaged citizens. But if public schooling can be credited with advancing the greatest experiment in self-government known in the modern world, the education it purveyed also has to share the blame for America's most glaring failures. If education is the currency for acquiring political power, then the uneven distribution of its benefits among distinct demographic groups is at the root of a political inequality that has beset the nation through the twentieth century. If the job of public education is to teach each of us how to live together amicably and productively in a pluralist society, then at least part of the responsibility for our inability to do so must be placed at the schoolhouse door. If Americans have become disenchanted with government and public life, as so many polls seem to indicate, then perhaps we need to start thinking seriously about other ways to cultivate the political culture of the republic.

There is a deep concern among contemporary social philosophers about the condition of American democracy. In one widely read book, Michael Sandel laments that we have lost our way as a people. We no longer have a vision of the good life; our politics is devoid of the civic virtue that defines the ideals of a healthy republic. Sandel finds that the great anxiety of our age is "the loss of self government and the erosion of community."[5] He describes liberal democracy as a procedural republic that does no more than mediate individual and group differences. He joins legal scholar Mary Ann Glendon and others who portray a nation of citizens more oriented to the rights and claims they can make against the polity than what they might contribute toward a common good.[6]

The reading of these doleful tracts undoubtedly brings to mind the moral relativism that shaped so much of the Progressive curriculum at various points in time and that still has a great influence on our public schools. These critical works also point to some fundamental contradictions that shape liberal education—on the one hand claiming value neutrality, and on the other hand promulgating a clearly formulated political agenda to actualize a certain vision of governance. An increasing emphasis has been placed on individual rights in the civic education curriculum that is taught in secondary schools.[7]

Yet with all the "rights talk" that occupies liberal social theory and education, the school curriculum has proven insensitive and even hostile to one of the first freedoms contained in our Constitution. Not only is there little room for the mention of religion within the public school, but there also exists an avid opposition to the very idea of enrolling children in private religious schools. What is it about religion that is so antithetical to the liberal view of education? Why, if we cannot figure out how to incorporate religion into public schooling in a nondiscriminatory and inoffensive way, must we take so prohibitive a stance against the support of religious schools that students attend as a matter of choice?

Aside from the constitutional arguments addressed earlier, the traditional response inherited from Enlightenment liberals is that religion can be divisive. It accentuates our differences and undermines our common identity. This argument against the support of religious education is worthy of attention not only for its apparent persuasiveness among the American people, but also because it is based on a conception of religion that is an intellectual curiosity—unusual among modern democracies and unique in its intensity even within our own political culture.

In no area of public spending is the separation between church and state so strictly enforced in the United States as in elementary and secondary education. Students at religious colleges have historically been eligible to receive federal grants under a variety of programs designed to address particular national priorities or assist individuals who qualified either as former veterans or on the basis of economic need.[8] It is common for the federal and state governments to channel public monies into social service programs run by churches and other sectarian institutions. One study found that a majority of the child and family service agencies operated by religious organizations derive more than 40 percent of their funding from government sources. In one year government revenue accounted for 65 percent of the budget for Catholic Charities, 75 percent of the budget for the Jewish Board of Family and Children's Services, and 55 percent of the budget for the Lutheran Social Ministries.[9]

As recently as 1996 Congress passed a welfare reform bill, signed by President Clinton, that allows the states to contract with private organizations or create voucher systems for the provision of social services. The "Charitable Choice" provision requires the states to consider religious organizations on an equal basis with others and guarantees that participating organizations would be permitted to express their religious orientations openly and without prejudice.[10]

Why is elementary and secondary education so different? There are two explanations. The political explanation is that teachers unions, which represent public school employees, have the influence to prevent state legislatures and Congress from directing public funds away from public schools. We have seen this played out in previous chapters, and there is not much more to say about it. The philosophical explanation put forward by many opponents of choice speaks to the special role that public schools play in inculcating democratic values. The presumption here is that private and religious schools do not have the capacity to convey those same democratic values, and, as the argument goes, the flourishing of private and religious schools would have a fragmenting effect on the body politic.

Notwithstanding the wide support that the argument enjoys among Americans, there is no evidence behind the claim that public schools are the only effective means for political socialization in a democracy, or that the robust development of private and parochial schools is anathema to our aspirations as a free democratic society. In fact, the evidence is to the contrary. Research shows that adults who have attended parochial schools display high levels of patriotism, tolerance, and civic involvement.[11] On the whole, religious institutions in the United States have played a positive role in advancing the democratic ethos, and the implementation of school choice could enhance their capacity to do so. If designed appropriately, school choice programs would be particularly beneficial to poor communities, not only extending educational opportunities, but also invigorating civic life and addressing the larger problem of political inequality that besets economically disadvantaged people.

America's Unfinished Assignment

Robert Putnam set off a somber discussion among political commentators in 1995 with the publication of his famous "bowling alone" essay, sounding the death knell for civil society in America. Putnam had marshaled an impressive and disturbing array of evidence to demonstrate that Americans were becoming disengaged from their communities.[12] Voter turnout, the simplest act of citizenship, had fallen off nearly a quarter between the early 1960s and 1990. Roper Organization surveys had shown that the number of Americans who reported having attended community meetings fell from 22 percent to 13 percent between 1973 and 1993. Similar declines were recorded for the proportion of people who had attended political rallies, served on local committees, or worked for a political party. Putnam's conclusion was unambiguous and disheartening:

> By almost every measure, Americans' direct engagement in politics and government has fallen steadily and sharply over the last generation, despite the fact that average levels of education—the best individual-level predictor of political participation—have risen sharply throughout this period.[13]

Putnam's investigation gave special attention to the extent of American engagement in voluntary activity. Data from the U.S. Department of Labor indicated that serious volunteer activity had eroded by one-sixth between 1974 and 1989. Participation in local PTAs had dropped from more than 12 million in 1964 to 5 million in 1982 and had recovered to only 7 million by the time he had written his disturbing article. The Harvard political scientist found a significant decline since 1970 in the number of volunteers who had come forward to work in such mainline civic associations as the Boy Scouts (26 percent) and the Red Cross (61 percent). So, too, was the trend in fraternal organizations: the Lions (down 12 percent since 1983), the Elks (down 18 percent since 1979), the Shriners (down 27 percent since 1979), the Jaycees (down 44 percent since 1979), and the Masons (down 39 percent since 1959). Even the proportion of Americans who reported having socialized with their neighbors had declined significantly (72 percent to 63 percent) between 1974 and 1993.

Putnam also discovered several stabilizing and countertrends. Religious affiliation remains the most common form of association among Americans. He explains that the United States continues to be "an astonishingly churched society," having more houses of worship per capita than any other nation on earth. However, Putnam is quick to point out that religious sentiment in America seems to be more personal and less tied to institutions than it used to be, an observation that is consistent with the "quiet faith" that Alan Wolfe came upon in his more recent survey. That is an important consideration if we are to understand the peculiar role that sectarian institutions can play in contemporary civil society. We will come back to it later.

The countertrends that Putnam uncovered in his inquiry seem to be a reflection of changing public attitudes and priorities apparent on the American scene. National environmental organizations like the Sierra Club had grown dramatically in size. While membership in traditional women's organizations such as the Federation of Women's Clubs and the League of Women Voters had shrunk, feminist groups like the National Organization of Women (NOW) had grown. (It appears that NOW's increasing membership numbers have reversed since the publication of Putnam's essay.) The quickest growing voluntary organization in the United States is the American Association of Retired Persons (AARP), much a function of changing demographics and the aging of the population. In support of his overall thesis, Putnam explains that the way men and women get involved in mass-membership organizations is different from the way in which they participated in the old community-based associations of which he wrote. Very often their only connection to the larger nationally directed organizations consists of writing a check. Their involvement is not personal or interactive, and it does not contribute to the social capital of their respective communities. This brings us to the major point of Putnam's work.

Drawing on the work of Coleman, Putnam used the term "social capital" to refer to the networks, norms, and trust that enable people to work together. These social connections link substantial sectors of a community and bridge existing social cleavages.[14] These connections are the aspect of community life that determines the performance of government and other social institutions. Putnam was not surprised to discover that education is by far the strongest correlate of all forms of civic engagement, including social trust and group membership. He was less prepared to find that the relative decline in social capital did not vary within each education category studied, and, in fact, that an overall decline in social capital occurred while the education level of the general population was on the rise.

Declining Public Trust

Putnam's contention about the sociability of the American people is not unchallenged. In a separate study, Verba, Schlozman, and Brady found that between 1967 and 1987 there was a significant increase in the number of respondents who claimed they were involved in problem-solving activities in their local communities.[15] In a World Values Survey completed in 1991, 82 percent of Americans claimed they belonged to at least one voluntary organization, a rate that exceeds most Western democracies.[16] Political scientist Everett Ladd has conducted a number of surveys showing that, while absolute numbers may be down, there has been no drop in the percentage of people volunteering; and he attributes the decline in PTA membership to comparable decreases in the school-age population.[17] Ladd also found that church attendance has remained stable, and he recorded an increase in charitable giving. His church attendance findings tend to corroborate Putnam's. While philanthropy may be an indication of public consciousness, it does not constitute the kind of civic involvement that Putnam had in mind when he warned about the erosion of social capital. In fact, money giving is the antithesis of the kind of interpersonal civic involvement that concerned Putnam.

Whether or not Putnam's prognosis of civic involvement can be believed—and I, like many political scientists, do believe it—there are certain facts about the condition of American democracy that are incontrovertible. One, already noted, is the drop in voter turnout, the most basic of civic responsibilities. Another commensurate trend is the plummeting of public confidence in government institutions and leaders. The rise of public cynicism has become so severe that it was the subject of a recent conference held by a large cross section of the Harvard faculty, the proceedings of which were published in a book entitled "Why People Don't Trust Government."[18] There are several manifestations of the downward spiral. In one essay, Gary Orren notes popular expressions of discontent through the tools of direct democracy like the initiative and referenda: the tax revolts of the late 1970s and the adoption of term limits in the 1990s.[19] More than half the states have passed ballot measures limiting the number of terms that an elected official can serve in a particular office.

The most compelling evidence of distrust is in the polls. In 1958 nearly three-fourths (73 percent) of Americans said that they trusted the government in Washington to "do the right thing" just about always or most of the time. By 1968 the figure dropped to 61 percent, in 1974 to 36 percent, and by 1980 it fell to 25 percent, where it has remained.[20] Since 1964 the proportion of the American people who believe that government is run by a few big interests looking out for themselves has climbed from 36 percent to 76 percent; those who say that the government does not care what the people think has grown from 36 percent to 66 percent; those who believe that quite a few people in charge of government are crooked has jumped from 29 percent to 51 percent.[21]

While the overall assessment of political institutions is quite negative, there are significant variations in attitudes based on the level of government. For example, a 1997 poll showed that only 22 percent of those questioned gave positive responses with regard to the federal government, whereas the responses for state and local governments were 32 percent and 38 percent respectively.[22] It appears that people are more trusting of public institutions that are closer to their communities.

Among the reasons people frequently offer for their eroding confidence in government are waste, inefficiency, and spending money on the wrong things. The public's disenchantment with government and its leaders has not grown uniformly over time. Political analysts have been able to tie dissatisfaction to particular episodes or events: the Vietnam War, Watergate, the pardoning of Nixon, Iran-Contra, economic recession. The overall downturn, nevertheless, has been steady. After a continued decline in the first two years of the Clinton presidency, confidence began to rebound during the second half of his first term. An assessment of the full damage inflicted by the Clinton impeachment will take some time.

The high degree of cynicism exhibited by the American public is not limited to government. Confidence levels have dropped by half with regard to a variety of major institutions that most people deem to be important. Over the past three decades, dramatic declines were recorded for universities (61 percent to 31 percent), corporations (55 percent to 21 percent), the medical profession (73 percent to 29 percent), and journalism (29 percent to 14 percent).[23] Banks, labor unions, lawyers, and, of course, public schools can be added to these. Analysts offer a variety of factors to explain our growing discontent: the declining significance of political parties, poor leadership, political mudslinging, negative media coverage, modern and postmodern values, animosity toward authority, anti-institutionalism, unreasonably high expectations, and, as already noted, the erosion of social capital.[24]

One of the problems with trying to explain this attitudinal phenomenon is that the data are not entirely consistent. To take our public schools, for example, most Americans express little confidence in public education generally, but they voice high levels of satisfaction with the particular schools that their own children attend.[25] On a similarly relevant note, contrary to the widespread cynicism that people show toward other institutions, confidence in religious institutions remains remarkably high. This is consistent with the high levels of church attendance that persist.

Blacks, Hispanics, and those who are at the lowest end of the income ladder—who historically have relied on government intervention to re-dress social grievances—have displayed slightly higher levels of confidence in the government than the rest of the population has. Even among these groups, however, only about one-third of those polled report that they trust the federal government always or most of the time.[26] While some-what confusing, the ambivalent attitude that the poor and racial minori-ties have toward government becomes more understandable when we dig deeper into the political behavior research. Since the beginning of the civil rights movement, government leaders, especially at the federal level, have expressed a great deal of sympathy toward disadvantaged populations. Public officials have even enacted numerous policies to reverse the effects of past discrimination. Racial minorities and the poor, nonetheless, have an unequal voice in the political process. Public policies that are enacted in the name of the poor are not always implemented in concert with their interests or desires. Sometimes the will of the poor is ignored by the same political leaders who claim to be acting on their behalf. The history of American education is replete with such examples. None is as glaring as the choice issue.

A Stubborn Inequality

Political equality is a fundamental assumption of democracy.[27] Trace-able to the Jeffersonian belief in the equal worth of all individuals, the principle of political equality enjoys wide support among the American people.[28] But translating this ideal into a reality has proven to be one of this country's most daunting challenges. First there were the legal obstacles. It was not until 1870 that an amendment was added to the Constitution prohibiting racial discrimination in voting. Only with the passage of the Voting Rights Act in 1965 did the nation begin to make real progress toward the egalitarian standard of one person, one vote; but the journey toward political equality would continue to be long, slow, and hazard-ous.[29] Although the elimination of poll taxes, literacy tests, and white pri-maries went a long way to remove legal impediments to political access, these critical steps would not address the underlying social causes of po-litical inequality. Implicit in the socioeconomic model of political re-search that goes so far in explaining the vitality of democracy is the powerful truth that personal resources determine who participates in politics and how well they do.[30] In the United States social inequality is very much associated with race. In 1997 the poverty rate for blacks and Hispanics was 26.5 percent and 27.1 percent, respectively, while that for whites was 8.6 percent.[31]

As we have seen in an earlier chapter, even the basic restructuring of political institutions cannot, in and of itself, raise the participation levels of the poor or significantly improve their political lot. In the end, the direct infusion of money into newly formed community-based corporations during the heyday of Lyndon Johnson's War on Poverty did not result in a significant redistribution of power at the local level. Turnout in local elections never exceeded 5 percent. Local activists often squandered resources on home-grown projects that rarely benefited the poor. When the dust finally settled, the control of funds and decisionmaking reverted back to city hall, where politics remained in the hands of the old ethnic coalitions. Chicago organizer Saul Alinsky, referring to the "stooges" who ran neighborhood poverty agencies on behalf of city hall, once described the Community Action Program as "political pornography."[32] The larger lesson to be gained from the episode is that you cannot jump start political development without furnishing the social requisites that make democracy work effectively.

I have already made the point, based on a substantial body of research, that education is among the key variables for creating the conditions of a healthy democracy. But I do not want to overstate the case of education's importance, nor do I mean to place the entire weight of the blame for our imperfect democracy on our public schools. The evidence on political socialization that takes place in our schools is mixed. Some of the research shows that most curricular materials used in the public schools are inadequate for developing an appreciation for the democratic process.[33] Delli Carpini and Keeter found that the disjuncture between the positive impression students come away with in the early grades and the realities of politics they become aware of in latter grades results in cynicism and withdrawal.[34] Recent research by Niemi and Junn, based on NAEP scores, is more encouraging, indicating that the civics courses students take in high school do enhance their knowledge of government. But the same study revealed significant knowledge gaps for black and Hispanic children.[35]

It is not my purpose here to impress the reader with the failure of either the political system or the education system. My limited objective—in this chapter at least—is to assess whether the implementation of school choice would have a negative effect on civic life in America. Before I can do that, I first need to reach some sort of conclusion about the current state of affairs. My review of the considerable evidence that exists suggests that there are two problems that stand out: a growing distrust of our major institutions that has been accompanied by a withdrawal from civic and community life, and a lasting inequality that not only defines the major dilemma of the present condition but also speaks to the primary subject of this book.

So now the question becomes more clear. How would the implementation of school choice, in the form of charter schools and vouchers for the poor, affect our growing disenchantment with public life (and with each other) and our continuing political inequality? If the answer to this question were to be as calamitous as opponents of school choice predict, then there would be no reason to go on with the discussion. If the answer to this question were to be "none" or "not very much at all," then there would be no conceivable reason to deny choice to the poor, once we get beyond our constitutional misperceptions. If the evidence were to suggest that school choice, as defined, might have an advantageous effect on one or both of the problems described, then it would provide a compelling argument for us to proceed. Before I can address this important question adequately, we need to spend a little more time understanding how democracy is made.

Growing Democracy

The concept of civil society has been so overused that it has come to mean different things to different people. For Benjamin Barber the term refers to "an independent domain of free social life where neither governments nor private markets are sovereign."[36] We create it for ourselves, according to Barber, in families, clans, churches, and communities. Michael Walzer uses the term to describe "the space of uncoerced human association and also a set of relational networks—formed for the sake of family, faith, interest—that fill this space."[37] Francis Fukuyama tells us that civil society is composed of "a complex welter of intermediate institutions, clubs, unions, media, charities, churches . . . by which people are socialized into their culture and given the skills that allow them to live in broader society."[38]

While somewhat different from each other, the common elements that appear in all these definitions are family, church, and, at least implicitly, community. Here we will focus on two essential functions that volunteer associations play in civil society: as training grounds for democracy and as mediating institutions between individuals and government. Family, church, and community play an important role in both.

Education for Citizenship

Among the foremost attributes that struck Tocqueville during his ponderous journey across a young nation was the propensity of its people to form organizations, which he perceived as a strong foundation for their democracy.[39] It was through personal associations made in such organizations that citizens would develop the "habits of the heart" that imbued them with solidarity, public spiritedness, and reciprocity; and it was these civic virtues that equipped them to take part in cooperative action. The natural development of these associations within communities of likeminded folks would serve as a counterpoint to the strong individualist spirit that characterized a free people and would even check the threat of majoritarian tyranny that so worried Madison.

The most important of all institutions, in Tocqueville's estimation, were religious. His observation bears witness not only to his insight on the role of religion in American civil society, but also to his keen understanding of the breadth and depth of religious sentiment among the people themselves. A great admirer of the separation of church and state that distinguished the United States from the governments of Europe, Tocqueville explains:

> Religion in America takes no direct part in the government of society, but it must be regarded as the first of their political institutions; for if it does not impart a taste for freedom, it facilitates the use of it. I do not know whether all Americans have a sincere faith in their religion for who can search the human heart?—but I am certain that they hold it to be indispensable to the maintenance of republican institutions.[40]

By the time James Coleman gave currency to the concept of "social capital" within the scholarly community, a prodigious volume of empirical research had accumulated across a variety of cultures to demonstrate the validity of Tocqueville's central thesis: members of voluntary institutions develop a higher aptitude for self-governance than others do.[41] Social capital, according to Coleman, is the ability of people to work together in groups and organizations. In addition to the acquisition of skills and knowledge, the capacity of people to associate depends on the degree to which communities share norms and values that enable them to subordinate individual interests to larger group or societal interests.[42]

At the core of all interpersonal transactions, the attribute that makes sociability achievable among separate individuals and groups is the ele-

ment of trust. Trust is a social virtue that emerges out of regularized interactions that are based on loyalty, honesty, and dependability. It is the infusion of this precious virtue from smaller social units, where they are
cultivated, to the larger societal context that makes democracy achievable. In his monumental exposition on the topic, Fukuyama emphasized
that the fountainhead of "trust" is the family structure. Like Aristotle,
Fukuyama understood the family to be the primary unit of human association. Human beings, however, are interdependent. To survive and pros-
per they need to go outside of the natural family unit and engage in
cooperative action, which they have learned to practice within the family.
The more elaborate forms of economic and political cooperation needed
to form societies are not meant to replace or compete with family, but to
build on it in the formation of communities.

A remarkably different view of political socialization can be obtained
by reading the research literature on civil society from that which we
became acquainted with under the framework of the common school.
Community-based institutions, including religious ones, are seen as the
foundation for a larger social cohesion that fortifies the health of the state,
rather than as a divisive force that jeopardizes the commonweal. Democracy forms through the natural evolution of institutions that begin small
and become large. Common values cannot be imposed through institutional mechanisms that foster an artificial process of political and social
homogenization, as Horace Mann sought to do. Social values are truly
"matters of the heart." They cannot be forced. It is not assumed that
schools, public schools in particular, are the only or the most effective
institutions for acculturating people to the ethos of democracy.

In a free society, education takes place in churches, union halls, club
houses, and workplaces; but most of all, it takes place in families. There is
nothing more obnoxious to a free society than the perpetration of conflict
between those institutions that pretend to educate for democracy and the
natural inclination of parents to raise their children in accord with their
own values. Then again, maybe there is. More hidebound is the proposition that when such differences ensue, they should, as a matter of course,
be settled in favor of government-operated institutions, or public schools.
Nobody has better explained the absurdity of the current formulation than
political theorist William Galston. He writes:

> Perhaps the most poignant problem raised by liberal civic education
> is the clash between the content of that education and the desire of

parents to pass on their way of life to their children. Few parents are unaware of or immune to the force of this desire. What could be more natural? . . . Conversely, who can contemplate without horror totalitarian societies in which families are compelled to yield all moral authority to the state?[43]

Galston's astute commentary introduces another dimension to the civil society discussion. It has to do with an important distinction to be made between harmony and conformity. While voluntary organizations can help induce social harmony by the way they involve citizens at the grass-roots level, conformity imposed by governmental institutions from above is counterproductive to democracy. Democracy is a form of governance that neither presumes nor calls for a universality of values.[44] It requires a healthy tension between government and the governed. Freedom is defined as the sphere of private action that is outside the realm of public authority. It is about the limits of government, the power to do as one pleases—as an individual and within groups, without suffering unreasonable constraints. This brings us to the second important function that voluntary associations perform in preserving the well-being of democracy.

Mediating Institutions

Peter Berger and Richard John Neuhaus describe mediating structures as organizations and institutions that mediate between an individual in his private life and the large institutions of public life.[45] Berger and Neuhaus were among the first social commentators of the late 1970s who were concerned with the weakening bonds of community in America and the effect it could have on the hardiness of our democracy. They were especially intrigued by the contribution that families, churches, and neighborhood organizations could make in improving the vitality of civic interaction. If only the influence of these "value generating and value maintaining" associations could more meaningfully be brought to bear in the policy arena, people would feel more "at home" in political life.

While Berger and Neuhaus's study of the American social landscape would alert us to the important role that mediating institutions play in a free society, the significance of these institutions would not be fully appreciated until seen in the context of societies where freedom was absent. The fall of the Soviet Union would spark a new interest in Eastern Europe and the heroic efforts that were being launched to create democracy in settings that were formerly dominated by totalitarian regimes. There the concept of civil society would have a different meaning. For people living under communism, civil society was both an alternative to and a refuge from politics. The instinct of the old order was to eliminate independent expressions of collective action. Like a child growing in a womb, civil society in Eastern Europe had sheltered the unseen but inevitable birth of new life. Under the rule of totalitarianism, civil society was the only sphere in which people could freely congregate to pursue common goals beyond the reach of government.[46] After the fall of communism, voluntary associations would form a counterweight to government power and create the tension needed to tone and strengthen these new democracies through their frail infancy.[47]

The struggle to reform education in Eastern Europe would be of particular consequence.[48] For more than a half-century, schooling had been controlled by an all-encompassing state bureaucracy. Education was used to impose a uniform system of thinking that was designed to promote loyalty to the state, bolster party control, and eradicate dissent. Thus one of the focal points of postcommunist reforms was to create alternative schools that were not operated by the government. This would be difficult in a culture where teachers and other educational professionals had been accustomed to functioning as part of an enormous government bureaucracy that discouraged innovation and demoralized the most talented individuals.

Many of the initial attempts to create nonpublic schools were brought by parents and teachers who had long been associated with anticommunist political activity. In some places, like Poland, where education had been closely identified with the secularization campaigns engineered by the state, many of the new schools would have a religious identity. In all places the fostering of educational alternatives was a manifestation of the new sense of freedom that had begun to grow. At first, these new options were available only to a small minority of families that could afford to pay the private school tuitions. The real sign of intellectual liberation would appear later, as governments began to adopt programs to support independent schools with public funding. By the time Charles Glenn completed his massive survey of education in the former Soviet-dominated territories in 1991, he could attest that more than a thousand such state-supported independent schools existed in places like Poland, Russia, and Hungary.[49] He was also keen to point out in his study, commissioned by the U.S. Department of Education, that such schools did not yet exist in the United States.

I do not mean to suggest, in alluding to the former Soviet states, that the education system of the United States is totalitarian in nature. The point I wish to make is that, contrary to the way some Americans think about it, most free societies cherish educational choice as an essential feature of democratic governance and liberty. It is common practice in the Western world. At this writing, government support for private and religious schools exists in one form or another in Australia, Belgium, Canada, Denmark, England, France, Germany, Holland, Iceland, Israel, Scotland, Spain, and New Zealand.[50] Since 1992 even socialist Sweden has instituted a system of publicly supported school vouchers in response to pleas from religious and language minorities whose educational needs were not being met by traditional public schools.[51] In most countries the principle of religious neutrality demands that no one creed be given priority over another and that a preference for nonreligion be honored in the same way. It is unusual among free-minded people to advocate giving preference to nonreligion over religion as a way to protect religious freedom. It is we Americans who are out of step.

There is an incredible irony here. From the church attendance figures that remain so high and the expressions of confidence that we express in our religious institutions, it can be claimed that Americans are among the most religious people in the western world. Of course, ours appears to be a quiet, demure kind of faith that does not insinuate itself into public life; but that speaks to the point that I am about to make. Some would argue that it is our particular political and legal culture that imposes such restrictive standards of separation and allows us to assume a common identity. But, the decade of *Lemon* and *Nyquist* aside, our political and legal culture is and always has been defined by pluralism. We are a nation of immigrants, and our diversity has been as pronounced as our unity.

On the religious front we are becoming even more diverse. The mainline Protestant consensus that once defined the culture of the common school is in a rapid state of flux. The old Episcopal, Presbyterian, and Methodist congregations that made up the mainstream of American Christianity are now equaled in membership by Catholics and evangelicals. While the size of the Jewish population has remained relatively steady, our diversity has been enhanced by the recent arrival of Muslims, Hindus, and Buddhists.[52] It is this raging pluralism that makes it so difficult for us to fit religion into our common schools in any other than either an antagonistic or trivial way. It is this same pluralism—political, legal, demographic— that will always remain the most significant safeguard against the threat of an established church.

The more vigilant we are about keeping religion out of the public schools, the stronger the argument becomes for providing options to the small minority of people who want their children to be educated according to teachings of their faith. Those opponents of choice who contend that giving more children an opportunity to receive a religious education will splinter society, foster separatism, or even endanger the republic, do not fully comprehend the nature of religious practice in contemporary America.

If we are to accept the picture of religion that Alan Wolfe and others have painted, it does not portray a population of zealots whose lifestyle or politics are defined by the doctrines of faith. For better or worse, most Americans are attracted to their churches and synagogues by the sense of community that they find there. Certainly, religious communities coalesce around common norms or values; but for the great majority of Americans, religious belief is not a source of antisocial behavior, disloyalty to the state, or even a rejection of the larger communities in which they live. As we approach the twenty-first century, our houses of worship are more likely to produce citizens than dissidents. After participating in one of the most extensive examinations of civil society ever undertaken in the United States, Galston and Levine echoed what Tocqueville had discovered more than a hundred and fifty years ago, when they recently concluded, "Church-affiliated groups are the backbone of civil society in America."[53]

But what about that small minority of people who are intensely religious, who live in self-contained communities and conduct their lives in ways that are detached from the customs and social mores that shape the so-called mainstream of American culture? Well, what about them? As a society that supposedly values religious freedom, we have an obligation to protect their right to be as different as they would be, so long as they live their lives within the law. The First Amendment was written for the benefit of people who are motivated by the dictates of their conscience; and sometimes those folks think, act, and even dress in very unusual ways. We do not have a constitutional obligation to provide these same folks with assistance for their children to attend sectarian schools, but we may. As a matter of public policy, the more the state uses public authority to impose secular values on these communities or burden them in the free exercise of their faith, the more likely it is that their religion will become a force for discord rather than harmony. That is one of the important lessons to be learned from Eastern Europe, and more recently from the culture wars being fought in public schools throughout the United States.

Will choice—public or private—install a process in which schools emerge from self-contained communities that form around particular norms or values? Lacking a great deal of experience with choice to draw from, I would concede to the opponents of choice that the answer to this question is most likely to be in the affirmative. The more important question though is whether the anticipated change would work to strengthen civil society or to weaken it. I would begin to address this question by returning to a point that was made at the very outset of the book. The fact is that most parents in America already exercise choice, and although our democracy is not what it can be, it has not served to divide us in an irreconcilable way. Should we expect that providing the poor with the same choices that most middle-class people enjoy would have a detrimental effect on the political order? I cannot imagine how anyone in good conscience could support that position. In the remainder of this chapter I will explain why I believe the opposite is true. I will argue that in addition to enhancing their educational opportunities, providing choice to the poor will help alleviate the political inequality that has held us all back for so long.

Liberating the Poor

First there is the obvious: how providing poor people access to better schools gives them the resources needed to pursue a fuller political and economic life. Then there is the less palpable sense of empowerment a mother or father acquires from being able to choose the school their child attends: the feeling of satisfaction that a parent gets after she has done something good for the most important person in her life; how a parent's power to act positively connects her to the larger society, both within and outside of her own depressed community; how the process of choosing, in and of itself, produces social capital in a community.[54] But to fully understand the effect that school choice can have on the poor, it is necessary to comprehend the central role that religion plays in their communities, and how past education policy has acted to undermine those same communities. Like Marx, many intellectuals view religion as the opiate of the masses—irrational, otherworldly, and, of course, patently anti-intellectual. If it is an addiction that has a particular hold over the poor, religion is also a drug that may relieve a pain from which the poor are more prone to suffer. It is, as proclaimed in the scriptures, a veritable source of salvation and redemption—in this world, if not the next.

The Wealth of the Poor

The centrality of the religious congregation in black communities has become the stuff of legend. In their landmark study on the topic, Lincoln and Mamiya remarked, "The Black Church has no challenger as the cultural womb of the black community."[55] Parallels between the African American and Eastern European experiences with religion as a cradle for civil society are remarkable. Under slavery the church was the only institution that permitted the oppressed to congregate and cultivate a sociability amongst themselves, beyond the purview of hostile authority. During the civil rights movement, the church was a storm center of protest against the established political order. After legislative and judicial victories were achieved under the banner of civil rights, the same church was transformed into an engine for the political and economic development of distressed urban neighborhoods.

Verba, Schlozman, and Brady published the results of their extensive investigation of civic voluntarism in the United States in 1995.[56] *Voice and Equality* begins with the socioeconomic model of political research as a premise, confirming the paramount role of education in fostering political activity and illustrating how the uneven distribution of social resources sets the conditions for political inequality. This ambitious analysis reaches further than any preceding it to explain how various social components interact to enhance participation. It examined a wide range of activities: voting, election campaigns, contributions, informal local activity, contacts with government officials, demonstrations, protests, and service on local governing bodies. Verba and his colleagues were particularly interested in finding out more about the consequences of such activities in terms of political efficacy: how these activities would enable people to communicate their preferences and needs to policymakers and exert pressure on officials to heed what they heard.

As might be anticipated, the authors found that different classes of citizens engage in different kinds of activity, depending on the bounty of resources they possess. Although education holds the premier position among social determinants, its relative importance in comparison to income and occupation varies according to the mode of participation. Wealthy people are more likely than poor people to make political and charitable contributions, and they are somewhat more inclined to make religious contributions. The less affluent, however, actually donate a much higher proportion of family income to their churches. The affluent are more prone than the poor to give time to political and charitable activity, but not to church activity. Like Tocqueville, Bellah, Galston, and a host of others before, Verba and his team paid special attention to the role of religion in civil society, not only to confirm its significance, but also to draw a more piercing conclusion concerning its leveling effect on the American polity. As they explain:

> Only religious institutions provide a counterbalance to this cumulative resource process. They play an unusual role in the American participatory system by providing opportunities for the development of civic skills to those who would otherwise be resource poor.[57]

African Americans are more inclined to get involved in their local churches than any other Americans—followed by Hispanics and then whites.[58] This study explains why. What stands out about religious institutions when compared to other voluntary associations is their democratic structure. While other organizations are stratified on the basis of class, race, and ethnicity, churches tend to be more egalitarian in their governance. The Protestant churches, to which a disproportionately high number of blacks belong, are especially organized so that all of their members can play a meaningful leadership role. This gives everyone an opportunity to develop participatory skills. Black churches also tend to be more politically oriented than other churches, largely because local congregations provide the most natural means for members to channel their political energies. Thus the contribution of churches to the political socialization of the disadvantaged is extraordinary. As Verba and his fellow researchers conclude, "Religious institutions play a much more important role in potentially enriching the stockpile of participatory factors for those who are otherwise disadvantaged."[59]

During the last quarter of the twentieth century, this incomparable resource, hatched in the nest of social deprivation, began to evolve in new ways. In the early 1960s several black scholars, impatient with the pace of progress, had speculated that the otherworldliness and political quiescence that characterized the black mainline denominations would lead to massive defections.[60] They predicted that upwardly mobile members would abandon the traditional black Baptist and Methodist congregations in favor of middle-class white churches, while more militant members would gravitate toward separatist movements like the Black Muslims. Another segment, it was believed, would give up on organized religion entirely. These predictions of widespread defections were never borne out, and the evidence suggests that it was the old mainline "Negro churches" that were at the forefront of political foment through the end of the century.[61]

One of the most encouraging stories to be told in America today depicts how church congregations have taken the lead in restoring the vitality of inner-city neighborhoods that might otherwise have been forsaken as hopeless.[62] While urban planners typically view development in economic and political terms, for many black and Hispanic leaders who work in the trenches, revitalization must also be seen in a spiritual sense. The differing perspectives between the two groups can be explained, at least in part, in terms of a large cultural gap that exists between whites and blacks. Over the last decade, outspoken black scholars have taken their white colleagues to task for a cultural myopia that leads them to impose a secularist agenda on a community of people whose spirituality is a source of great strength.

Cornel West criticizes liberal social scientists for their discomfort with moral and cultural concepts that would permit them to acknowledge fundamental social pathologies that must be dealt with in order to remove the greatest threats to distressed communities. He rebukes those who fail to nurture children morally and spiritually and who leave them unequipped to withstand the inevitable disappointments that life has in store for them. He identifies the church as the most important single institution to replace moral emptiness with the values of love, care, service, sacrifice, and justice.[63] In support of West's claim, there is a growing body of research evidence that demonstrates a negative correlation between religiosity and social deviance.[64] Adolescents who become connected with faith-based institutions are less likely to become involved with crime, violence, drug abuse, illegitimacy, and other forms of harmful behavior.

Among the black ministers who have taken the lead in working with inner-city youths is Reverend Eugene Rivers III of Boston. A Pentecostal pastor, Rivers collaborated with Catholic, Jewish, and other black religious leaders in his city to launch a successful campaign against juvenile violence that includes family counseling, summer recreation programs, and the reclamation of parks and other public places where young people congregate. Rivers has capitalized on local success by working with the Reverend Kevin Cosby of Louisville and the Reverend Harold Dean Trulear of Philadelphia to help mobilize a national campaign to replicate his program in a thousand inner-city churches located in twenty-five cities around the country.[65] There is much to be learned from that experience, but perhaps the most important lesson of all is the one that Rivers himself learned from a young heroin dealer he got to know in his program.

The young man seemed to be perplexed by the initial strategy the clergy had adopted. Why, he asked, if you are doing all this for the sake of God, do you never mention him by name? Rivers admits, "All this time we had been doing our good works, we were worried about being offensively religious. We didn't want folks to know too much about our faith." He goes on to explain:

> We realized the hard way . . . that secular solutions could never work in these forgotten pockets of despair. We realized that therapeutic institutions such as government, foundations, public schools and the whole panoply of non-faith-centered self-help outfits could not speak to the depth of psychic and moral decay that plagued our inner cities.[66]

I do not mean to suggest here that the role of the church has been limited to a moral or spiritual one. What Princeton political scientist John DiIulio refers to as "spiritual capital" has been invested wisely to transform inner-city neighborhoods into viable entities that employ, house, educate, and care for the people who reside in them. Based on the social networks of trust cultivated within and between religious congregations, cooperative efforts have been launched to bring economic and social resources into these communities so that they can be more self-reliant. In San Antonio, for example, Catholic parishes proved to be a crucial organizational factor in transforming the once powerless Hispanic community into a major political force on both the local and state levels of government.[67]

Meredith Ramsey reports that there are now five thriving national networks of faith-based coalitions: Direct Action Research and Training (DART) in Florida and the Midwest, with twelve affiliates; Gamaliel Foundation in Chicago, with thirty-five affiliates; the Industrial Areas Foundation, with sixty-five affiliates; the Organization and Leadership Training Center (OLTC) in New England, with six affiliates; and the Pacific Institute for Community Organizing in California, with twenty-nine affiliates. When these coalitions are added to a host of unaffiliated groups that also exist, Ramsey counts more than one hundred and seventy-five church-based institutions involved in developmental activities.[68]

Few local ministers in the United States have done more to advance the political, economic, and social renewal of their communities than the Reverend Floyd Flake of New York. Flake, the pastor of the Allen African Methodist Episcopal Church, served for six terms in the House of Representatives until 1998, when he resigned to give full attention to his ministry. He is a shining example of the potential that faith-based institutions have in serving as a catalyst for integrating local entrepreneurship with the intelligent leveraging of public and private resources. When one drives around his community in Eastern Queens, the fruits of Flake's labors are evident in a large stock of low- and middle-income housing, a senior citizen residence, a day care center, a credit union, a health clinic, a prenatal and postnatal clinic, a shelter for women and children who are the victims of domestic violence, and a multiservice community center. Allen has also launched an economic development effort with tithes and offerings and the establishment of nonprofit entities that have been able to tap public and private funding to get business started. The result is a small commercial strip that will house eighteen new businesses.[69]

Since 1982 the congregation has been operating the Allen Christian School, a facility where 480 children attend classes from prekindergarten through the eighth grade.[70] The school is financed through tuition and a subsidy from the church. Its students consistently surpass their peers in neighboring public schools on state standardized tests, and it has a long waiting list of applicants that continues to grow each year.[71]

Flake was one of the first Democratic members of Congress to take a strong public position in support of school choice. That move upset many of his party colleagues, but he offers no apologies for his position on the issue and continues to speak out forcefully on it. In his words,

> We can not offer our children any hope for the future, if we do not first furnish them with a quality education. The public schools in the city have not been able to provide that opportunity for the great majority of poor children.[72]

Countering Educational Neglect

The Allen School in New York is part of a growing phenomenon beginning to show a presence in American cities, the black independent school. According to a survey completed by the Institute for Independent Education in Washington, D.C., 350 of these institutions had come into existence by 1993, enrolling more than 52,700 students.[73] A separate survey conducted by the Toussaint Institute in New York identifies seventy-one such schools in the New York-New Jersey metropolitan area.[74] Another survey counts eighteen Christian and one Muslim school in the District of Columbia as of 1998.[75] Many of these institutions—like the one affiliated with the Concord Baptist Church in Brooklyn, the

Bethel AME Church in Baltimore, and a school started by the Reverend Richard Tolliver in Chicago's Washington Park neighborhood—are connected to urban ministries. All suffer from the same financial dilemma inherent in their mission to cater to the educational needs of the poor, who by definition are unable to afford the cost of tuition. The reach and effectiveness of these institutions is stifled by a system of school funding that refuses to support the educational preferences of parents who choose to send their children to private or parochial schools, but invests valuable public resources in government-run institutions that have failed generations of minority children. The strict separationist philosophy that has dominated educational policy in America for more than a century is so out of step with the culture and needs of racial minorities that it must share a large part of the blame for the years of educational neglect that has been visited on poor communities.

Toussaint director Gail Foster argues that black independent schools represent "a powerful alternative" to concerned parents, where "(t)he spiritual context of life is acknowledged even among most of the secular schools."[76] It all seems to make reasonable sense. When James Coleman wrote about the extraordinary success of Catholic schools in educating inner-city youths, he emphasized the community-building structure of these value-generating institutions. If Catholic schools are able to create social capital by integrating religious values with education, then schools associated with black ministries could become one of the most potent forces for growth in the urban environment. Describing such institutions, Joan Ratteray of the Institute for Independent Education writes, "This community becomes functional if students and families in the school share common experiences such as attending the same church or living in the same community."[77]

What about those single-parent families that, because of poverty and an assortment of social deficits, are in disarray? Again Coleman is instructive. In the latter part of his career the distinguished sociologist wrote a thoughtful essay where he mused about the changing family structure in the United States and its implications for education.[78] As a general rule, the role of the family has changed. As America has passed through the transition from an agricultural society to an industrial one, the family is no longer a unit of production, and the upbringing of children has been moved to institutions outside of it. With women joining the work force, we have become even more dependent on external entities for the care and nurturing of our offspring. Is the common school up to it? Coleman expressed concern with the failure of public schools to provide the moral and character education that were once bred within the family. He reflected on his own research thirty years past, which showed how the active involvement of families was so crucial to the academic success of children and speculated that the changing nature of family life would place even heavier burdens on the schools than ever before.

At the end of his essay Coleman turned his attention to the plight of poor children whose households might not be well equipped to provide the support needed for academic success. His own research had shown that all schools succeed less well with children whose parents are single and poorly educated. A disproportionate number of children who fit these categories are black or Hispanic. Searching for a remedy, he then returned to his research on Catholic schools, which showed that the dropout rate for single-parent children who attend these schools are no higher than those of other children. He then reviewed some new data showing that the "Catholic school effect" had been replicated in other secular schools. From this observation he concluded that "religious sector schools supply something that is deficient in many single-parent families, something that is not supplied by schools outside of the religious sector, whether public or private."[79]

Coleman explained that "something" in terms of social capital. Gail Foster offered a similar account when writing on the contribution of black independent schools. Foster runs a scholarship program in New York for students who were formerly enrolled in public schools, many of whom were placed in special education programs before their parents pursued other alternatives. Commenting on the orderly environment, clearly defined mission, caring staff, and high expectations that define the core values of the private institutions where she works, Foster confides:

> For many children in crisis, whose families are also in crisis, special education class in the context of a bureaucratic public school, even with a class size of seven children and two adults, is no match for the kind of surrogate parenting these historically black independent schools are willing and able to offer in their mainstream classrooms, even with 20 or 25 students and one teacher.[80]

In reviewing the history of black independent schools, Joan Ratteray regretfully remarks how these institutions have historically been undermined by a mentality that defined a generation of racial policy. The underlying assumption among desegregation advocates, she asserts, was that white schools are superior, and in order for black children to receive a proper education, they need to attend white schools. When considered in the context of community building, the implications of this policy are more disturbing, since it was understood that the white schools black children would attend were not in their own neighborhoods. If church-state separation and forced secularism were a grave offense committed against black civil society by education policymakers, it was forced busing that completed the harm. Together these policies landed a crippling blow on the two institutions that are the bedrock of any local community, the neighborhood church and the neighborhood school.

One of the most redeeming features of the charter school concept is that it provides an institutional mechanism for the natural formation of public schools within the bosom of real communities. They are schools of character rather than a figment of the bureaucracy. They are schools of choice, where students and teachers are present by their own accord rather than through coerced assignment. The future promises to offer a wide spectrum of educational institutions in urban areas that would have stunned the imagination of those who were at the forefront of the common school movement a century ago. The great hope of years to come is that such a large proportion of these new institutions are appearing in disadvantaged neighborhoods, where the quality of education has proven to be chronically inadequate.

Many of the new charter schools, like the Johnson Elementary School in San Diego, will have traditional curriculums. Others, like the Sankofa Shule in Lansing, Michigan, where teachers and children don traditional West African dress, will have an ethnic theme to their curriculum. There are some educators who will find the sight of these teachers and children incompatible with their image of the American melting pot. They confuse cultural identity with separatism. Children in African garb are no more of a threat to the health of American democracy and its underlying pluralism than were the legions of plaid-skirted girls who attended Catholic parochial schools in years past, or the sons of the privileged who appear on the campuses of elite prep schools uniformed in blue blazer and tie. They are just different. In the end, Sankofa's students will be expected to pass the same standardized tests that are given by the state of Michigan to hold other public schools accountable.

A furor broke out in New York during the winter of 1998, about a week after the state passed its charter school law, when several black ministers declared an interest in starting schools in their communities. Even though the pastors promised that the schools they had in mind would be secular, the chair of the state assembly's education committee (who had reluctantly supported the law) expressed public alarm, alleging that the religious leaders were on "shaky ground . . . thinking that they could organize and operate public schools."[81] The head of the local civil liberties union warned that "charter schools can't be a pretext for religious indoctrination," as he pledged to keep an watchful eye.

It was another dramatic exhibit of the cultural dissonance that sometimes appears between the white political establishment and the black community. Black church leaders sought to seize the opportunity to reverse a horrible pattern of educational neglect among the children in their communities; others were preoccupied with drawing an abstract line of separation between church and state. Very often even the most well-meaning white public officials and political actors are incapable of appreciating the unique and complex role the church plays in poor communities beyond the religious mission. The museums, civic associations, and cultural institutions that initiate charter schools elsewhere are hard to come by in the poorest urban neighborhoods; they have their churches instead.

Given the social structure of minority communities, it is inevitable that local churches will have a hand in the development of charter schools. Long before the debate broke out in New York, black ministers had already launched successful charter schools in Newark, Grand Rapids, and Tallahassie—all with little fanfare.[82] I discern no evidence that these ministers have used their schools to proselytize religion, or that they have done anything to offend the sensibilities of children who attend them. As creative people go about the business of identifying new opportunities for underserved populations, we can expect to see a blossoming of novel relationships between religious communities and public institutions that is unprecedented in American education. One example that comes to mind is a public high school I recently visited in the South Bronx. The Bronx Leadership Academy (BLA) is the brainchild of South Bronx Churches, an affiliate of the Industrial Areas Foundation, the oldest and largest community organizing institution in the United States. The South Bronx coalition is made up of thirty congregations representing nine Christian denominations and a mosque.

BLA was opened in 1986. Its students, reflecting the composition of the South Bronx, are mostly Hispanic and black. The school distinguishes itself within the burned-out neighborhood that is among the poorest in the nation by its high academic standards and an innovative curriculum built around the theme of community service. Perhaps the most miraculous aspect of the BLA story (if one believes in such things) is that it was able to produce itself out of the Byzantine structure of the New York City school bureaucracy. At the time it was created, New York did not have a charter school law. But South Bronx Churches has extraordinary and determined leadership, which explains how BLA came about.[83]

Equally fascinating is how this coalition of faith-based communities has been able to carry out its educational agenda within the legal boundaries required of a public school. As Lee Stuart, the lead organizer for the group, explains, the church-state conundrum was never a serious issue. With the wide diversity of groups that shaped their coalition, it would have been impossible to agree on a program of religious doctrine to teach even if the leaders were inclined to do so. As Madison would have it, pluralism proved to be the best defense against chauvinism. This did not mean, however, that religion would be treated as taboo, as is often the case in public schools. Religion is appreciated, not only as an important aspect of life within the South Bronx community, but as a normative cohort to the civic virtue that the school seeks to instill in its students. As Stuart explains,

> The thirty congregations involved in SBC [South Bronx Churches] had long ago agreed that their solidarity was around the issues of public life and social justice values common to their religious traditions, not doctrine nor place on the partisan political spectrum. . . . SBC never intended to establish anything but a public school, consistent with the laws of the United States with respect to the separation of church and state. This did not mean, however, a surrender to common assumptions that have too often removed religion from public life. SBC assumed that in their school, values would be taught and that faith and religious traditions would be lifted up as important factors in personal and societal decisions.[84]

Church, State, and Civil Society

There is no discernible evidence extant that the implementation of public or private school choice would have a negative influence on civil society in America. Nor do I see any logical connection between the strict separation of church and state urged by choice opponents and the health of democracy. I believe that most democratic societies view public support for religious education as a key ingredient of the freedom they cherish. It is one of the great ironies of twentieth-century civilization that America—

which was founded by European émigrés in pursuit of religious liberty and which remains one of the most religious countries in the world—has taken such a preemptive view toward providing faith-based communities with an opportunity to educate their children in accord with their own values. This restrictive approach is especially counterintuitive in a society with such a diversity of religious orientations and a tradition of moderation that defines the way the great majority of Americans practice their faith.

If there is any danger inherent in the relationship between religious institutions and government that pertains in the United States, it has little to do with the eventuality of an established church. Our great risk arises from the fact that because so few Americans live their lives according to the strict dictates of their faith, the majority of us do not appreciate the strength of the moral obligations that compel devout observers. We need to be reminded that such people exist, and that it was for their sake that the First Amendment was written. We should not expect them to accept the secularist ethos that most Americans are comfortable with, or to deal with their faith on the same terms that the rest of us do. The promise of the framers was to protect people of conscience from oppression by the majority. The Constitution was not designed to protect the majority from the sound of disparate voices, or to ensure an unanimity of values in terms of religion or any other aspect of private life. Democracy is by nature a contentious form of governance.

If there is anything we can be sure of about religion in American society, it is that communities of faith are the giant rocks on which civil society rests. The house of worship—whether in the form of a church, a synagogue, or mosque—is an invaluable resource for overcoming the widespread public cynicism that discourages people from becoming active members of civil society. The church is a special source of strength in poor communities. A rigid standard of separation limits the role that these bedrock institutions can play in the schooling of inner-city youths, and it curtails their potential effect in promoting educational, social, and political equality. Education policy in America has been out of touch with the culture and spirit of the nation's most disadvantaged communities largely because it has been formulated by individuals and groups who are not of those communities. If there is any hope of translating the principle of equality into a reality, then poor people must be given the opportunity to make their own choices when it comes to the welfare of their children. They must be free to achieve self-reliance on their own terms.

CHAPTER EIGHT

Choosing Equality

W E ARE NOW IN THE second generation of debate on school choice in America. During the first generation, discussion revolved around the pure market model identified with Milton Friedman. This approach acquired traction in the policy community with the publication in 1990 of Chubb and Moe's controversial book espousing a similar model; but support at the time came mostly from Republicans and people identified with the political right. During the first generation, there seemed to be more certainty among opponents that providing aid for students to attend religious schools runs afoul of the First Amendment. Now opponents act as though they are less certain of these legal claims, and they are more apt to rest their challenges on state constitutional arguments.

The second generation of policy proposals has been shaped to target specific populations in need: the poor and children consigned to failing schools. This approach first saw the light of day in the writing of liberal scholars like Ted Sizer, Christopher Jencks, John Coons, and Stephen Sugarman. But it did not fully blossom until bipartisan coalitions of white liberals, blacks, and conservatives got the state legislatures of Wisconsin and Ohio to pass revolutionary legislation that allowed disadvantaged children to attend private and parochial schools with public support. A plan adopted by the Florida legislature in 1999 at the urging of a similar coalition is designed to provide relief to students at failing schools.

209

It is not difficult to understand why minorities want to escape from deplorable institutions to which they are habitually assigned. More intriguing is the growing consensus that seems to be emerging among people of different political persuasions, a shared belief among advocates on both the left and the right, that supports a policy of targeted choice designed specifically to benefit economically disadvantaged children.

In an early part of this volume I explained the distinct political perspectives of contemporary liberals and conservatives by their differing definitions of equality. In the general realm of public policy, conservatives (once referred to as classical liberals) tend to favor a more neutral state role in resolving social inequities. Ever protective of individual freedom, conservatives are more comfortable with a conception of equal opportunity that restricts the role of government in intervening on behalf of the less fortunate. They believe that the social hierarchy should be structured on the basis of competition, albeit a contest among individuals endowed with distinct advantages, abilities, ambition, and industry. Contemporary liberals are more inclined to define equality in terms of outcomes. Mindful of the economic and social advantages that some enjoy over others, they champion an activist state as an agent for moderating class differences.

A policy that allows poor families to use public dollars to acquire private services appears more consistent with the redistributive agenda of liberal social theorists than the laissez-faire predilections of free market economists. But education has a unique place in the realm of American public policy. It is a basic social good to which all people need access in order to ensure equality of opportunity in even a minimal sense. As a unanimous Supreme Court reminded us in *Brown*, a decent education is the indispensable ingredient for vigorous citizenship, economic well-being, and acculturation. On this there appears to be wide agreement across the political spectrum. In real terms, the opportunity to acquire a decent education can best be marked by the outcomes achieved by students. If children are unable to read, write, compute, and think clearly, they cannot hope to function or compete in the complex world of the twenty-first century. If large segments of society do not possess these requisite skills, the result cannot be passed off as personal inadequacy or parental neglect. America must come to terms with the fact that it has failed to provide the most disadvantaged members of its national community with a proper education; and we all live lesser lives because of it.

As the second generation of dialogue takes shape, there is little mention—except among choice opponents—of eliminating public schools. To the contrary, market advocates remain persuaded that competition will lead to improvements in public education, allowing it to thrive. Nor is there a strong disposition among most choice advocates to obliterate the regulatory role of government in education. If Milwaukee and Cleveland are any indication of what the future holds, the state will play an important part in setting educational standards and evaluating the performance of private schools that participate in choice programs. Granted, there is risk inherent in this proposition. There is the risk that those who control education policy will use their influence to encumber the implementation of choice programs (private or public), and some may even do their best to undermine the enforcement of high standards for regular public schools. Government, nonetheless, has a justifiable responsibility to monitor public programs supported by taxpayer dollars. And if parents are truly empowered to vote with their feet when it comes to the selection and support of schools, it is they who will ultimately enforce the high standards of accountability.

Old arguments precipitated by Friedman nearly fifty years ago about the desirability of choice have become outmoded by the realities of the new generation. Charter schools, tuition scholarships, and market competition—conceived by Chubb and Moe less than a decade ago as remote possibilities—are already being realized. The more relevant question of our time is not whether to enact choice, but how to enact it to achieve desirable public objectives.

From the outset of this book I have contended that education policy must be designed to benefit the most disadvantaged members of society—those who are underserved by the current system. The point is to improve the lot of the poor so that their level of opportunity more closely resembles that which is available to the middle class. If we can raise the lowest tier of academic achievement in American education, then we will have elevated the entire enterprise. This requires that each and every child, regardless of family income, have access to a school that equips him or her with the tools needed to succeed in life. It also means that all parents should have the chance to choose a school—public, private, or religious—that reflects their own values.

For nearly a half-century Americans have been experimenting with a variety of approaches for attaining educational equity. Nonetheless, the achievement gap between the races remains wide. After years of experimentation with judicial oversight, forced busing, magnet schools, and controlled choice, black and white children still attend separate schools. The segregation of Hispanics is even more striking. Presuming that black or Hispanic children need to take leave of their communities to get a good education, social planners have struck a damaging blow to the viability of the neighborhood school—a vital component of community life that most middle-class parents would not compromise in their own towns and localities. Poor people, like those of the middle class, want their children to attend good local schools with strong instructional programs and high academic standards.

Over the last twenty years we have made notable progress in achieving financial parity between rich and poor school districts, in part because of successful litigation, complemented by aggressive compensatory spending programs adopted by the federal and state governments. While in principle the idea of financial parity is fair, pouring more money into hidebound systems has not led to better schooling for the poor. Unless spending is coupled with meaningful reform, it will not improve the effectiveness of schools that disadvantaged children typically attend. The resource approach to educational equality, as enacted thus far, is one of the stark examples of a public policy promulgated in the name of poor people that does not usually result in any tangible educational benefits for their children. The money spent has created elaborate programs, generated more jobs, and swelled the ranks of the education bureaucracy, but the schools that poor children attend continue to fail.

School choice places educational resources directly in the hands of parents. It blends economic empowerment with political empowerment in a way never before tried in disadvantaged communities. It allows parents who are economically handicapped to make decisions on behalf of their own children, and, in so doing, it increases the probability that decisions will be responsive to the learning needs of students. School choice surely is not a magic wand that will singularly reverse the pattern of educational deprivation that has held back racial minorities for generations. But if properly designed and implemented, choice could move the nation in the right direction and bring us closer to the ever elusive goal of educational equality.

However much we may perceive the ongoing crisis in education as a national dilemma, education is primarily a state function in America. While it might be helpful for Congress and the president to exercise moral leadership by supporting innovative demonstration projects and experiments, the real solutions to our educational problems will need to emerge from the states in the form of far-reaching legislation. In the remaining pages, I will outline ten general principles to guide policymakers in the design and implementation of school choice programs. These guidelines flow from nine premises derived from a substantial body of existing research on the subject. Although Americans have had only a limited experience with school choice in its various manifestations, we already know enough to formulate policies that will improve the educational opportunities of our most deprived citizens.

Premises

1. *A diverse demand.* Based on the evidence we have from charter schools, privately supported voucher programs, and the experiments in Milwaukee and Cleveland, it appears that parents exercise choice for different reasons. A large portion of those who exercise choice do so out of dissatisfaction with the quality of instruction provided for their children in regular public schools. Since the public schools located in minority communities are generally inferior to the public schools found elsewhere, a disproportionate number of parents attracted to charter schools and private schools are black and Hispanic. This has raised concerns that choice may have a segregating effect. Unfortunately, most blacks and Hispanics already attend school in segregated settings. Many of the parochial schools that would become available to poor minorities as a result of choice are better integrated than traditional public schools. Furthermore, most minority parents, if allowed to make a choice, would place a higher priority on having their children attend schools that are academically rigorous than having them sit in a classroom that is racially integrated. Most, unfortunately, do not have the chance to choose either.

A second segment of the population inclined to exercise choice includes parents who want to have their children attend schools that reflect a particular educational philosophy, theme, or approach not commonly found in public schools. Such value preferences may or may not be religiously motivated. While devout religious observers may be more apt to choose sectarian schools, other parents may find their preferences met in charter schools or other public or private schools of choice. These may encompass, for example, a Montessori or Waldorf school with a unique curriculum or schools that emphasize such programmatic specializations as public service, the arts, or medical science. The motivation of parents who make philosophical choices may not be as intense as those who are fleeing academically deficient institutions. One might expect, however, that this second segment of the choice population would also have a disproportionate number of economically disadvantaged people, since many of the more fortunate families already have the means to exercise such value-based choices on their own.

2. *A limited demand.* If we are to believe the public opinion polls conducted on the topic, most American families will prefer to have their children remain in the schools they already attend. This is particularly true of the middle class, who, for the most part, are content with the schools that their children attend. To assert that these satisfied parents would not exercise choice, though, is somewhat inappropriate. Many have already exercised choice on their own, and their determination to remain where they are even with the passage of legislatively enacted choice programs is indeed a choice in itself. We should not commit the error of measuring the success of choice by the number of families who use it as a vehicle to exit traditional public schools. Success is more accurately signaled when those who are searching for alternatives are given a chance to move their children without the usual financial and bureaucratic impediments that are put in the way.

If opting out is a choice that will be taken by a relatively small portion of public school parents, the evacuation scenarios predicted by choice opponents are greatly exaggerated. Ironically, if the level of dissatisfaction with public education in its present form were so widespread as to provoke a large-scale exodus, then the argument for choice would be even more compelling. The real danger inherent in the present situation is that the great majority of parents who are satisfied with their children's schools will not appreciate the gnawing educational and value-based concerns of those who are not. Insensitivity makes it easier for the majority to dismiss the subject out of hand or to fall prey to the alarms sounded by groups that have a stake in maintaining the status quo.

The demand for choice among the economically disadvantaged is variable, and it is responsive to the financial burdens that choosing imposes on parents. We already know from the evaluation data on several privately funded programs that requiring parents to pay part of the tuition costs or substantial fees at nonpublic schools can serve as a disincentive for the poorest of the poor to participate. This is not necessarily as much a measure of their motivation to secure new educational options for their children as it is a function of their ability to afford even marginal expenses that result from opting out.

3. *Inadequate supply.* There is an inadequate supply of classroom space available to accommodate the number of students who would choose to

opt out of the public schools they currently attend. We know this from the long waiting lists that have sprung up at most charter schools and the similar backlog of applications from those who have expressed interest in public and privately funded scholarship programs. Even in those local and statewide jurisdictions where public school choice has been implemented on a grand scale, long waiting lists persist for entry into the best schools. The problem is most severe in the inner city, where the relatively small supply of high-quality institutions drives up the demand and puts students in competition for a limited number of desirable placements. The creation of new charter schools should help alleviate the supply problem, but this relief will come slowly and with limited effect. Most charter schools are small. In the normal scheme of things, it will take several charter schools to accommodate a population of students who want to transfer out of one average-sized public school that is struggling academically.

4. *Demand induces supply.* As more families become economically enabled to acquire a private school education for their children, a larger number will do so. This will provide an incentive for existing institutions to expand their enrollments and will eventually induce innovative educators and entrepreneurs to open new schools. While the evidence to support this assertion remains limited with regard to elementary and secondary education, the claim is based on sound economic reasoning concerning normal market functions. Many private and parochial schools in urban areas have been forced to cut back their enrollment because of financial constraints at a time when there is a growing demand for educational alternatives among people who lack the means to afford tuition in a private school. The passage of charter school laws in over thirty-five states already has brought into existence a new kind of hybrid arrangement where privately owned and run corporations enter into contracts with public authorities to operate public schools. The educational marketplace is undergoing a serious restructuring. Public education—or more specifically, our national commitment to provide each and every child with a decent education—no longer needs to be defined solely in terms of schools run and operated by the government. The promise of public education can be fulfilled by providing all families with the means to select from a wide array of institutions.

5. *Competition will improve public education.* Choice advocates like to tell the story of the Giffen Elementary School in Albany, New York, where philanthropist Virginia Gilder offered to pay 90 percent of the private school tuition costs for any child who wanted to leave the failing institution. Approximately 20 percent of the students in the impoverished com-

munity took up the offer. Within a year the school became a showcase for innovation. The principal, two top administrators, and twelve teachers were replaced; the new leaders launched a variety of programs to retain their client base and attract other students.

While Giffen is a powerful example of how competition can motivate professionals to do a better job, it is hardly a scientific experiment. Until now, most of the economic models developed to forecast the effect choice will have on public schools have existed only in the abstract. Even with the emergence of charter schools, privately funded voucher programs, and the scholarship programs in Milwaukee and Cleveland, real competition has been inhibited. Policymakers have made sure that the number of options available to parents who want to choose charter schools or private schools is limited. They have acted to guarantee that schools of choice have not received the level of funding regular public schools enjoy. As a result, the market has not been allowed to assume its natural course.

Economists have not yet been able to conduct controlled experiments from actual experience. Based on an understanding of normal market functions and the findings derived from theoretical models conceived by scholars, it is reasonable, nevertheless, to expect that real competition will induce public schools to improve. To believe otherwise is the ultimate act of cynicism toward public education. If public schools were unwilling to improve or incapable of improving in the face of real competition, then the system is truly bankrupt.

6. *A private school advantage.* There is a tangible academic advantage to be derived by poor children who attend private schools. This is indicated by a substantial body of empirical research that began with the Coleman studies of the early 1980s and continues to appear in a wide-ranging set of evaluations that have been conducted to assess public and privately supported scholarship programs. Some of the evidence is based on standardized test scores. More compelling evidence is found in the high school graduation rates of students who attend Catholic schools—all pointing to the fact that parochial schools are more effective at modifying the empirical connection between student demographics and academic performance. Additional evidence of a private school advantage is found in surveys of parents who have exercised choice, many of whom have not selected Catholic schools. Among the positive factors cited by the latter in comparing the private and public school experience are more rigorous academic programs, a safer school environment, increased opportunities for parental involvement, core values, and, for some, a religious orientation.

7. *Schools as communities.* As a rule, the best schools are those that emerge as natural communities. They have an underlying value structure to which professionals, parents, and children adhere. They are voluntary associations that participants have joined as a matter of their own free will. We understand this cultural phenomenon from the work Coleman and others have conducted on Catholic schools. Catholic schools are unusually effective in educating disadvantaged youths because they are caring communities that believe in the fundamental equality of all children. The research on Catholic schools is not just relevant because Catholic schools represent a significant alternative for inner-city children who want to flee failing public schools. While there is not yet a similarly significant body of research to support the claim, it is reasonable to suggest that other nonpublic schools designed around a commitment to serve the needs of the poor are capable of fostering the same kind of caring environments found in Catholic schools. This is especially the case with regard to schools that have emerged from urban ministries in minority communities and a small crop of similarly placed independent schools struggling to maintain their financial independence.

The research on Catholic schools is relevant also because it presents us with a model for the redesign of public schools. Public schools, especially those found in large metropolitan areas, represent the organizational antithesis of the Catholic school model. They are not, for the most part, voluntary associations with regard to their professionals or clients. Inner-city public schools function as part of an enormous administrative structure that sets policy from on high and determines what teachers and principals can and should do. These massive bureaucracies do have a culture of their own; but anyone who has studied large organizations knows that the guiding principles of the bureaucracy are hierarchy, order, predictability, control, and uniformity. Concepts such as creativity and autonomy do not quite fit the scheme. It is amazing that we have entrusted our most vulnerable and precious family members to a type of organizational structure that is depersonalized by design.

Max Weber, the famous student of bureaucracy, was convinced that the advantage gained from such stupefying mechanization is efficiency. Weber's undeniable brilliance aside, modern management theory has long abandoned the bureaucratic model. Educators, for the most part, have not. Charter schools are an exception. They allow institutions of learning to evolve from communities of professionals and parents that share certain core values. They reside outside the administrative structure that governs regular public schools, providing an organizational form that until recently was available only in the private and parochial sectors. In this way charter schools have the potential to serve as a viable alternative to both public and nonpublic schools as we know them.

8. *Constitutional limitations: religious schools.* The First Amendment of the Constitution as interpreted by the Supreme Court through most of twentieth century does not allow government to give direct financial assistance to religious schools. This is an unusual approach to the protection of religious freedom. Most modern democratic states perceive public support for sectarian schools as a manifestation of religious freedom, provided that attendance at schools is a matter of individual choice. Nonetheless, in America a prohibition against direct aid is the law. A body of case law handed down by the Rehnquist Court over the last fifteen years suggests that it is permissible to provide assistance to parents who freely choose to send their children to religious schools so long as the aid is rendered in a neutral manner. This more accommodationist approach to church-state relations is consistent with a long-standing constitutional tradition in the United States that was temporarily interrupted during a brief period of time in the 1970s.

States are permitted to set their own constitutional standards of separation so long as these standards do not infringe on federally protected rights. Thus, in principle states may proscribe tuition assistance to parents who choose to send their children to religious schools; but to specifically exclude religious schools from choice programs that involve the participation of other private institutions raises serious questions regarding the free exercise and equal protection rights of parochial school parents and students.

9. *Constitutional limitations: public schools.* The Constitution prohibits public schools from teaching religion in a way that proselytizes one or another faith, but it poses no limit on teaching about religion as part of a cultural, historical, or philosophical course of study. Most constitutional scholars agree that the Constitution prohibits organized school prayer in the public schools. The determination of some religious leaders to pass an amendment to change that seems ill advised and impractical. It would be difficult, if not impossible, to write a prayer that has significant spiritual meaning to a substantial portion of the school population without offending the sensibilities of others. The implementation of a school choice plan that allows children to attend religious schools with public support should reduce the pressure for prayer in the public schools.

Principles

1. *Full choice for the poor*. State governments should implement a program of school choice for economically and educationally deprived children that includes public schools, independent private schools, and religious schools. This will furnish poor parents with the widest range of options in choosing an appropriate school for their children. A program that included only public schools would be too limiting and incapable of accommodating parents who want a religious education for their children. A program that involved only religious schools would be unsuitable for those who do not want their children educated in a sectarian setting and would be unlikely to pass constitutional scrutiny. In principle, a plan that does not favor one form of schooling over another is fair and is most likely to accommodate the diverse needs of parents.

2. *Eligibility: public school choice*. Charter schools and other public schools of choice should be open to all on a first come, first served basis so long as adequate space is available to accommodate the demand. If demand exceeds supply, priority should be given to students who attend failing public schools, as determined by an objective standard of academic performance. For example, any school in which fewer than 35 percent of the children read at grade level might be deemed a failing school. This standard could be raised as more schools of choice open and additional seats become available. Once applications from students attending failing schools are accommodated, excess demand should be met through a lottery.

3. *Eligibility: private school choice*. Participation in the private (and parochial) school choice program should be limited to families that can meet a predetermined objective standard of economic need. For example, one commonly used measure in existing public and private scholarship programs is qualification for a free or subsidized school lunch as currently prescribed under the guidelines set by the federal government. In the event that the program is oversubscribed, priority should be given to children who attend failing institutions, as defined above. The goal would be to provide every poor parent with an alternative to having their child remain in a school that most middle-class parents would not allow their own children to attend.

There is an implicit priority in the "failing school" criterion that needs to be made explicit. It holds that children who would opt out of their regular public schools for academic reasons should be given a preference over those who would choose another school for philosophical or religious reasons. This is not meant to understate the considerations of the latter population so much as to recognize the absolute necessity to furnish each and every child with access to a decent school. In those cases where demand continues to exceed the supply of available spaces in acceptable schools, scholarships should be granted on the basis of a lottery.

4. *Charter schools.* A robust charter school law should be adopted as part of the choice initiative to improve the quantity and diversity of institutions available to families. These schools should be granted the maximum degree of autonomy so that they are allowed to develop their own character generated on the basis of a core philosophy and values that define them as institutions. Such schools should be released from all state and local regulations that do not relate to the health, safety, or civil rights of anyone (including employees, students, and parents) belonging to or wishing to become a part of the school community. These institutions should have a maximum degree of autonomy on budgetary and personnel matters, within the bounds of fiscal probity as warranted through a periodic state audit. While teachers and staff might be permitted to form collective bargaining units at the school level and to maintain membership in their unions and professional organizations, such schools should not be governed by collective bargaining agreements in effect in their respective local or state jurisdictions. A mechanism should be provided for meaningful parental involvement. Parents should be consulted on all academic issues and be granted access to information involving the financial management of the school.

5. *High academic standards.* In exchange for autonomy, charter schools must be held to high academic standards set by the state. These standards should include content requirements in basic skill and subject areas, as well as an objective system of assessment that evaluates whether students are learning at acceptable levels. Standardized tests should be administered on an annual basis. While some professional educators continue to emphasize the limitations of such instruments, standardized tests remain the most objective method for assessing student (and school) performance. They are the currency of academic distinction. Relatively few middle-class parents would send their children to a school where a majority of students do not do well on standardized tests. There is no reason to believe that poor parents would want to either. It is assumed here that if a majority of the children in a given school are not performing at an acceptable level over an extended period of time, the fault lies with the school and not the children. If we truly believe in the fundamental equality of all people, then

we must assume that most children (excepting those with special disabilities) are capable of performing well in school.

Under the eligibility criteria set above, many, if not most, of the students entering charter schools and other schools of choice will arrive with the academic deficits that are inherent in an inferior education. Their performance should initially and temporarily be assessed in terms of their own individual progress (commonly referred to as a value-added approach), with the period of transition set in accord with the amount of time the student has spent in a failing school. Any charter school that does not meet the academic standards set by the state should have its charter revoked and be closed. Any private or parochial school that elects to participate in the choice program must be held to the same academic standards set for charter schools to become and to remain eligible.

6. *Real competition.* There should be no cap on the number of charter schools that can be created so long as these institutions meet the established standards of performance. Approval authority for the creation of new charters or the conversion of regular public schools should not reside with local districts that may have a stake in limiting competition. Several agencies should be empowered by the state (for example, the state education department, the state university, or a newly created board) for granting charters.

Private entrepreneurs that qualify should be permitted to set up charter schools. Charter schools should receive a full complement of funding equivalent to what is provided for regular public schools, including per capita state and local expenditures as well as capital costs. Regular public schools that do not meet the same standards of performance set for charter schools should also be forced to close. The most effective response to the so-called skimming problem is real competition. The skimming thesis is based on the presumption that incompetent institutions will be permitted to survive. It stands to reason that as long as failing institutions persist, students with the poorest, least informed, and least motivated parents will continue to occupy their classrooms. The best way to ensure that no student ends up in an unsatisfactory school is to put such institutions out of existence.

7. *Admission to nonpublic schools.* Any nonpublic school that elects to participate in the choice program must accept each child who applies under its auspices without regard to race, ethnicity, or religion. This means that if religious schools elect to participate, they should not be allowed to refuse admission to students based on the religious orientation of their families.

Single-sex schools should be allowed to maintain their normal admissions policies. For many individuals—especially women, but increasingly young men—attending a single-sex institution carries benefits that are not found in a coeducational setting. Economically disadvantaged boys and girls should have the same chance to avail themselves of opportunities that have worked so well for the middle and upper classes over time.

8. *Private school tuition.* Tuition allotments for students attending private schools should not exceed the per capita cost equivalent set for charter schools (and other public schools) or the normal costs of the private school under consideration. As with charter schools, this amount should include state and local expenses as well as capital costs. A nonpublic school participating in the program must be required to accept the state allocation as full payment for tuition. No family should be asked to accept a financial penalty for attending a private or parochial school under the auspices of a publicly supported choice program. While families might be allowed to make personal donations to their children's schools or become involved in fund-raising drives, they should not be forced to contribute money as a requirement for admission or retention.

9. *Religion in public schools.* Public schools must remain wholly secular institutions. Any organized activity that appears to promote religious beliefs must be deemed impermissible. There is no reason, however, to treat religion as a taboo within the context of the school curriculum. This kind of restrictive policy makes for neither good law nor good pedagogy. Religion has an important place in civil society and is of particular significance in the lives of many children who grow up with serious economic and social disadvantages. It is an essential aspect of human civilization that deserves attention within the general course of humanistic studies.

10. *Religion in private schools.* Religious schools participating in the choice program should be permitted to maintain their sectarian orientation and to purvey the values that define their unique institutional culture. As participants in a public program, these institutions should be open to all children, regardless of their faith (or lack of it). To accommodate a diverse population of children, families should be given an opportunity to opt out of religious instruction and exercises; but these institutions should not be forced to compromise the generally pervasive religious climate that makes them what they are. As schools of choice, nobody is required to attend these sectarian institutions. The very character of these places is what that makes them attractive to so many people and fills a need that cannot be met in public schools.

Final Thoughts

Yes, we know enough about school choice to fit it to a more egalitarian public agenda. The burning question is whether we have the political will to do so. Are state legislative bodies that are accustomed to doing business at the behest of powerful interests and ruling majorities capable of responding to the needs of the weakest and ill served? The resolution to the problem defies political logic because it requires governmental bodies to do what they are rarely inclined to do; the historical record is not encouraging. In this case, the action is an especially tall order, demanding nothing less than a redefinition of public education in America so that it is customer driven rather than producer driven.

As with all crucial political issues, choice is a moral question. It speaks to who we are as a people and to our capacity to think beyond ourselves. The most compelling argument for school choice in America remains an egalitarian one: education is such an essential public good for living life in a free and prosperous society that all people deserve equal access to its benefits regardless of race, class, or philosophical disposition. There should be no exceptions to the rule or excuses for the contrary.

When the political and legal issues are laid aside, there are many decent people who are reluctant to endorse choice because they sincerely do not believe it will help the poor gain access to better schools. They are doubtful that parents burdened with the hardships of social deprivation are prepared to make the best decisions on behalf of their children when the time comes to choose an education. The doubters are more comfortable leaving those important decisions in the hands of others, whether they be school administrators, judges, or political advocates. Their inclination, though well meaning, contradicts experience. They have missed the essential lesson on equality from which this book began, which is worth repeating as the book comes to a close: we cannot aspire to equality as a societal objective unless we believe in it as the fundamental truth in the human equation. All individuals should be treated equally because they are all equal in the most fundamental of ways.

In the most recent of his many highly regarded books, *On Democracy*, the eminent Yale political scientist Robert Dahl discusses the concept of "intrinsic equality." He explains that, except for a very strong showing to the contrary, in rare circumstances protected by law, it must be assumed that every adult subject to the laws of the state is sufficiently well qualified to participate in the process of governing the state. This is the egalitarian spirit that inspires democracy. Professor Dahl's insight is directly on the point here; for if we are to believe that every individual, no matter how humble their existence, is equipped to deal with the complex affairs of governing the state, then it must be assumed that each has the capacity to decide which school is most appropriate for her own child.

Yes, poor parents have much to overcome in trying to secure the best education for their children, not the least of which is the limited financial resources they have at their disposal as they do their bidding. But they are like all mothers and fathers. There is nobody who loves their children more than they do; there is no institution that is more willing to put the interests of their children ahead of all others as they are; and there is no one who will share the joy of their children's triumphs or the disappointment of their failures as they will. Poor people understand the meaning of educational equality so well because they have been confronted with the realities of inequality for so long. We should let them choose for themselves.

Notes

Chapter One

1. Milton Friedman, "The Role of Government in Education," in Robert A. Solo, ed., *Economics and the Public Interest* (Rutgers University Press, 1955).

2. See Andrew J. Coulson, *Market Education: The Unknown History* (Transaction Press, 1999); David K. Kirkpatrick, *Choice in Schooling: A Case for Tuition Vouchers* (Loyola University Press, 1990); Myron Lieberman, *Privatization and Educational Choice* (St. Martin's Press, 1989).

3. See Theodore Sizer, "The Case for a Free Market," *Saturday Review,* January 11, 1969; Christopher Jencks, "Giving Parents Money to Pay for Schooling: Education Vouchers," *New Republic,* July 4, 1970; John E. Coons and Stephen D. Sugarman, "Family Choice in Education: A Model State System for Vouchers," *California Law Review,* vol. 59 (1971).

4. Albert Shanker, "Restructuring Our Schools," *Peabody Journal of Education,* vol. 65 (1988).

5. James W. Gutherie, "School Finance: Fifty Years of Expansion," *The Future of Children: Financing the Schools,* vol. 7 (Winter 1997), p. 9.

6. Eric A. Hanushek, "Conclusions and Controversies about the Effectiveness of School Resources," *Economic Policy Review,* vol. 4 (March 1998).

7. Organization for Economic Cooperation and Development, *Education at a Glance: OECD Indicators (1997)* (Washington, D.C., 1997).

8. "Pursuing Excellence: A Study of U.S. Twelfth Grade Mathematics and Science Achievement in an International Context," Third International Mathematics and Science Study, 1998. See Deborah Viadaro, "U.S. Seniors near Bottom in World Test," *Education Week*, March 4, 1998.

9. Some of the more positive assessments of the current condition can be found in David C. Berliner and Benjamin J. Biddle, *The Manufactured Crisis: Myths, Fraud and the Attack on America's Public Schools* (Adison-Wesley, 1995); Richard Rothstein, *The Way We Were: The Realities of America's Student Achievement* (Washington, D.C.: Century Foundation, 1998); Gerald Bracey, "Are U.S. Students Behind?" *American Prospect*, vol. 37 (March–April 1998). See also William Raspberry, "The Good News About U.S. Schools," *Washington Post*, March 6, 1998.

10. Lawrence C. Stedman, "International Achievement Differences: An Assessment of a New Perspective," *Educational Researcher*, vol. 26 (April 1997).

11. Christopher Jencks and Meredith Phillips, "The Black-White Test Score Gap: An Introduction," in Jencks and Phillips, eds., *The Black-White Test Score Gap* (Brookings, 1998), p. 1. See also Christopher Jencks and Meredith Phillips, "America's Next Achievement Test: Closing the Black-White Test Score Gap," *American Prospect* (September–October 1998).

12. Susan E. Mayer and Paul E. Peterson, eds., *Earning and Learning: Why Schools Matter* (Brookings, 1999). See also William R. Johnson and Derek Neal, "Basic Skills and the Black-White Earnings Gap," in Jencks and Phillips, *The Black-White Test Score Gap*; Derek Neal and William R. Johnson, "The Role of Premarket Factors in Black-White Wage Differences," *Journal of Political Economy*, vol. 104 (October 1996).

13. Jencks and Phillips, "The Black-White Test Score Gap," p. 4.

14. In 1998 support grew to 51 percent (versus 45 percent) against. "Phi Delta Kappa/Gallup Poll of Parents Attitudes towards Public Schools, 1998."

15. Lowell C. Rose, Alec M. Gallup, and Stanley M. Elam, *The 29th Annual Phi Delta Kappan Gallup Poll of Public Attitudes toward the Public Schools*, (September 1997), pp. 48–49.

16. David Bositis, *1997 National Opinion Poll—Children's Issues* (Joint Center for Political and Economic Studies, 1997), p. 7.

17. Ibid., p. 6.

18. In a national survey of public school parents taken in 1994, 80 percent of black parents indicated that drugs and violence are serious problems in their public schools, as compared to 58 percent of white parents. Jean Johnson and John Immerwahr, *First Things First: What Americans Expect from the Public Schools* (Public Agenda, 1994). In a national survey published in 1995, 7.1 percent of black high school students (as opposed to 3 percent white), admitted that they "felt too unsafe to go to school." *Digest of Education Statistics* (National Center for Education Statistics, 1995), p. 275.

19. Diane Ravitch and Joseph P. Viteritti, "Introduction," in Ravitch and Viteritti, eds., *New Schools for a New Century: The Redesign of Urban Education* (Yale University Press, 1997).

20. "Quality Counts.'98: The Urban Challenge," *Education Week*, vol. 17 (January 8, 1998), p. 12.

21. Public Agenda, *Time to Move On: African-American and White Parents Set an Agenda for Public Schools* (New York, 1998).

22. Johnson and Immerwahr, *First Things First.*

23. Lisa Delpit, *Somebody Else's Children: Cultural Conflict in the Classroom* (New Press, 1995).

24. Among the major scholarly studies that are critical of school choice and vouchers are Kevin V. Smith and Kenneth J. Meier, *The Case against School Choice: Politics, Markets and Fools* (M. E. Sharpe, 1995); Peter Cookson, *School Choice: The Struggle for the Soul of American Education* (Yale University Press, 1994); Jeffrey R. Henig, *Rethinking School Choice: The Limits of the Market Metaphor* (Princeton University Press, 1994); Amy Stuart Wells, *Time to Choose: America at the Crossroads of School Choice Policy* (Hill & Wang, 1993); Edith Rassell and Richard Rothstein, eds., *School Choice: Examining the Evidence* (Washington, D.C.: Economic Policy Institute, 1993); Timothy Young and Evans Clinchy, *Choice in Public Education* (Teachers College Press, 1992).

25. Bruce Fuller and Richard E. Elmore, eds., *Who Chooses? Who Loses? Culture, Institutions and the Unequal Effects of School Choice* (Teachers College Press, 1996); Terry M. Moe, ed., *Private Vouchers* (Hoover Institution Press, 1995); Sabrina Lutz, "The Impact of School Choice in the United States and the Netherlands on Ethnic Segregation and Equal Educational Opportunity," *Equity in Education*, vol. 29 (1996).

26. See, for example, Leo Pfeffer, *Church, State and Freedom* (Beacon Press, 1967), which remains one of the most cogent legal arguments against vouchers.

27. See, for example, *Committee on Public Education and Religious Liberty* v. *Nyquist*, 413 U.S. 756 (1973); *Sloan* v. *Lemon*, 413 U.S. 825 (1973).

28. See Joseph P. Viteritti, "Blaine's Wake: School Choice, the First Amendment, and State Constitutional Law," *Harvard Journal of Law & Public Policy*, vol. 21 (1998).

29. Benjamin R. Barber, "Education for Democracy," *The Good Society*, vol. 7 (Spring 1997); Mary Jane Guy, "The American Common School: An Institution at Risk," *Journal of Law & Education*, vol. 21 (1992).

30. See Thomas J. Nechyba and Robert P. Strauss, "Community Choice and Local Public Services: A Discrete Choice Approach," *Regional Science and Urban Economics*, vol. 28 (1998), based on an economic public choice model; Margot Slade, "First the Schoolhouse, Then the Home," *New York Times*, March 8, 1998, sec. 11, for a more journalistic treatment of the issue.

31. National Center for Education Statistics, "National Household Education Survey," *The Condition of Education, 1997* (1997).

32. Rose, Gallup, and Elam, *Phi Delta Kappan Gallup Poll*, p. 48.

33. See Ellis Sandoz, *A Government of Laws: Political Theory, Religion, and the Founding* (Louisiana State University Press, 1990); Thomas J. Curry, *The First Freedoms: Church and State in America to the Passage of the First Amendment* (Oxford University Press, 1986); Patricia U. Bonomi, *Under the Cope of Heaven: Religion, Society and Politics in Colonial America* (Oxford University Press, 1986).

34. See John G. West, *The Politics of Revelation and Reason: Religion and Civic Life in the New Nation* (University Press of Kansas, 1996); Barry Allen Shain, *The Myth of American Individualism: The Protestant Origins of American Constitutional Thought* (Princeton University Press, 1994); Barbara Allen, "Alexis de Tocqueville on the Covenantal Tradition of American Federal Democracy," *Publius*, vol. 28 (Spring 1998).

35. See Bernard Bailyn, *Education and the Forming of American Society* (Vintage Books, 1960).

36. Charles Glenn, *Choice of Schools in Six Nations: France, Netherlands, Belgium, Britain, Canada, West Germany* (Department of Education, 1989).

37. *Everson v. Board of Education*, 330 U.S. 1 (1947).

38. Michael W. McConnell, "Religious Participation in Public Programs: Religious Freedom at the Crossroads," *University of Chicago Law Review*, vol. 59 (1992), pp. 127–34.

39. See Joseph P. Viteritti, "Choosing Equality: Religious Freedom and Educational Opportunity under Constitutional Federalism," *Yale Law & Policy Review*, vol. 15 (1996), pp. 137–42, 187–91; Carl H. Esbeck, "A Restatement of the Supreme Court's Law of Religious Freedom: Coherence, Conflict, or Chaos?" *Notre Dame Law Review*, vol. 70 (1995); Michael A. Paulsen, "Religion, Equality, and the Constitution: An Equal Protection Approach to Establishment Clause Adjudication," *Notre Dame Law Review*, vol. 61 (1986).

40. *Jackson v. Benson*, 578 N.W. 2d 602 (Wis. 1998), cert. denied, 119 S. Ct. 466 (1998).

41. *Cochran v. Board of Education*, 281 U.S. 370 (1930).

42. See Leonard Levy, *The Establishment Clause: Religion and the First Amendment* (Duke University Press, 1994).

43. See, for example, Sidney Verba, Kay Lehman Schozman, and Henry Brady, *Voice and Equality: Civic Voluntarism in American Politics* (Harvard University Press, 1995), pp. 75–79.

44. See Jay P. Green, "Civic Values in Public and Private Schools," in Paul E. Peterson and Bryan C. Hassel, eds., *Learning from School Choice* (Brookings, 1998).

45. Robert D. Putnam, "Bowling Alone: America's Declining Social Capital," *Journal of Democracy*, vol. 6 (January 1995).

46. Robert D. Putnam, "Turning In, Turning Out: The Strange Disappearance of Social Capital in America," *PS: Political Science and Politics*, vol. 28 (Decem-

ber 1995); Joseph S. Nye, Jr., Philip Z. Zelikow, and David C. King, eds., *Why People Don't Trust Government* (Harvard University Press, 1997); E. J. Dionne, *Why Americans Hate Politics* (Simon & Schuster, 1996).

47. C. Eric Lincoln and Lawrence H. Mamiya, *The Black Church in the African-American Experience* (Duke University Press, 1990) remains the authoritative study on the subject. See also Judith Crocker Burris and Andrew Billingsley, "The Black Church in the Community: Antebellum Times to Present," *National Journal of Sociology*, vol. 8 (Summer–Winter 1994).

48. Taylor Branch, *Parting the Waters: America in the King Years, 1954–63* (Simon & Schuster, 1988); David Garrow, *Bearing the Cross: Martin Luther King and the Southern Christian Leadership Conference* (Morrow, 1986); Aldon M. Morris, *The Origins of the Civil Rights Movement: Black Communities Organizing for Change* (Free Press, 1984); Hart M. Nelson and Ann K. Nelson, *The Black Church in the Sixties* (University Press of Kentucky, 1975).

49. See Robert Woodson, *The Triumphs of Joseph: How Today's Community Healers Are Reviving Our Streets and Neighborhoods* (Free Press, 1998); Robert D. Carle and Louis A. DeCarlo, eds., *Signs of Hope in the City: Ministries of Community Renewal* (Judson Press, 1997); Samuel G. Freedman, *Upon This Rock: The Miracle of a Black Church* (HarperCollins, 1993).

Chapter Two

1. "Equality, Moral and Social," in Paul Edwards, ed., *The Encyclopedia of Philosophy* (Collier Macmillan, 1972).

2. "We hold these truths to be self evident, that all men are created equal, that they are endowed by their Creator with certain inalienable rights; that among these are Life, Liberty and the pursuit of Happiness." Declaration of Independence, 1776.

3. There recently has been some debate regarding the exact role that Jefferson played in drafting the momentous document. See Pauline Maier, *American Scripture: Making the Declaration of Independence* (Knopf, 1997).

4. See R. H. Tawney, *Equality* (Allen and Unwin, 1952); J. L. Lukas, "Equality," in Richard Flathman, ed., *Concepts in Political and Social Philosophy* (Macmillan, 1973).

5. Alexis de Tocqueville, *Democracy in America*, vol. 1, Phillips Bradley, ed. (Random House, 1945), p. 56.

6. Ibid., p. 99.

7. For a historic overview of the equality principle, see Sanford Lakoff, *Equality in Political Philosophy* (Beacon Press, 1964), which focuses on theory; J. R. Pole, *The Pursuit of Equality in American History* (University of California Press, 1978), which focuses on policy and practice.

8. For a further explanation, see Richard Flathman, "Equality and Generali-

zation: A Formal Analysis," in J. Roland Pennock and John W. Chapman, eds. *Nomos IX: Equality* (Atherton, 1967).

9. See John Schaar, "Equality of Opportunity and Beyond," in Pennock and Chapman, *Nomos*; Robert Nozick, *Anarchy, State and Utopia* (Basic Books, 1974).

10. Milton Friedman and Rose Friedman, *Free to Choose: A Personal Statement* (Harcourt Brace, 1980); Milton Friedman, *Capitalism and Freedom* (University of Chicago Press, 1962).

11. Ernest Barker, ed., *The Politics of Aristotle* (Oxford University Press, 1962), pp. 65, 204–05, 258–60. See also Aristotle, *The Nichomachean Ethics*, trans. W. D. Ross (Oxford University Press, 1925).

12. The classic statement on liberal democracy in contemporary political theory remains John Rawls, *A Theory of Justice* (Harvard University Press, 1971). But see also John Rawls, *Political Liberalism* (Columbia University Press, 1993); Michael Walzer, *Spheres of Justice* (Basic Books, 1983); Bruce Ackerman, *Social Justice in the Liberal State* (Yale University Press, 1980); Amy Gutman, *Liberal Equality* (Cambridge University Press, 1980).

13. *Brown v. Board of Education*, 347 U.S. 483 (1954). There is voluminous literature on *Brown* and its effect. One of the most comprehensive is Richard Kluger, *Simple Justice: The History of Brown v. Board of Education and Black America's Struggle for Equality* (Knopf, 1975).

14. See William E. Nelson, *The Fourteenth Amendment: From Political Principle to Judicial Doctrine* (Harvard University Press, 1988), which provides an account of the original thinking behind the amendment and its subsequent reinterpretation by the courts.

15. This outcome has stirred considerable debate among constitutional scholars. For a variety of responses, moving from positive to negative, see Michael K. Curtis, *No State Shall Abridge: The Fourteenth Amendment and the Bill of Rights* (Duke University Press, 1986); Michael J. Perry, *The Constitution in the Courts: Law or Politics* (Oxford University Press, 1994); Raoul Berger, *Government by Judiciary: The Transformation of the Fourteenth Amendment* (Harvard University Press, 1977).

16. *New Orleans City Park Improvement Association v. Detiege*, 358 U.S. 54 (1958); *Gayle v. Browder*, 352 U.S. 903 (1956); *Holmes v. Atlanta*, 350 U.S. 879 (1955); *Mayor of Baltimore v. Dawson*, 350 U.S. 877 (1955); *Boynton v. Virginia*, 364 U.S. 903 (1956); *Burton, v. Wilmington Parking Authority*, 365 U.S. 715 (1961); *Johnson v. Virginia*, 373 U.S. 61 (1963); *Brown v. Louisiana*, 383 U.S. 131 (1966).

17. See Chandler Davidson, "The Voting Rights Act: A Brief History," in Bernard Grofman and Chandler Davidson, eds., *Controversies in Minority Voting: The Voting Rights Act in Perspective* (Brookings, 1992); Joseph P. Viteritti, "Unapportioned Justice: Local Elections, Social Science and the Evolution of the Voting Rights Act," *Cornell Journal of Law & Public Policy*, vol. 4 (1994).

18. See Gerald N. Rosenberg, *The Hollow Hope: Can Courts Bring about Social Change?* (University of Chicago Press, 1991), which makes a convincing argument that court decisions did not really realize significant social change until they were bolstered by political action undertaken by the other branches of government.

19. *Brown* v. *Board of Education*, at 493.

20. See Rosemary C. Salomone, *Equal Education under Law: Legal Rights and Federal Policy in the Post-Brown Era* (St. Martin's, 1986), which outlines a variety of approaches undertaken to achieve equal educational opportunity by the various branches of government.

21. 42 U.S.C. 2000c-1, sec. 402.

22. James S. Coleman and others, *Equality of Educational Opportunity* (Office of Education, National Center for Education Statistics, 1964). See also the discussion of the report in Frederick Mosteller and Daniel P. Moynihan, eds., *On Equality of Educational Opportunity* (Vintage Books, 1972).

23. *Plessy* v. *Ferguson*, 163 U.S. 537 (1896). See Nelson, *The Fourteenth Amendment*, pp. 185–87, which suggests that while the Supreme Court bowed to segregation to protect state prerogatives under federalism as it was then understood, the Court had also expected that the distinct systems of schools available to blacks and whites would be comparable. See also Charles A. Lofgren, *The Plessy Case: A Legal-Historical Interpretation* (Oxford University Press, 1987).

24. Christopher Jencks and others, *Inequality* (Basic Books, 1972).

25. Jencks himself contended that improving minority achievement itself would not reduce economic inequality—a position he later reversed. See Christopher Jencks and Meredith Phillips, "The Black-White Test Score Gap: An Introduction," in Christopher Jencks and Meredith Phillips, eds., *The Black-White Test Score Gap* (Brookings, 1998), p. 4.

26. See Ronald R. Edmonds, "Advocating Inequity: A Critique of the Civil Rights Attorney in Class Action Desegregation Suits," *Black Law Journal*, vol. 3 (1974); Ronald R. Edmonds, "Effective Schools for the Urban Poor," *Educational Leadership*, vol. 37 (October 1979). For an overview of Edmonds's work, see Joseph P. Viteritti, "Agenda Setting: When Politics and Pedagogy Meet," *Social Policy*, vol. 15 (Fall 1984).

27. See Diane Ravitch, *The Troubled Crusade* (Basic Books, 1983) for a critical review of federal policy.

28. *Brown* v. *Board of Education*, 349 U.S. 294 (1955).

29. Salomone, *Equal Education Under Law*, pp. 45–46.

30. U. S. Commission on Civil Rights, *With Liberty and Justice for All* (1959). See also Stephen L. Wasby, Anthony D'Amato, and Mary Metrailler, *Desegregation From Brown to Alexander* (Southern Illinois University Press, 1977).

31. See Jeffrey R. Henig, *Rethinking School Choice: Limits of the Market Metaphor* (Princeton University Press, 1994), pp. 102–06; Amy Stuart Wells, *Time*

To Choose: America at the Crossroads of School Choice Policy (Hill & Wang, 1993), pp. 63–72; Benjamin Muse, Ten Years of Prelude (Viking, 1964).

32. Griffen v. County School Board of Prince Edward County, 377 U.S. 218, 234 (1968). See also Norwood v. Harrison, 413 U.S. 455 (1973).

33. Green v. County School Board, 391 U.S. 430, 437–38 (1968). In Alexander v. Holmes County Board of Education, 396 U.S. 19, 20 (1969), the Court confirmed the obligation of every school district "to terminate dual school systems at once and to operate now and hereafter unitary school systems."

34. Swann v. Charlotte-Mecklenburg Board of Education, 402 U.S. 1 (1971). Here the Court also prescribed that in such cases the remedy must fit the violation, imposing some restraints on the extent of lower court action. For a sympathetic analysis of the case and its impact, see Bernard Schwartz, Swann's Way: The School Busing Case and the Supreme Court (Oxford University Press, 1986).

35. Reviewing a Denver case, the Court found that, even absent a history of de jure segregation, a finding of intentional segregative policy in a substantial number of schools could be grounds for presuming intentional segregation in the entire district. The burden of proof to avoid remedial action would then be placed on district officials. Keys v. School District No.1, 413 U.S. 189 (1973).

36. See J. Anthony Lukas, Common Ground: A Turbulent Decade in the Lives of Three Families (Knopf, 1985), which provides personal accounts of three families that had been affected by the busing decision in Boston.

37. For two well-argued but divergent commentaries on the busing issue, see Gary Orfield, Must We Bus? Segregated Schools and National Policy (Brookings, 1978)(for busing) and Lino Graglia, Disaster By Decree: The Supreme Court Decisions on Race and the Schools (Cornell University Press, 1976)(against busing).

38. See Robert A. Dentler and Marvin B. Scott, Schools on Trial: An Inside Account of the Boston Case (Abt Books, 1981); Emmett H. Buell, School Desegregation and Defended Neighborhoods: The Boston Controversy (Lexington Books, 1981); J. Brian Sheehan, The Boston School Integration Dispute: Social Change and Legal Maneuvers (Columbia University Press, 1984); Ronald F. Formisano, Boston against Busing: Race, Class, and Ethnicity in the 1960s and 1970s (University of North Carolina Press, 1991).

39. James S. Coleman, Sara D. Kelly, and John A. Moore, Trends in School Segregation 1968–1973 (Urban Institute, 1975).

40. See Diane Ravitch, "The 'White Flight' Controversy," Public Interest, no. 51 (1978), for a commentary on the episode.

41. Diane Ravitch, "The Coleman Reports and American Education," in Aage B. Sorensen and Seymour Spilerman, Social Theory and Social Policy: Essays in Honor of James S. Coleman (Praeger, 1993), p. 137.

42. Compare Christine H. Rossell, "School Desegregation and White Flight," Political Science Quarterly, vol. 90 (1975) and Thomas F. Pettigrew and Robert L. Green, "School Desegregation in Large Cities: A Critique of the Coleman 'White

Flight' Thesis," *Harvard Educational Review*, vol. 46 (1976) with Reynolds Farley and C. Wurdock, *Can Government Policies Integrate Public Schools?* (Population Studies Center, University of Michigan, 1977) and Christine H. Rossell, "The Unintended Impacts of Public Policy: School Desegregation and Resegregation," report to the National Institute of Education, Boston University, 1978.

43. Among the early studies were Franklin D. Wilson, "The Impact of School Desegregation Programs on White Public School Enrollment, 1968–1976," *Sociology of Education*, vol. 58 (1985), and Finis Welch and Audrey Light, *New Evidence on School Desegregation* (U.S. Commission on Civil Rights, 1987).

44. David J. Armor, *Forced Justice: School Desegregation and the Law* (Oxford University Press, 1995), p. 170. See also Laura Steel and others, *Magnet Schools and Issues of Desegregation, Quality and Choice* (American Institutes for Research, 1993).

45. See Henig, *Rethinking School Choice*, pp.106–10; Wells, *Time to Choose*, pp. 72–91; Peter W. Cookson, *School Choice: The Struggle for the Soul of American Education* (Yale University Press, 1994), pp. 58–64.

46. Christine H. Rossell, *The Carrot or the Stick for Desegregation Policy? Magnet Schools vs. Forced Busing* (Temple University Press, 1990); Christine H. Rossell and David J. Armor, "The Effectiveness of School Desegregation Plans, 1968–1991," *American Politics Quarterly*, vol. 24 (July 1996).

47. 20 U.S.C., sec. 1601–19 (1972)(repealed 1978). See Susan L. Greenblat and Charles V. Willie, *Community Politics and Educational Change: Ten School Systems under Court Order* (Longman, 1981).

48. 20 U.S.C., sec. 1701 (1994).

49. 20 U.S.C., sec. 1701(a)(2) (1994).

50. *Miliken* v. *Bradley*, 418 U.S. 717 (1974). A year earlier the Court, in a one-sentence opinion, struck down an interdistrict busing plan in Richmond, Virginia. *Bradley* v. *State Board of Education*, 411 U.S. 913 (1973)(per curiam). For an analysis of the political context, see George R. Metcalf, *From Little Rock to Boston: The History of School Desegregation* (Greenwood Press, 1983), pp. 162–92.

51. *Board of Education* v. *Dowell*, 498 U.S. 237, 249–50 (1991). As early as 1976, the Court allowed the Pasadena school board to adopt its own voluntary integration plan, freeing the district from four years of judicial intervention. *Pasadena Board of Education* v. *Spangler*, 427 U.S. 424 (1976).

52. *Freeman* v. *Pitts*, 503 U.S. 467 (1992).

53. See Brian K. Landesberg, "Equal Educational Opportunity: The Rehnquist Court Revisits Green and Swann," *Emory Law Journal*, vol. 42 (1993).

54. *Missouri* v. *Jenkins*, 515 U.S. 70, 114 (1995) (Justice Thomas concurring).

55. See Chris Hansen, "Are the Courts Giving Up? Current Issues in School Desegregation," *Emory Law Journal*, vol. 42 (1993).

56. In St. Louis, which eventually enacted a voluntary program that transported students to neighboring suburbs, the experience with busing has been some-

what more positive. See Amy Stuart Wells and Robert L. Crain, *Stepping over the Color Line: African American Students in White Suburban Schools* (Yale University Press, 1997); Christine H. Rossell, "School Desegregation in the St. Louis Public Schools," a report to the Court in the Case of *Liddell* v. *St. Louis Board of Education, et. al.,* November 29, 1995.

57. See Christine Rossell, "School Desegregation in the Kansas City, Missouri, District, 1954–1996," a report to the Court in the case of *Jenkins, et. al.* v. *State of Missouri, et. al.,* January 20, 1999.

58. Raymond Hernandez, "Neither Separate Nor Equal: Yonkers Integrates Its Schools, to Little Effect," *New York Times,* December 29, 1995.

59. Christine H. Rossell, "The Convergence of Black and White Attitudes on School Desegregation Issues during the Four Decade Evolution of the Plans," *William & Mary Law Review,* vol. 36 (1995); Richard A. Pride and J. David Woodward, *The Burden of Busing: The Politics of Desegregation in Nashville, Tennessee* (University of Tennessee Press, 1985), pp. 145–64.

60. Public Agenda, *Time to Move On* (Washington, D.C.: August 1998).

61. Derrick A. Bell, Jr., "Serving Two Masters: Integration Ideals and Client Interests in School Litigation," *Yale Law Journal,* vol. 85 (1976). See also Edmonds, "Advocating Inequity."

62. See Stephen K. Bailey and Edith K. Mosher, *ESEA: The Office of Education Administers a Law* (Syracuse University Press, 1968), pp. 37–71, which provides a legislative history of the law. See also Julie Ray Jeffrey, *Education for Children of the Poor: A Study of the Origins of the Elementary and Secondary Education Act of 1965* (Ohio State University Press, 1978).

63. Elementary and Secondary Education Act of 1965, sec. 201, 79 Stat. 27 (repealed 1978).

64. Eugene Eisenberg and Roy D. Morey, *An Act of Congress: The Legislative Process and the Making of Education Policy* (Norton, 1969), pp. 75–95.

65. Bailey and Mosher, *ESEA,* p. 33. See also Ravitch, *Troubled Crusade,* pp. 3–42, for an overview of postwar federal initiatives in education.

66. *Aguiler* v. *Felton,* 473 U.S. 402 (1985).

67. Joseph Berger, "Limit on Remedial Education Appealed," *New York Times,* August 31, 1996; Mark Walsh, "NYC Seeks to Overturn Limits on Title I at Religious Schools," *Education Week,* February 28, 1996.

68. *Agostini* v. *Felton,* 521, U.S. 203 (1997).

69. See Launor F. Carter, "The Sustaining Effects Study of Compensatory and Elementary Education," *Educational Researcher* (August–September 1984); David J. Hoff, "Tracking Title I," *Education Week,* October 22, 1997.

70. Michael Puma and others, *Prospects: Final Report on Student Outcomes* (Abt Associates, April 1997); David J. Hoff, "Chapter I Aid Failed to Close Learning Gap," *Education Week,* April 2, 1997. See also Geoffrey D. Borman and Jerome

V. D'Agostino, "Title I and Student Achievement: A Meta-Analysis of Federal Evaluation Results," *Education Evaluation and Policy Analysis,* vol. 18 (Winter 1996).

71. Sam Stringfield and others, *Special Strategies for Educating Disadvantaged Children: Final Report* (Abt Associates, 1997).

72. Department of Education, *Promising Results, Continuing Challenges: The Final Report of the National Assessment of Title I* (1999).

73. See Allan Odden and others, "The Story of the Education Dollar: No Fiscal Academy Awards and No Fiscal Smoking Gun," *Phi Delta Kappan,* vol. 77 (1995).

74. Arthur Wise, *Rich Schools, Poor Schools* (University of Chicago Press, 1968); John E. Coons, William H. Clune and Stephen D. Sugarman, *Private Wealth and Public Education* (Harvard University Press, 1970).

75. *Serrano v. Priest,* 5 Cal.3d 584 (1971).

76. *San Antonio Independent School District v. Rodriguez,* 411 U.S. 1, 24 (1973).

77. Ibid., at 25.

78. Ibid., at 44.

79. *Robinson v. Cahill,* 303 A.2d 273, 294 (N.J. 1973).

80. These included Illinois (1968), West Virginia (1969), Minnesota (1971), Maryland (1972), Texas (1973). Robert Inman, "Introduction, Special Issue— *Serrano v. Priest:* 25th Anniversary," *Journal of Policy Analysis and Management,* vol. 16 (Winter 1997).

81. The states where the courts ordered reforms include New Jersey (1973 and 1990), Kansas (1976), California (1976), Wisconsin (1976), Washington (1978), West Virginia (1979), Wyoming (1980), Arkansas (1983), Texas (1989), Montana (1989), Kentucky (1989), Alabama (1993), Massachusetts (1993), Tennessee (1993), Arizona (1994), Connecticut (1997). Inman, "*Serrano v. Priest:* 25th Anniversary," p. 2.

82. Fabio Silva and Jon Sonstelie, "Did *Serrano* Cause a Decline in School Spending?" *National Tax Journal,* vol. 47 (June 1995); Neil D. Theobald and Lawrence O. Picus, "Living with Equal Amounts of Less: Experiences of States with Primary State Funded School Systems," *Journal of Education Finance,* vol. 17 (Spring 1991).

83. Sheila E. Murray, William N. Evans, and Robert M. Schwab, "Education Finance Reform and the Distribution of Education Resources," unpublished paper, Departments of Economics, University of Maryland and University of Kentucky, March 1996; William N. Evans, Sheila E. Murray, and Robert M. Schwab, "Schoolhouses, Court Houses, and Statehouses after *Serrano,*" *Journal of Policy Analysis and Management,* vol. 16 (Winter 1997).

84. Paul Courant and Susanna Loeb, "Centralization of School Finance in Michigan," *Journal of Policy Analysis and Management,* vol. 16 (Winter 1997).

85. William Duncombe and John Yinger, "Why It Is So Hard to Help Central City Schools," *Journal of Policy Analysis and Management*, vol. 16 (Winter 1997); Neil D. Theobald and Faith Hanna, "Ample Provision for Whom? The Evolution of State Control over School Finance in Washington," *Journal of Education Finance*, vol. 17 (1991).

86. Stephen J. Goetz and David L. Debertin, "Rural Areas and Educational Reform in Kentucky: An Early Assessment of Revenue Equalization," *Journal of Education Finance*, vol. 18 (1992).

87. Linda Hertert, Carolyn Busch, and Allan Odden, "School Financing Inequities among the States: The Problem from a National Perspective," *Journal of Education Finance*, vol. 19 (1994); Kern Alexander and Robert Salmon, *American School Finance* (Allyn & Bacon, 1995).

88. See Michael Heise, "Equal Educational Opportunity, Hollow Victories, and the Demise of School Finance Equity Theory: An Empirical Perspective and Alternative Explanation," *Georgia Law Review*, vol. 32 (1998); John Dayton, "Examining the Efficacy of Judicial Involvement in Public School Funding Reform," *Journal of Educational Finance*, vol. 22 (1996); G. Alan Hickrod, "The Effect of Constitutional Litigation on Educational Finance: A Preliminary Analysis," *Journal of Educational Finance*, vol. 18 (1992); Note, "Unfulfilled Promises: School Finance Remedies and State Courts," *Harvard Law Review*, vol. 104 (1991).

89. The term first appeared in William Thro, "The Third Wave : The Impact of the Montana, Kentucky and Texas Decisions on the Future of Public School Finance Reform," *Journal of Law & Education*, vol. 19 (1990). See also Michael Heise, "State Constitutions, School Finance Litigation and the 'Third Wave': From Equity to Adequacy," *Temple Law Review*, vol. 68 (1995); Julie K. Underwood and William E. Sparkman, "School Finance Litigation: A New Wave of Reform," *Harvard Journal of Law & Public Policy*, vol. 14 (1991); Gail F. Levine, "Meeting the Third Wave: Legislative Approaches to Recent Judicial Finance School Rulings," *Harvard Journal on Legislation*, vol. 28 (1991).

90. See Peter Enrich, "Leaving Equality Behind: New Directions in School Finance Reform," *Vanderbilt Law Review*, vol. 48 (1995); William E. Thro, "Judicial Analysis during the Third Wave of School Finance Litigation," *Boston College Law Review*, vol. 35 (1994).

91. *Rose v. Council for Better Education, Inc.*, 790 S.W.2d 186, 215 (Ky 1989).

92. *Leandro v. State of North Carolina*, 346 N.C. 336, 488 S.E.2d. 249 (N.C. 1997). See Robert C. Johnson, "N.C. Court Targets Adequacy in Equity Ruling," *Education Week*, August 6, 1997.

93. *Abbott v. Burke*, 149 N.J. 145, 693 A.2d 417 (N.J. 1997).

94. Abby Goodnough, "Judge Offers Specific Plans for Schools: State Court Could Force New Jersey to Comply," *New York Times*, January 23, 1998, p. B1.

95. Caroline Hendrie, "For the 4th Time, Court Rejects N.J. Formula: Says Poorest Districts Need More Money," *Education Week*, May 21, 1997, p. 1.

96. See *Abbott* v. *Burke*, remedial relief order, May 21, 1998. See also Caroline Hendrie, "N.J. Schools Put Reform to the Test: Verdict Still Out on 'Whole School' Models," *Education Week*, April 21, 1999.

97. Rob Greenwald, Larry V. Hedges, and Richard Laine, "The Effect of School Resources on Student Achievement," *Review of Educational Research*, vol. 66 (Fall 1996), pp. 361–96; Ronald F. Ferguson and Helen Ladd, "How and Why Money Matters: An Analysis of Alabama Schools," in Helen Ladd, ed., *Holding Schools Accountable* (Brookings, 1996); David Card and Alan Krueger, "Does School Quality Matter? Returns to Education and the Characteristics of Public Schools in the United States," *Journal of Political Economy*, vol. 100 (1992).

98. Odden and others, "The Story of the Education Dollar"; Hamilton Lankford and James Wyckoff, "Where Has the Money Gone? An Analysis of School Spending in New York," *Educational Evaluation and Policy Analysis*, vol. 17 (1995).

99. Jacob E. Adams, Jr., "Spending School Reform Dollars in Kentucky: Familiar Patterns and New Programs, but Is This Reform?" *Educational Evaluation and Policy Analysis*, vol. 16 (1994); William A. Firestone and others, "Where Did the $800 Million Go? The First Year of New Jersey's Quality Education Act," *Education Evaluation and Policy Analysis*, vol. 16 (1994).

100. James W. Guthrie, "School Finance: Fifty Years of Expansion," *The Future of Children: Financing Schools*, vol. 7 (Winter 1997).

101. Eric Hanushek, "Assessing the Effects of School Resources on Student Performance: An Update," *Education Evaluation and Policy Analysis*, vol. 19 (Summer 1997); Eric A. Hanushek, Stephen G. Rivkin, and Lori L. Taylor, "Aggregation and the Estimated Effects of School Resources," *Review of Economics and Statistics*, vol. 78 (November 1996).

102. Richard Cloward and Lloyd Ohlin, *Delinquency and Opportunity: A Theory of Delinquent Gangs* (Free Press, 1960).

103. Daniel Patrick Moynihan, *Maximum Feasible Misunderstanding: Community Action in the War on Poverty* (Free Press, 1969), p. 147.

104. Francis Fox Piven and Richard A. Cloward, *Regulating the Poor: The Functions of Public Welfare* (Vintage Books, 1971), p. 261.

105. See, generally, Sar Levitan, *The Great Society's Poor Law* (Johns Hopkins University Press, 1969); John Donovan, *The Politics of Poverty* (Pegasus, 1967).

106. See Carole Patemen, *Participation and Democratic Theory* (Cambridge University Press, 1970).

107. For a general critique of the thinking behind the participatory ideology, see Joseph P. Viteritti, *Bureaucracy and Social Justice* (Kennikat Press, 1979).

108. The classic statement on this phenomenon remains Stokeley Carmichael and Charles V. Hamilton, *Black Power: The Politics of Liberation in America* (Vintage Books, 1967).

109. See Alan A. Altshuler, *Community Control: The Black Demand for Participation in Large American Cities* (Pegasus, 1970); Milton Kotler, *Neighborhood Government: The Local Foundations of Political Life* (Bobbs-Merrill, 1969).

110. See, generally, Joseph P. Viteritti, "The City and the Constitution: A Historical Analysis of Institutional Evolution and Adaptation," *Journal of Urban Affairs*, vol. 12 (1990), for a historical overview of the creation of municipal institutions and the thinking behind their design; and Joseph P. Viteritti, "The Urban School District: Towards an Open Systems Approach to Leadership and Governance," *Urban Education*, vol. 21 (1986).

111. David Tyack and Elizabeth Hansot, *Managers of Virtue: Public School Leadership, 1820–1980* (Basic Books, 1982), pp. 129–66. See also David Tyack, *The One Best System* (Harvard University Press, 1974); Raymond Callahan, *Education and the Cult of Efficiency* (University of Chicago Press, 1962).

112. See Diane Ravitch and Joseph P. Viteritti, "New York: The Obsolete Factory," in Diane Ravitch and Joseph P. Viteritti, eds., *New Schools for a New Century: The Redesign of Urban Education* (Yale University Press, 1997) for a contemporary portrait of the New York City school system.

113. See Diane Ravitch, *The Great School Wars: New York City, 1805–1973* (Basic Books, 1974), pp. 251-86; David Rogers, *110 Livingston Street: Politics and Bureaucracy in the New York City School System* (Random House, 1968); Clarence Taylor, *Knocking at Our Own Door: Milton Galamison and the Struggle to Integrate New York City Schools* (Columbia University Press, 1997).

114. See Viteritti, *Bureaucracy and Social Justice*, pp. 59–88; Robert F. Pecorrella, *Community Politics in a Postreform City: Politics in New York City* (M. E. Sharpe, 1994).

115. Ravitch, *The Great School Wars*, pp. 287–404.

116. See Jeffrey Mirel, *The Rise and Fall of an Urban School System: Detroit, 1907–1981* (University of Michigan Press, 1993), pp. 338–44, 359–68.

117. See Ravitch and Viteritti, "The Obsolete Factory," in Ravitch and Viteritti, *New Schools for a New Century*, pp. 27–32.

118. See "State of the City Schools, '98: A Performance Report on the New York City Public Schools" (Public Education Association, 1998).

119. For three distinct accounts of the reform campaign, see G. Alfred Hess, *Restructuring Urban Schools: A Chicago Perspective* (Teachers College Press, 1995); Jeffrey Mirel, "School Reform, Chicago Style: Educational Innovation in a Changing Urban Context, 1976–1991," *Urban Education*, vol. 28 (July 1993); Michael B. Katz, "Chicago School Reform as History," *Teachers College Record*, vol. 94 (Fall 1992).

120. See Saul Alinsky, *Rules for Radicals* (Vintage Books, 1971), which is Alinsky's signature piece on organizing. For a more historical approach, see Julia Wrigley, *Class, Politics and Public Schools: Chicago, 1900–1950* (Rutgers Uni-

versity Press, 1982); Michael Herrick, *The Chicago Schools: A Social and Political History* (Sage Publications, 1981).

121. Quoted in Anthony S. Bryk, David Kerbow, and Sharon Rollow, "Chicago School Reform," in Ravitch and Viteritti, *New Schools for a New Century*, p. 164.

122. Quoted in Bryk, Kerbow, and Rollow, "Chicago School Reform," in Ravitch and Viteritti, *New Schools for a New Century*, pp. 174–200.

123. Priscilla Wohlstetter, Susan Albers Mohrman, and Peter J. Robertson, "Successful School-Based Management: A Lesson for Restructuring Urban Schools," in Ravitch and Viteritti, *New Schools for a New Century*, pp. 201–25; Betty Malen, Rodney T. Ogawa, and Jennifer Kranz, "What Do We Know about School-Based Management," in William H. Clune and John F. Witte, eds., *Choice and Control in American Education*, vol. 2, *The Practice of Choice, Decentralization and School Restructuring* (Falmer Press, 1990), pp. 289–42.

124. Bryk, Kerbow, and Rollow, "Chicago School Reform," in Ravitch and Viteritti, *New Schools for a New Century*, p. 187.

125. See Paul G. Vallas, "Saving Public Schools," presentation at the Manhattan Institute, New York, December 9, 1998; Pam Bellard, "In Chicago, the Story behind the Test Scores," *New York Times*, January 21, 1999.

126. National School Boards Association, *Still Separate, Still Unequal? Desegregation in the 1990's* (1995), pp. 19, 26–27.

127. Armor, *Forced Justice*, pp. 171–73.

128. Gary Orfield and others, "Deepening Segregation in the American Public Schools," Harvard Project on School Desegregation, April 5, 1997, p. 11.

129. Gary Orfield and Susan E. Eaton, *Dismantling Desegregation: The Quiet Reversal of Brown v. Board of Education* (New Press, 1997).

130. See Armor, *Forced Justice*, pp. 77–98; Meredith Phillips, "Does School Desegregation Explain Why African-Americans and Latinos Score Lower than Whites on Academic Achievement Tests?" paper prepared for the Annual Meeting of American Sociological Association, 1997; Thomas Cook and others, *School Desegregation and Black Achievement* (Department of Education, 1984); Robert Crain and Rita Mahard, "Desegregation and Black Achievement, a Review of the Research," *Law & Contemporary Problems*, vol. 42 (1978), pp. 17–58; Nancy St. John, *School Desegregation: Outcomes for Children* (John Wiley, 1978).

131. Armor, *Forced Justice*, pp. 99–101; William B. Stephan, "The Effects of School Desegregation: An Evaluation 30 Years after Brown," in M. Saxe and L. Saxe, eds., *Advances in Applied Social Psychology* (Erlbaum, 1986); Judith R. Porter and Robert E. Washington, "Black Identity and Self-Esteem," *Annual Review of Sociology*, vol. 5 (1979), pp. 53–74; St. John, *School Desegregation*; Morris Rosenberg and Roberta G. Simmons, *Black and White Self-Esteem: The Urban School Child* (American Sociological Association, 1971).

132. Orfield and others, "Deepening Segregation," p. 20.

133. General Accounting Office, *School Finance: State and Federal Efforts to Target Poor Students* (1998). See also William M. Evans, Sheila Murray, and Robert Schwab, "School Houses, Court Houses, and State Houses After Serrano," *Journal of Policy Analysis and Management*, vol. 16 (January 1997).

134. Diane Ravitch, *National Standards in American Education* (Brookings, 1995), pp. 59–97; Stephen Thernstrom and Abigail Thernstrom, *America in Black and White: One Nation Indivisible* (Simon & Schuster, 1997), pp. 352–57; Christopher Jencks and Meredith Phillips, eds., *The Black-White Test Score Gap* (Brookings, 1998).

135. Thernstrom and Thernstrom, *America in Black and White*, p. 19; Meredith Phillips and others, "Family Background, Parenting Practices, and the Black-White Test Score Gap," in Jencks and Phillips, *The Black-White Test Score Gap*.

136. Department of Education, *No More Excuses: The Final Report of the Hispanic Dropout Project* (1998).

Chapter Three

1. Milton Friedman, "The Role of Government in Education," in Robert A. Solo, ed., *Economics and the Public Interest* (Rutgers University Press, 1955), revised as Milton Friedman, *Capitalism and Freedom* (University of Chicago Press, 1962), chapter 6. For a critique of the market model in education, see Jeffrey R. Henig, *Rethinking School Choice: Limits of the Market Metaphor* (Princeton University Press, 1994).

2. See Diane Ravitch and Joseph P. Viteritti, eds., *New Schools for a New Century: The Redesign of Urban Education* (Yale University Press, 1997).

3. Milton Friedman and Rose Friedman, *Free to Choose: A Personal Statement* (Harcourt Brace, 1980), chaps. 1, 2, 5.

4. Ibid., chap. 6.

5. Theodore Sizer and Philip Whitten, "A Proposal for a Poor Children's Bill of Rights," *Psychology Today* (August 1968); Theodore Sizer, "The Case for a Free Market," *Saturday Review,* January 11, 1969 .

6. Christopher Jencks, *Education Vouchers: A Report on Financing Education by Payments to Parents* (Cambridge, Mass.: Center for the Study of Public Policy, 1970).

7. Christopher Jencks, "Is Public School Obsolete?" *Public Interest* (Winter 1966).

8. Christopher Jencks, "Giving Parents Money to Pay for Schooling: Education Vouchers," *New Republic*, July 4, 1970.

9. The others included Gary, Kansas City, Milwaukee, Minneapolis, and Rochester. John L. Puckett, "Educational Vouchers: Rhetoric or Reality?" *Educational Forum*, vol. 47 (Summer 1983).

10. R. G. Bridge and J. Blackman, *Family Choice in Schooling: A Study of Alternatives in American Education* (Rand Corporation, 1978); Frank Cappel, *A Study of Alternatives in American Education. Volume 6: Student Outcomes in Alum Rock, 1974–1976* (Rand Corporation, 1978).

11. Testimony before the House Committee on Education and Labor, April 2, 1971, 92d Cong., 1st sess. (Government Printing Office, 1971).

12. John E. Coons and Stephen D. Sugarman, "Family Choice in Education: A Model State System for Vouchers," *California Law Review*, vol. 59 (1971). The proposal is more fully developed in John E. Coons and Stephen D. Sugarman, *Education By Choice: The Case for Family Control* (University of California Press, 1978). See also John E. Coons and Stephen D. Sugarman, "The Scholarship Initiative: A Model State Law for Elementary and Secondary School Choice," *Journal of Law & Education*, vol. 21 (1992); Stephen D. Sugarman, "Using Private Schools to Promote Public Values," *University of Chicago Legal Forum* (1991).

13. John E. Coons, William H. Clune, and Stephen D. Sugarman, *Private Wealth and Public Education* (Harvard University Press, 1970).

14. See Dominick Cirelli, "Utilizing School Voucher Programs to Remedy School Financing Problems," *Akron Law Review*, vol. 30 (1997); Greg D. Andes, "Private School Voucher Remedies in Education Cases," *University of Chicago Law Review*, vol. 62 (1995).

15. Henig, *Rethinking School Choice*, pp. 71–73.

16. Nancy Paulu, *Improving Schools and Empowering Parents: Choice in American Education* (Department of Education, 1989), p. 14.

17. Ibid., pp.78–80.

18. Rolf K. Blank, Roger E. Levine, and Lauri Steel, "After 15 Years: Magnet Schools in Urban Education," in Bruce Fuller and Richard F. Elmore, eds., *Who Chooses? Who Loses? Culture, Institutions and the Unequal Effects of School Choice* (Teachers College Press, 1996); Adam Gamoran, "Student Achievement in Public Magnet, Public Comprehensive, and Private City High Schools," *Educational Policy Analyses*, vol. 18 (Spring 1996).

19. Blank, Levine, and Steel, "Magnet Schools," in Fuller and Elmore, *Who Chooses? Who Loses?*; Rolf Blank, "Educational Effects of Magnet High Schools," in William H. Clune and John F. Witte, eds., *Choice and Control in American Education*, vol. 2, *The Practice of Choice, Decentralization and School Restructuring* (Falmer Press, 1990); Christine H. Rossell, *The Carrot or the Stick for School Desegregation Policy? Magnet Schools vs. Forced Busing* (Temple University Press, 1990).

20. Jeffrey R. Henig, "The Local Dynamics of Choice: Ethnic Preferences and

Institutional Responses," in Fuller and Elmore, *Who Chooses? Who Loses?*; Donald R. Moore, "Voice and Choice in Chicago," in Clune and Witte, *Choice and Control in American Education*, vol. 2.

21. Moore, "Voice and Choice in Chicago," in Clune and Witte, *Choice and Control in American Education*, vol. 2.

22. Mary H. Metz, "Potentialities and Problems of Choice in Desegregation Plans," in Clune and Witte, *Choice and Control in American Education*, vol. 2, pp. 111–18.

23. Kerry H. White, "Suit Challenges Integration Plan in Louisville," *Education Week*, May 6, 1998.

24. Christine H. Rossell and David Armor, "The Effectiveness of Desegregation Plans," *American Politics Quarterly*, vol. 24 (July 1996).

25. Quoted in Peter W. Cookson, *School Choice: The Struggle for the Soul of American Education* (Yale University Press, 1994), p. 59. See also Christine H. Rossell and Charles Glenn, "The Cambridge Controlled Choice Plans," *Urban Review*, vol. 20 (1988).

26. Michael J. Alves and Charles V. Willie, "Controlled Choice Assignments: A New and More Effective Approach to School Desegregation," *Urban Review*, vol. 19 (1987); Michael J. Alves and Charles V. Willie, "Choice, Decentralization and Desegregation: The Boston 'Controlled Choice' Plan," in Clune and Witte, *Choice and Control in American Education*, vol. 2; Charles C. Glenn, "Controlled Choice in Massachusetts Public Schools," *Public Interest*, no. 103 (Spring 1991).

27. Amy Stewart Wells, *Time to Choose: America at the Crossroads of School Choice Policy* (Hill & Wang, 1993), p. 91.

28. Christine H. Rossell, "Controlled-Choice Desegregation Plans: Not Enough Choice, Too Much Control," *Urban Affairs Review*, vol. 31 (September 1995).

29. Christine H. Rossell, "The Convergence of Black and White Attitudes on School Desegregation Issues during the Four Decade Evolution of the Plans," *William & Mary Law Review*, vol. 36 (1995).

30. Caroline Hendrie, "Pressure for Community Schools Grows as Court Oversight Wanes," *Education Week*, June 17, 1998.

31. Rossell, "Controlled-Choice Desegregation Plans."

32. For personal accounts by two of the main actors in the experiment, see Seymour Fliegel and James MacGuire, *Miracle in East Harlem: The Fight for Choice in Public Education* (Times Books, 1993) and Deborah Meier, *The Power of Their Ideas* (Beacon Press, 1995).

33. Raymond Domonico, "Model for Choice: A Report on Manhattan's District 4," Education Policy Paper 1, Center for Educational Innovation, Manhattan Institute for Policy Research, 1989.

34. Deborah Meier, "Central Park East: An Alternative Story," *Phi Delta Kappan* (June 1987), pp. 753–57.

35. Mary Anne Raywid, "Family Choice Arrangements in Public Schools: A Review of the Literature," *Review of Educational Research*, vol. 55 (Winter 1985).

36. Cookson, *School Choice*, pp. 77–79; Richard Elmore, "Public School Choice as a Policy Issue," in William T. Gormley, ed., *Privatization and its Alternatives* (University of Wisconsin Press, 1991).

37. Diane Harrington and Peter Cookson, "School Reform in East Harlem: Alternative Schools vs. Schools of Choice," in G. Alfred Hess, ed., *Empowering Teachers and Parents* (Bergin and Garvey, 1992).

38. David Kirp, "What School Choice Really Means," *Atlantic Monthly* (November 1992), p. 127.

39. Paul Teske and others, "Evaluating The Effects of Public School Choice in District 4," unpublished report, January 16, 1998.

40. Mark Schneider and others, "Shopping for Schools: In the Land of the Blind, the One Eyed Parent May Be Enough," *American Journal of Political Science*, vol. 42 (1998).

41. See, generally, Wells, *Time to Choose*, pp. 96–128; Tim Mazzoni and Barry Sullivan, "Legislating Educational Choice in Minnesota: Politics and Prospects," in William L. Boyd and Herbert Walberg, eds., *Choice in Education: Potential and Problems* (McCutchan, 1990).

42. Joe Nathan and Wayne Jennings, *Access to Opportunity: Experiences of Minnesota Students in Four Statewide School Choice Programs* (Center for School Change, Hubert H. Humphrey Institute of Public Affairs, University of Minnesota, 1990); Judith Pearson, *The Myths of Educational Choice* (Praeger, 1993); Policy Studies Associates, *Minnesota's Educational Options for At-Risk Youth: Urban Alternative Schools and Area Learning Centers* (1992).

43. Janie Funkhouser and Kelly W. Colopy, *Minnesota's Open Enrollment Option: Impacts on School Districts* (Department of Education, 1994).

44. Nina H. Shokraii and Sarah E. Youssef, *School Choice Programs: What's Happening in the States, 1998 Edition* (Heritage Foundation, 1998).

45. Carnegie Foundation for the Advancement of Teaching, *School Choice: A Special Report* (1992).

46. Ernest L. Boyer, "School Choice in Perspective," in Carnegie Foundation for the Advancement of Teaching, *School Choice*, p. 1.

47. See Joe Nathan, *Charter Schools: Creating Hope and Opportunity for American Education* (Jossey-Bass, 1996); "Breaking Away: The Charter School Revolution," *Education Week, Special Report*, November 29, 1995.

48. Peter Schmidt, "Citing Debts, L.A. Board Revokes School's Charter," *Education Week*, December 14, 1994; Peter Applebome, "Start of Charter School Shows Flaws in Concept," *New York Times*, March 6, 1996.

49. Michael Janofsky, "Suspension of School Principal Saves Charter School," *New York Times*, November 7, 1997.

50. Center for Education Reform, *Charter Schools: A Progress Report: Part II, The Closures* (Washington, D.C.: February 1999).

51. On the issue of site-based management, see Priscilla Wohlstetter and others, "Successful School-Based Management: A Lesson for Restructuring Urban Schools," in Ravitch and Viteritti, *New Schools for a New Century*; Susan Mohrman and others, eds., *School-Based Management: Organizing for High Performance* (Jossey-Bass, 1994); Betty Malen, Rodney T. Ogawa, and Jennifer Kranz, "What Do We Know about School-Based Management? A Call for Research," in Clune and Witte, *Choice and Control in American Education*, vol. 2.

52. Shokraii and Youssef, *School Choice Programs*, p. 5.

53. See Chester E. Finn, Louann A. Bierlein, and Bruno V. Manno, "Charter Schools in Action: A First Look," Hudson Institute, January 1996; "Charter Schools: What Are They Up To?" Education Commission of the States and the Center for School Change, University of Minnesota, 1994.

54. On the development of Edison, see John E. Chubb, "Lessons in School Reform from the Edison Project," in Ravitch and Viteritti, *New Schools for a New Century*.

55. "Edison Project Schools," the Edison Project (http://www.edisonproject. com/intro.html [April 5, 1999]).

56. Mark Walsh, "Baltimore Vote Ends City Contract with EAI," *Education Week*, December 6, 1995; George Judson, "Baltimore Ends City Experiment," *New York Times*, November 23, 1995; George Judson, "Education Company Banned from Hartford Public Schools," *New York Times*, February 1, 1996.

57. "Annual Report on School Performance," the Edison Project, December 1997. This evaluation has been contested in a separate evaluation performed by the American Federation of Teachers (AFT), "Student Achievement in Edison Schools: Mixed Results in an Ongoing Enterprise" (May 1998). Edison responded to the AFT report with a point-by-point rebuttal. See Mark Walsh, "AFT Report Disputes Claims by Edison Project," *Education Week*, April 13, 1998. See also John Chubb, "The Performance of Privately Managed Schools: An Early Look at the Edison Project," in Paul E. Peterson and Bryan C. Hassel, eds., *Learning from School Choice* (Brookings, 1998); "Second Annual Report on School Performance," the Edison Project, February 1999.

58. See Paul Hill, Lawrence C. Pierce, and James W. Guthrie, *Reinventing Public Education: Contracting Can Transform America's Schools* (University of Chicago Press, 1997).

59. Somini Sengupta, "Edison Project Gets Aid to Open New Schools," *New York Times*, May 27, 1998.

60. Bess Keller, "Dayton Union Nixes Plan for Edison to Run Charters," *Education Week*, April 13, 1998.

61. Robert Johnson, "1993 Mich. Charter School Statute Is Legal, High Court Declares," *Education Week*, August 6, 1997.

62. Jordana Hart, "Marblehead School Backers Say They Are Harassed," *Boston Globe*, August 23, 1995.

63. Tom Loveless and Claudia Jasin, "Starting from Scratch: Political Organizational Challenges Facing Charter Schools," *Education Administration Quarterly*, vol. 34 (1988).

64. Joseph Pereira, "Storm over Cambridge Charter School: Parents Assail the Toll on Public System," *Wall Street Journal*, April 26, 1996.

65. See David J. Dent, "Diversity Rules Threaten North Carolina Charter Schools that Aid Blacks," *New York Times*, December 23, 1998; Lynne Schnaiberg, "Predominantly Black Charters Focus of Debate in N.C., *Education Week*, August 5, 1998.

66. Mark Pitsch, "Riley Announces First Charter-School Grants, New Study," *Education Week*, October 4, 1998.

67. See Stella Cheung, Mary Ellen Murphy, and Joe Nathan, "Making a Difference? Charter Schools, Evaluation and Student Performance," Center for School Change, Hubert H. Humphrey Institute for Public Affairs, University of Minnesota, March 1998. This survey of thirty-one charter schools in eight states provides preliminary evidence of improved student achievement in twenty-one schools.

68. The locations included Phoenix, San Diego, Atlanta, Colorado Springs, and Linikai, Hawaii. Ann Bradley, "NEA Seeks to Help Start Five Charter Schools," *Education Week*, April 24, 1996.

69. "Charter School Laws: Do They Measure Up?" American Federation of Teachers, 1996.

70. See Chester Finn and Diane Ravitch, "Charter Schools—Beware Imitations," *Wall Street Journal*, September 7, 1995.

71. RPP International and the University of Minnesota, *A Study of Charter Schools: First Year Report* (Department of Education, 1997); RPP International, *A National Study of Charter Schools* (Department of Education, 1998).

72. RPP International, *A National Study of Charter Schools.*

73. Gregg Vanourek and others, *Charter Schools as Seen by Those Who Know Them Best* (Hudson Institute, 1997).

74. Carnegie Foundation for the Advancement of Teaching, *School Choice.*

75. Schneider and others, "Shopping for Schools in the Land of the Blind." See also Mark Schneider and others, "School Choice and Culture Wars in the Classroom: What Different Parents Seek from Education," *Social Science Quarterly*, vol. 79 (September 1998).

76. Bryan C. Hassel, "Charter Schools: Politics and Practice in Four States," in Peterson and Hassel, *Learning from School Choice*, p. 259.

77. Eric Rofes, "How Are School Districts Responding to Charter Laws and Charter Schools," policy analysis for California Education, April 1998. Three of the states (California, Georgia, Wisconsin) had restrictive laws that allowed only local school districts to serve as a charter sponsor; the remainder (Arizona, Colo-

rado, Massachusetts, Michigan, Minnesota, District of Columbia) had nonrestrictive laws that provided for more than one chartering authority. Every jurisdiction had at least two years of experience with charter schools.

78. Ibid., p. 5.

79. Ibid., pp. 6–7.

80. See Robert Maranto and others, "Do Charter Schools Improve District Schools? Three Approaches to the Question," in Robert Maranto and others, eds., *The Frontiers of Public Education: Lessons from Arizona Charter Schools* (Westview Press, forthcoming); "Los Angeles Unified School District Charter School Evaluation," West End Regional Laboratory, 1998.

Chapter Four

1. James S. Coleman, Thomas Hoffer, and Sally Kilgore, *High School Achievement* (Basic Books, 1982).

2. For a review of the episode, see Diane Ravitch, "The Meaning of the New Colemen Report," *Phi Delta Kappan* (June 1981); Diane Ravitch, "The Coleman Reports and American Education," in Aage B. Sorensen and Seymour Spilerman, eds., *Social Theory and Social Policy* (Praeger, 1993), pp. 137–41.

3. Cited in Ravitch, "The Coleman Reports," in Sorensen and Spilerman, *Social Theory*, p. 139.

4. Ibid., p. 140.

5. T. C. Hunt and N. M. Kunkel, "Catholic Schools: the Nation's Largest Alternative School System," *New Catholic World*, vol. 6 (1988).

6. Jay Noell, "Public and Catholic Schools: A Reanalysis of Public and Private Schools," *Sociology of Education*, vol. 55 (1982); Arthur Goldberger and Glen G. Cain, "The Causal Analysis of Cognitive Outcome in the Coleman, Hoffer, and Kilgore Report," *Sociology of Education*, vol. 55 (1982); Karl L. Alexander and Aaron M. Pellas, "Private Schools and Public Policy: New Evidence on Cognitive Achievement in Public and Private Schools," *Sociology of Education*, vol. 56 (1983); Richard Murnane, Stuart Newstead, and Randall J. Olsen, "Comparing Public and Private Schools: The Puzzling Role of Selectivity Bias," *Journal of Business and Economic Statistics*, vol. 3 (1985); and the entire edition of the *Harvard Educational Review*, vol. 51 (1981).

7. James S. Coleman and Thomas Hoffer, *Public, Catholic and Private Schools: the Importance of Community* (Basic Books, 1987).

8. See also Christopher Jencks, "How Much Do High School Students Learn?" *Sociology of Education*, vol. 58 (1985).

9. For an excellent review of this literature, see Darlene Eleanor York, "The Academic Achievement of African Americans in Catholic Schools: A Review of

the Literature," in Jacqueline Jordan Irvine and Michele Foster, eds., *Growing Up African American in Catholic Schools* (Teachers College Press, 1996).

10. National Center for Education Statistics, *Digest of Education Statistics* (1997). About 10 percent of the students in the United States attend private schools, 85 percent of which are religious.

11. Valerie E. Lee, "Catholic Lessons for Public Schools," in Diane Ravitch and Joseph P. Viteritti, eds., *New Schools for a New Century: The Redesign of Urban Education* (Yale University Press, 1997), p. 148.

12. Derek Neal, "The Effects of Catholic Schooling on Educational Achievement," *Journal of Labor Economics*, vol. 15 (1997), pp. 100–02.

13. Jeanne Ponessa, "Catholic School Enrollment Continues to Increase," *Education Week*, April 17, 1996.

14. See Adam Gamoran, "Student Achievement in Public Magnet, Comprehensive, and Private City High Schools," *Education Evaluation and Policy Analysis*, vol. 18 (Spring 1996); William Sander, "Catholic Grade School and Academic Achievement," *Journal of Human Resources*, vol. 31 (1996).

15. Andrew M. Greeley, *Catholic High Schools and Minority Students* (Transaction Books, 1982). See also James Cibulka, Timothy J. O'Brien, and Donald Zewe, *Inner City Catholic Elementary Schools: A Study* (Marquette University Press, 1982).

16. William N. Evans, Amanda A. Honeycutt, and Robert M. Schwab, "Who Benefits from a Catholic School Education," Department of Economics, University of Maryland, November 1998, unpublished.

17. See Neal, *Effects of Catholic Schooling*; William N. Evans and Robert M. Schwab, "Finishing High School and Starting College: Do Catholic Schools Make a Difference?" *Quarterly Journal of Economics* (November 1995); William Sander and Anthony C. Krautman, "Catholic Schools, Dropout Rates, and Educational Attainment," *Economic Inquiry*, vol. 33 (1995); Timothy Z. Keith and Ellis B. Page, "Do Catholic Schools Really Improve Minority Achievement?" *American Educational Research Journal*, vol. 22 (1985).

18. See, for example, Henry M. Levin, "Educational Vouchers: Effectiveness, Choice, and Costs," *Journal of Policy Analysis and Management*, vol. 17 (1998).

19. Anthony S. Bryk, Valerie E. Lee, and Peter B. Holland, *Catholic Schools and the Common Good* (Harvard University Press, 1993)

20. Peter Rossi, "Book Review," *American Journal of Education*, vol. 102 (May 1994), p. 351.

21. Bryk, Lee, and Holland, *Catholic Schools*, p. 312. See also Paul T. Hill, Gail E. Foster, and Tamar Gendler, *High Schools with Character* (Rand Corporation, 1990).

22. Janice E. Jackson, "Foreword," in Irvine and Foster, *African American in Catholic Schools*, p. x.

23. National Center for Education Statistics, *The Condition of Education, 1997* (1998).

24. Bryk, Lee, and Holland, *Catholic Schools,* p. 33.

25. For a fuller treatment of the concept, see James S. Coleman, "Social Capital in the Creation of Human Capital," *American Journal of Sociology,* vol. 94 (1988).

26. John E. Chubb and Terry M. Moe, *Politics, Markets, and America's Schools* (Brookings, 1990).

27. See, for example, Arthur F. Bentley, *The Process of Government* (University of Chicago Press, 1908); David Truman, *The Governmental Process* (Knopf, 1960); Robert Dahl, *Who Governs?* (Yale University Press, 1966).

28. Joseph P. Viteritti, *Across the River: Politics and Education in the City* (Holmes & Meier, 1983). See also Joseph P. Viteritti, "Public Organization Environments: Constituents, Clients and Urban Governance," *Administration and Society,* vol. 21 (February 1990).

29. Chubb and Moe, *Politics, Markets, and America's Schools,* p. 11.

30. See, for example, Amy Stuart Wells, "Choice in Education: Examining the Evidence on Equity," *Teachers College Record,* vol. 93 (1991); James S. Liebman, "Voice, Not Choice," *Yale Law Journal,* vol. 101 (1991); Anthony Bryk and Valerie E. Lee, "Is Politics the Problem and Markets the Answer? *Economics of Education Review,* vol. 11 (1992); John F. Witte, "Private School versus Public School Achievement: Are There Findings That Should Affect the Educational Choice Debate?" *Economics of Education Review,* vol. 11 (1992).

31. Myron Lieberman, *The Teacher Unions: How the NEA and the AFT Sabotage Reform, and Hold Students, Parents, Teachers and Taxpayers Hostage to Bureaucracy* (Free Press, 1997), p. 92. Voucher initiatives have been defeated in Michigan (1978) and Washington (1981).

32. See David S. Broder, "Awaiting a School Choice Showdown," *Washington Post,* July 24, 1996.

33. See, generally, Robert C. Johnston, "D.C. Budget Bill Includes School Voucher Plan," *Education Week,* November 8, 1995; Mark Pitsch, "Voucher Fight Shows New Political Dynamics," *Education Week,* April 10, 1996.

34. John Leo, "NEA Sabotages School-Choice Issue," *Staten Island Advance,* April 5, 1996.

35. "Children in Crisis: Statistics, Facts, and Figures," report of the District of Columbia Financial Responsibility and Management Assistance Authority, November 1996.

36. Lieberman, *The Teacher Unions,* p. 66.

37. Ibid., p. 92.

38. There is an extensive literature on the decline of the old Democratic coalition. See, for example, Samuel Freedman, *The Inheritance: How Three Families and America Moved from Roosevelt to Reagan and Beyond* (Simon & Schuster,

1996); Thomas Byrne Edsall and Mary D. Edsall, *Chain Reaction: The Impact of Race, Rights, and Taxes on American Politics* (W. W. Norton, 1991); Kevin P. Phillips, *The Emerging Republican Majority* (Arlington House, 1969). For a thoughtful and sympathetic set of essays on the inherent contradictions of liberal politics, see Alan Brinkley, *Liberalism and Its Discontents* (Harvard University Press, 1998).

39. "Phi Delta Kappa/Gallup Poll of the Public's Attitudes toward the Public Schools, 1998."

40. "Sidwell Liberals," *Wall Street Journal*, September 8, 1997.

41. Nina H. Shokraii, "How Members of Congress Practice School Choice," The Heritage Foundation, no. 147 (September 9, 1997).

42. Brent Staples, "Showdown in Milwaukee: How Choice Changes Public Schools," *New York Times*, May 15, 1997. See also "Schoolyard Brawl: The New Politics of Education Casts Blacks in a Starring Role," *New York Times*, Education Life Section, January 4, 1998.

43. William Raspberry, "Let's at Least Experiment with School Choice," *Washington Post*, June 16, 1997. See also William Raspberry, "Not Enough Lifeboats," *Washington Post*, March 9, 1998.

44. William A. Galston and Diane Ravitch, "Scholarships for Inner-City School Kids," *Washington Post*, December 17, 1997.

45. See Diane Ravitch, "Somebody's Children: Educational Opportunity for All Children," in Ravitch and Viteritti, *New Schools for a New Century*, pp. 251–73.

46. See, generally, the relevant essays in Terry Moe, ed., *Private Vouchers* (Hoover Institution Press, 1995); Paul E. Peterson and Bryan C. Hassel, eds., *Learning from School Choice* (Brookings, 1998).

47. See "Just Doing It, 3: 1996 Annual Survey of the Private Voucher Movement in America," survey for the Washington Scholarship Fund, 1997.

48. Among the key founders were Peter Flanigan, Richard Gilder, Roger Hertog, Bruce Kovner, Leslie Quick, Thomas Rhodes, and Thomas Tisch. SCS gave another thousand scholarships in the 1998–99 school year.

49. Ted Forstmann, *Restoring Equal Opportunity: How Competition Can Save American Education* (Children's Scholarship Fund, September 28, 1998).

50. Anemona Hartocollis, "Private School Choice Plan Draws a Million Aid-Seekers," *New York Times*, April 21, 1999.

51. Anemona Hartocollis, "Scholarship Winners Gather in Celebration," *New York Times*, April 22, 1999.

52. Mark Walsh, "Group Offers $50 Million for Vouchers," *Education Week*, April 29, 1998, p. 22.

53. *San Antonio Independent School District* v. *Rodriguez*, 411 U.S. (1973). See discussion in chapter 2 of this book.

54. See Michael Heise, Kenneth D. Colburn, and Joseph P. Lambert, "Private Vouchers in Indianapolis: The Golden Rule Program"; Janet R. Beals and Maureen

Wahl, "Private Vouchers in San Antonio"; Valerie Martinez, Kenneth Godwin, and Frank R. Kemerer, "Private Vouchers in Milwaukee: the PAVE Program"; and Paul T. Hill, "Private Vouchers in New York City: The Student/Sponsor Partnership Program," in Moe, *Private Vouchers*.

55. Performance data was not available in Indianapolis.

56. Paul E. Peterson and others, "Initial Findings from an Evaluation of School Choice Programs in Washington, D.C., and Dayton, Ohio," Program on Education Policy and Governance, Harvard University, 1998.

57. See David J. Weinschrott and Sally Kilgore, "Evidence from the Indianapolis Voucher Program" and Kenneth Goodwin, Frank Kemerer, and Valerie Martinez, "Comparing Public Choice and Private Voucher Programs in San Antonio," in Peterson and Hassel, *Learning from School Choice*. Also see Sammis B. White, "Milwaukee's Partners Advancing Values in Education (PAVE) Scholarship Program," unpublished manuscript.

58. Paul Peterson, David Meyers, and William Howell, "Research Design for the Initial Findings from an Evaluation of the New York School Choice Scholarship Program," paper prepared for presentation before the Association of Public Policy and Management, Washington, D.C., November 7, 1997. In a separate study of privately funded programs in Washington and Dayton, Peterson and his colleagues found that scholarship applicants coming from public schools were more disadvantaged than those applicants who were already attending private school. Peterson and others, "Initial Findings from and Evaluation of School Choice Programs in Washington, D.C. and Dayton, Ohio."

59. Paul Peterson, David Meyers, and William G. Howell, "An Evaluation of the New York City School Choice Scholarship Program: The First Year," Program in Education Policy and Governance, Harvard University, 1998.

60. Hill, "Private Vouchers in New York City," in Moe, *Private Vouchers*.

61. Moe, *Private Vouchers*, p. 29.

62. Blue Ribbon Panel on Catholic Programs, "Report to State Education Commissioner Thomas Sobel," New York State Education Department, 1993.

63. According to David Armor, about a thousand white suburban students attended magnet schools in Milwaukee, but the long-term effect of desegregation efforts was white flight. David Armor, *Forced Justice: School Desegregation and the Law* (Oxford University Press, 1995), pp. 192, 225.

64. David A. Bennett, "Choice and Desegregation," in William H. Clune and John F. Witte, eds., *Choice and Control in American Education: The Practice of Choice, Decentralization and School Restructuring*, vol. 2 (Falmer Press, 1990); George A. Mitchell, "An Evaluation of State Financed School Integration in Metropolitan Milwaukee," *Wisconsin Policy Research Institute Report*, vol. 2 (June 1989).

65. Mitchell, "State Financed School Integration," *Wisconsin Policy Research Institute Report*; Howard Fuller, "The Impact of the Milwaukee Public School

System's Desegregation Plan on Black Students and the Black Community (1976–1982)," Ph.D dissertation, Marquettte University, 1985.

66. Michael Stolee, "The Milwaukee Desegregation Case," in John L. Rury and Frank A. Cassell, eds., *Seeds of Crisis: Public Schooling in Milwaukee since 1920* (University of Wisconsin Press, 1993).

67. Quoted in Daniel McGroarty, *Break These Chains: The Battle for School Choice* (Prima Publishing, 1996), p. 65.

68. "'Voucher' No Longer Dirty Word," *New York Times*, June 10, 1990, cited in McGroarty, *Break These Chains*, p. 71.

69. Charles Sykes, "Fuller's Choice," *Wisconsin Interest* (Winter–Spring 1992), cited in McGroarty, *Break These Chains,* pp. 29–30.

70. Michael Fisher, "Fiscal Accountability in Milwaukee's Public Elementary Schools: Where Does the Money Go?" *Wisconsin Policy Research Institute Report,* September 1990, cited in McGroarty, *Break These Chains,* p. 21.

71. See Susan Mitchell, Testimony before the Subcommittee on Oversight and Investigations of the House Committee on Economic and Educational Opportunities, October 23, 1995, 104th Cong., 1st sess. (Government Printing Office, 1995), which provides an informative overview of the political dynamics that surrounded the choice debate.

72. See, generally, Jim Carl, "Unusual Allies: Elite and Grass-Roots Origins of Parental Choice in Milwaukee," *Teachers College Record*, vol. 98 (Winter 1996).

73. McGroarty, *Break These Chains,* p. 60.

74. *Milwaukee Journal,* July 23, 1990, cited in Paul E. Peterson and Chad Noyes, "School Choice in Milwaukee," in Ravitch and Viteritti, *New Schools for a New Century,* p. 134.

75. WIS. STAT. sec. 119.23 (2) (a). See, generally, Peterson and Noyes, "School Choice in Milwaukee," in Ravitch and Viteritti, *New Schools for a New Century,* pp. 128–36.

76. Howard L. Fuller and Sammis B. White, "Expanded School Choice in Milwaukee: A Profile of Eligible Students and Schools," *Wisconsin Policy Research Institute Report,* vol. 8, no. 5 (July 1995).

77. *Davis v. Glover,* 166 Wis. 2d 501, 480 N.W. 2d. 460 (1992).

78. Carnegie Foundation for the Advancement of Teaching, *School Choice: A Special Report* (1992), p. 22.

79. *Miller v. Benson,* 878 F. Supp. 1209 (E.D. Wis. 1995).

80. 1995 Wis. Act. sec. 4002, amending WIS. STAT. sec. 119.23 (2) (a).

81. *Thompson v. Jackson,* no. 95-2153, L.C. numbers 95CV1982 and 95CV1997.

82. Peter Applebome, "Milwaukee Forces Debate on Vouchers," *New York Times,* September 1, 1995.

83. Correspondence from Howard Fuller to the author, December 30, 1998.

84. Statement by Howard Fuller, Ph.D., superintendent of Milwaukee Public Schools, April 18, 1995. See also Joanna Richardson, "Citing Board Politics, Milwaukee's Fuller Resigns," *Education Week*, April 26, 1995; "Milwaukee School Superintendent Is Resigning," *New York Times*, April 20, 1995; Neil Peirce, "How a Teachers' Union Blocked Education Reform," *Philadelphia Inquirer*, July 17, 1995.

85. See McGroarty, *Break These Chains,* pp. 130–52.

86. John F. Witte, "First Year Report: Milwaukee Parental Choice Program," University of Wisconsin, Department of Political Science, November 1991.

87. Peterson and Noyes, "School Choice in Milwaukee," in Ravitch and Viteritti, *New Schools for a New Century,* p. 137–38.

88. David Ruenzel, "A Choice in the Matter," *Education Week*, September 27, 1995, p. 25.

89. See Fuller and White, "Expanded School Choice in Milwaukee."

90. Witte's official evaluation appeared in the form of four annual reports. John F. Witte, "First Year Report: Milwaukee Parental Choice Program," Department of Political Science and Robert M. LaFollette Institute of Public Affairs, University of Wisconsin-Madison, November 1991; John F. Witte and others, "Second Year Report: Milwaukee Parental Choice Program," Department of Political Science and Robert M. LaFollette Institute of Public Affairs, University of Wisconsin-Madison, December 1992; John F. Witte and others, "Third Year Report: Milwaukee Parental Choice Program," Department of Political Science and Robert M. LaFollette Institute of Public Affairs, University of Wisconsin-Madison, December 1993; John F. Witte and others, "Fourth Year Report: Milwaukee Parental Choice Program," Department of Political Science and Robert M. LaFollette Institute of Public Affairs, University of Wisconsin-Madison, December 1994.

91. Witte and others, "Fourth Year Report," p. 28.

92. See Bob Davis, "Dueling Professors Have Milwaukee Dazed over School Vouchers," *Wall Street Journal*, October 11, 1996.

93. Paul E. Peterson, "A Critique of the Witte Evaluation of Milwaukee's School Choice Program," Center for American Political Studies, Harvard University, Occasional Paper 95-2, February 1995.

94. Jay P. Greene, Paul E. Peterson, and Jiangtao Du, "The Effectiveness of School Choice in Milwaukee: A Secondary Analysis of Data from the Program's Evaluation," paper prepared for presentation before the Panel on the Political Analysis of Urban Systems at the August–September meetings of the American Political Science Association, San Francisco, August 30, 1997.

95. Howard L. Fuller, "The Real Evidence: An Honest Update on School Choice Experiments," *Wisconsin Interest* (Fall–Winter 1997), pp. 25–30.

96. Cecilia Elena Rouse, "Lessons from the Milwaukee Choice Program," *Policy Options* (July–August 1997); Cecilia Elena Rouse, "Private School Vouchers and

Student Achievement: An Evaluation of the Milwaukee Parental Choice Program," Department of Economics, Princeton University, December 1996.

97. John F. Witte, "Achievement Effects of the Milwaukee Voucher System," paper presented at the American Economics Association meeting, New Orleans, January 4–6, 1997.

98. See John F. Witte, "The Milwaukee Voucher Experiment," *Education and Policy Analysis*, vol. 20 (Winter 1998), pp. 243–44; Levin, "Educational Vouchers," p. 377.

99. *Warren v. Benson*, 578 N.W. 22 602 (Wis. 1998)

100. People for the American Way Foundation, press release, December 8, 1998.

101. Joe Williams, "2 Rallies, 2 Views on School Choice Programs," *Milwaukee Journal Sentinel*, December 9, 1998.

102. Joe Williams, "Poll Finds More Support for School Vouchers," *Milwaukee Journal Sentinel*, December 17, 1998.

103. Caroline Hendrie, "Judge Ends Desegregation Case in Cleveland," *Education Week*, April 8, 1998.

104. Ibid.

105. Ohio Department of Education, *District Profile for Fiscal Year 1995* (1996).

106. Ohio Rev. Code Ann. sec 3313.974-979 (Anderson).

107. Drew Lindsay, "Wisconsin, Ohio Back Vouchers for Religious Schools," *Education Week*, July 12, 1995, p. 14.

108. Kimberley J. McLarin, "Ohio Paying Some Tuition for Religious School Students," *New York Times*, August 28, 1996.

109. Curt W. Olsen, "Children, Parents Tout Voucher Plan," *The News-Herald*, September 13, 1997, p. A3.

110. Jay P. Greene, William G. Howell, and Paul E. Peterson, "An Evaluation of the Cleveland Scholarship Program," Program on Education Policy and Governance, Harvard University, September 1997.

111. *Gatton v. Goff*, no. 96CVH-01-193 (C.P. Franklin County, 1996).

112. *Gatton v. Goff*, no. 96APE08-982 and 96APE08-991 (Ohio, 1997).

113. Greene, Howell, and Peterson, "An Evaluation of the Cleveland Scholarship Program."

114. Ibid.

115. Kim K. Metcalf and others, "A Comparative Evaluation of the Cleveland Scholarship and Tutoring Grant Program: Year One: 1996–97," a project of the School of Education, Smith Research Center, Indiana University, March 1998.

116. Paul E. Peterson and Jay P. Greene, "Assessing the Cleveland Scholarship Program: A Guide to the Indiana University School of Education Evaluation," occasional paper, Program on Education Policy and Governance, Harvard University, March 1998.

117. Paul E. Peterson, Jay P. Greene, and William Howell, "New Findings from the Cleveland Scholarship Program: A Reanalysis of Data from the Indiana University School of Education Evaluation," Program on Education Policy and Governance, Harvard University, May 6, 1998.

118. Kim K. Metcalf and others, "Evaluation of the Cleveland Scholarship Program: Second Year Report (1997–98)," Indiana Center for Evaluation, Smith Research Center, Indiana University, November, 1998.

119. Caroline M. Hoxby, "The Effects of Private School Vouchers on Schools and Students," in Helen F. Ladd, ed., *Holding Schools Accountable: Performance-Based Reform in Education* (Brookings, 1996); Caroline M. Hoxby, "Do Private Schools Provide Competition for Public Schools?" Working Paper 4978 (Cambridge, Mass.: National Bureau of Economic Research, 1994, rev.); Caroline M. Hoxby, "Analyzing School Choice Reforms That Use America's Traditional Forms of Parental Choice," in Peterson and Hassel, *Learning from School Choice*. See also Thomas J. Nechyba, "Public School Finance in a General Equilibrium Tiebot World: Equalization Programs, Peer Effects and Private School Vouchers," Working Paper 5642 (Cambridge, Mass.: National Bureau of Economic Research, 1997). For a critique of Hoxby, see Thomas J. Kane, "Comments on Chapters Five and Six," in Ladd, *Holding Schools Accountable*.

120. Melven Borland and Roy Howsen, "Student Academic Achievement and the Degree of Market Concentration in Education," *Economics of Education Review*, vol. 11 (1992); J. Couch, William Shugart, and A. Williams, "Private School Enrollment and Public School Enrollment," *Public Choice*, vol. 76 (1993).

Chapter Five

1. "Congress shall make no law respecting the establishment of religion or prohibiting the free exercise thereof."

2. Mark DeWolfe Howe, *The Garden and the Wilderness: Religion and Government in American History* (University of Chicago Press, 1965), pp. 5–6.

3. It reads, "Believing with you that religion is a matter which lies solely between man and his God, that he owes account to none other for his faith or his worship, that the *legislative powers of government reach actions only, and not opinions,* I contemplate with solemn reverence that act of the whole American people which declared that their legislature should 'make no law respecting an establishment of religion, or prohibiting the free exercise thereof,' thus building a wall of separation between church and state" (emphasis added). Letter from Thomas Jefferson to A Committee of the Danbury Baptist Association, in the State of Connecticut (January 1, 1802), in Saul K. Padover, ed., *The Complete Jefferson* (Duell, Sloan, and Pierce, 1943), pp. 518–19.

4. Perry Miller and Thomas A. Johnson, eds., *The Puritans: A Sourcebook of the Writings*, vol. 1, (Harper & Row, 1963), p. 186.

5. See also the "Bill for Establishing Religious Freedom," which Jefferson presented to the Virginia Assembly in 1777, reading, "All men shall be free to profess, and by argument to maintain their opinion in matters of religion, and . . . *the same shall in no wise, diminish, enlarge or affect their civic capacities*" (emphasis added), in Padover, *Complete Jefferson*, pp. 946–47.

6. See Michael W. McConnell, "The Origins and Historical Understanding of Free Exercise of Religion," *Harvard Law Review*, vol. 103 (1990), pp. 1430–36; Sanford Kessler, "Locke's Influence on Thomas Jefferson's 'Bill for Establishing Religious Freedom,'" *Journal of Church & State*, vol. 25 (1983); J. R. Pole, *The Pursuit of Equality in American History* (University of California, 1978), pp. 59–86.

7. McConnell explains, "For Locke, the field left to untrammeled conscience could only extend to that in which the civil magistrate had no particular interest—principally, to things pertaining to the world to come. Religious liberty could only be defined negatively; any broader definition would be pointless, since the magistrate would be judge of his own powers." McConnell, "Origins and Historical Understanding of Free Exercise," p. 1444.

8. Lorraine Smith Pangle and Thomas L. Pangle, *The Learning of Liberty: The Educational Ideas of the American Founders* (University of Kansas Press, 1993), p. 20.

9. See, generally, Peter Gay, *The Enlightenment: An Interpretation* (Knopf, 1966), which focuses on the European experience; Henry A. May, *The Enlightenment in America* (Oxford University Press, 1976), which explains its influence on America.

10. See Walter Berns, "Religion and the Founding Principle," in Robert H. Horwitz, ed., *The Moral Foundations of the American Republic* (University Press of Virginia, 1986).

11. Daniel L. Dreisbach, "Thomas Jefferson and Bills Number 82-86 of the Revision of the Laws of Virginia, 1776–1786: New Light on the Jeffersonian Model of Church-State Relations," *North Carolina Law Review*, vol. 69 (1990).

12. A. James Reichley, *Religion in American Public Life* (Brookings, 1985), p. 94.

13. See Carl J. Friedrich, *Constitutional Government and Democracy*, rev. ed. (Ginn and Co., 1950); J. Roland Pennock and John W. Chapman, *Nomos XX: Constitutionalism* (New York University Press, 1979).

14. For an exposition on the liberal position explained in the context of contemporary constitutional law, see Kathleen Sullivan, "Religion and Liberal Democracy," *University of Chicago Law Review*, vol. 59 (1992).

15. James Madison, *Detached Memoranda* (1817). See, generally, Ronald F. Thiemann, *Religion in Public Life: A Dilemma for Democracy* (Georgetown University Press, 1996), pp. 19–41, 72–95; Reichley, *Religion in American Public Life*, pp. 85–96; Pangle and Pangle, *The Learning of Liberty*, pp. 187–94.

16. See Dreisbach, "Thomas Jefferson and Bills Number 82-86 of the Revision of the Laws of Virginia, 1776–1786," p. 201.

17. James Madison, "Memorial and Remonstrance against Religious Assessments," (1785), reprinted in Saul K. Padover, ed., *The Complete Madison* (Harper, 1953).

18. See John T. Noonan Jr., *The Lustre of Our Country: The American Experience of Religious Freedom* (University of California Press, 1998), pp. 59–92, which argues that Madison's commitment to religious freedom was the outcome of his own deeply held religious beliefs.

19. There is a burgeoning literature of the influence of republican thought on the writing of the Constitution. See Thomas L. Pangle, *The Spirit of Modern Republicanism: The Moral Vision of the American Founders and the Philosophy of Locke* (University of Kansas, 1988); Morton J. Horowitz, "Republicanism and Liberalism in American Constitutional Thought," *William & Mary Law Review*, vol. 29 (1987); Donald S. Lutz, "The Intellectual Background of the American Founding," *Texas Tech Law Review*, vol. 21 (1990); Lance Banning, *The Sacred Fire of Liberty: James Madison and the Founding of the Federal Republic* (Cornell University Press, 1995); Richard R. Beeman, "Deference, Republicanism and the Emergence of Popular Politics in Eighteenth-Century America," *William & Mary Quarterly*, vol. 49 (1992); Daniel T. Rogers, "Republicanism: the Career of a Concept," *Journal of American History*, vol. 79 (1992); Robert E. Shalhope, "Republicanism and Early American Historiography," *William & Mary Quarterly*, vol. 39 (1982); Cass R. Sunstein, "Interest Groups in American Public Law," *Stanford Law Review*, vol. 38 (1985–86); Cass R. Sunstein, "Beyond the Republican Revival," *Yale Law Journal*, vol. 97 (1988); M. N. S. Sellers, *American Republicanism: Roman Ideology in the United States Constitution* (New York University Press, 1994).

20. "Extend the sphere and you take in a variety of parties and interests; you make it less probable that the majority of the whole will have a common motive to invade the rights of other citizens." *The Federalist, No. 10*, Clinton Rossiter, ed. (Random House, 1961). See David F. Epstein, *The Political Theory of the Federalist* (University of Chicago Press, 1984), pp. 59–146; Robert A. Dahl, *A Preface to Democratic Theory* (Yale University Press, 1956), pp. 4–33; Peter S. Onuf, "James Madison's Extended Republic," *Texas Tech Law Review*, vol. 21 (1990); Jack N. Rakove, *Original Meanings: Politics and Ideas in the Making of the Constitution* (Random House, 1996), pp. 35–36, 310–16, 330–36.

21. See Thiemann, *Religion in Public Life*, pp. 72–144; James Davidson Hunter, "Religious Freedom and the Challenge of Modern Pluralism," in James Davidson Hunter and Os Guinness, eds., *Articles of Faith, Articles of Peace: The Religious Liberty Clauses and the American Public Philosophy* (Brookings, 1990); Robert Audi, "The Separation of Church and State and the Obligations of Citizenship," *Philosophy & Public Affairs*, vol. 18 (Summer 1989).

22. Thiemann, *Religion in Public Life*, pp. 149–50.

23. Cited in Steven B. Epstein, "Rethinking the Constitutionality of Ceremonial Deism," *Columbia Law Review*, vol. 96 (1996).

24. Reprinted in Philip Kurland and Ralph Lerner, eds., *The Founder's Constitution*, vol. 5 (University of Chicago Press, 1987).

25. Reichley, *Religion in American Public Life*, p. 99.

26. George Washington, "Farewell Address," September 17, 1796.

27. See Patricia U. Bonomi, *Under the Cope of Heaven: Religion, Society and Politics in Colonial America* (Oxford University Press, 1986); Paul Kauper, *Religion and the Constitution* (Louisiana State University Press, 1964); Ellis Sandoz, *A Government of Laws: Political Theory, Religion and the American Founding* (Louisiana State University Press, 1990).

28. Bernard Bailyn, *Education in the Forming of American Society* (Vintage Books, 1960); Richard J. Gabel, *Public Funds for Church and Private Schools* (Catholic University of America, 1937).

29. Alexis de Tocqueville, *Democracy in America*, vol. 1, Philips Bradley, ed. (Knopf, 1945), p. 320, n. 4.

30. Thomas J. Curry, *The First Freedoms: Church and State in America to the Passage of the First Amendment* (Oxford University Press, 1986).

31. Northwest Ordinance, Article 3, Articles of Confederation, July 13, 1787.

32. See David Tyack, Thomas James, and Aaron Benavot, *Law and the Shaping of Public Education, 1785–1954* (University of Wisconsin Press, 1987), pp. 26–27.

33. Jefferson's letter to Congress seeking ratification of a treaty with the Kaskaskia Indians, accompanied by the articles, is worth quoting at length: "And whereas the greater part of the said tribe have been baptized and received into the Catholic church, to which they are much attached, the United States will give annually, for seven years, one hundred dollars toward a priest of that religion, who will engage to perform for said tribe the duties of his office, and so to instruct as many of their children as possible, in the rudiments of literature. And the United States will further give the sum of three hundred dollars, to assist the said tribe in the erection of a church." Cited in Robert Cord, *The Separation of Church and State* (Lambeth Press, 1982), pp. 261–63.

34. *Worcester v. Georgia*, 31 U.S. (6 Pet) 515 (1832).

35. *Cantwell v. Connecticut*, 310 U.S. 296 (1940).

36. *Everson v. Board of Education*, 330 U.S. 1 (1947).

37. A notable exception was the *Reynolds* case, where the Supreme Court upheld a state law prohibiting polygamy that was challenged by the Mormons. *Reynolds v. United States*, 98 U.S. 145, (1879).

38. *Meyer v. State of Nebraska*, 262 U.S. 390 (1923).

39. *Bartels v. Iowa*, 262 U.S. 4904 (1923).

40. *Pierce v. Society of Sisters*, 268 U.S. 510, 535 (1925).

41. *Cochran v. Board of Education*, 281 U.S. 370, 374–75 (1930).

42. *Everson v. Board of Education*, at 15–16. See Jo Renee Formicola and Hubert Morken, eds., *Everson Revisited: Religion, Education and Law at Crossroads* (Rowman & Littlefield, 1997). This was not the first time that the Court

had invoked Jefferson's metaphor. It was used in an 1879 case upholding a federal law against polygamy. Here the Court opined that while the wall protects individual rights of conscience, it does not shield the actions that violate public standards of behavior. *Reynolds* v. *United States*, 98 U.S. 145 (1879).

43. *Everson* v. *Board of Education*, at 16.

44. *Illinois* v. *Board of Education*, 333 U.S. 203 (1948).

45. *Zorach* v. *Clauson*, 343 U.S. 306 (1952).

46. *McGowan* v. *Maryland*, 366 U.S. 420, 448–49 (1961). Two years later the Court upheld the right of Seventh Day Adventists to observe the Sabbath on Saturday in an employment suit. *Sherbert* v. *Verner*, 374 U.S. 398 (1963). The Court also protected the rights of nonbelievers when it struck down a Maryland law requiring officeholders to declare a belief in God, *Torcaso* v. *Watkins* 367 U.S. 488 (1961); and it recognized the rights of nonreligious conscientious objectors to avoid conscription in the military, *United States* v. *Seeger*, 380 U.S. 163 (1965); *Welsh* v. *United States*, 398 U.S. 333 (1970); *Gillette* v. *United States*, 401 U.S. 437 (1971).

47. *Wisconsin* v. *Yoder*, 406 U.S. 205, 232 (1972).

48. *Engel* v. *Vitale*, 370 U.S. 421 (1962).

49. *Abington School District* v. *Schempp*, 374 U.S. 203 (1963).

50. *Board of Education* v. *Allen*, 392 U.S. 236 (1968).

51. *Walz* v. *Tax Commission*, 397 U.S. 664, 669 (1970).

52. Ibid., at 696 (Justice Harlan concurring).

53. Ibid., at 689 (Justice Brennan concurring).

54. *Lemon* v. *Kurzman*, 403 U.S. 602 (1971).

55. Ibid., at 614–15.

56. A year earlier the Court had sustained a lower court decision invalidating a Connecticut decision that would have paid a portion of the salaries of private school teachers who taught secular subjects. *Saunders* v. *Johnson*, 403 U.S. 955 (1971).

57. *Lemon* v. *Kurzman*, at 665 (Justice White dissenting).

58. Ibid., at 614.

59. Ibid., at 614–15, citing *Walz* v. *Tax Commission*, at 674–76.

60. *Committee for Public Education and Religious Liberty* v. *Nyquist*, 413 U.S. 756, 793 (1973). Issuing another dissent, Justice White argued that denying aid to parents who send their children to religious schools made it "difficult, if not impossible, for parents to follow the dictates of their conscience and seek a religious as well as secular education for their children." *Nyquist*, at 814.

61. *Sloan* v. *Lemon*, 413 U.S. 825, 830, 832 (1973).

62. Ibid., at 832.

63. *Levitt* v. *Committee for Public Education and Religious Liberty*, 413 U.S. 472, 480 (1973).

64. See *Marburger* v. *Public Funds for Public Schools*, 413 U.S. 916 (1973);

Grit v. *Wolman*, 413 U.S. 901 (1973); *Cathedral Academy* v. *Committee for Public Education and Religious Liberty*, 413 U.S. 472 (1973).

65. For a discussion of these confused distinctions, see Jesse H. Choper, "The Religion Clauses and the First Amendment: Reconciling the Conflict," *University of Pittsburgh Law Review*, vol. 41 (1980). For a finely tuned conceptual analysis on interpreting the First Amendment, see Jesse H. Choper, *Securing Religious Liberty: Principles for Judicial Interpretation of the Religious Clauses* (University of Chicago Press, 1995).

66. Compare *Meek* v. *Pittenger*, 421 U.S. 349 (1975); *Marburger* v. *Public Funds for Public Schools*, 417 U.S. 229 (1977).

67. *Leutkemeyer* v. *Kaufman*, 419 U.S. 888 (1974).

68. *Wolman* v. *Watters*, 433 U.S. 229 (1977).

69. *Franchise Tax Board* v. *United Americans for Public Schools*, 419 U.S. 890 (1974); *Byrne* v. *Public Funds For Public Schools*, 442 U.S. 907 (1979).

70. *Committee for Public Education and Religious Liberty* v. *Regan*, 444 U.S. 646 (1980).

71. *Meuller* v. *Allen*, 463 U.S. 387, 399 (1983). During the same term, the Court upheld Nebraska's practice of paying a chaplain to open its legislative sessions with a prayer, describing the practice as "a tolerable acknowledgment of beliefs widely held among the people of this country." *Marsh* v. *Chambers*, 463 U.S. 783, 792 (1983).

72. *Meuller* v. *Allen*, at 393. A year later Chief Justice Burger declared that neither the *Lemon* test nor any other "fixed per se rule" was appropriate in reviewing First Amendment cases. *Lynch* v. *Donnelly*, 465 U.S. 668, 678 (1984). In the same case, Justice Sandra Day O'Connor proposed an alternative "endorsement test." In 1992 Justice Kennedy introduced a less rigorous "coercion standard." *Lee* v. *Weisman*, 505 U.S. 577(1992).

73. *Wallace* v. *Jaffree*, 472 U.S. 38, 106 (1985) (Justice Rehnquist dissenting).

74. Ibid., at 112 (Justice Rehnquist dissenting).

75. There were two notable exceptions to the emerging pattern. In *Aguilar* v. *Felton*, 473 U.S. 402 (1985), the Court held that public employees could not provide remedial services to poor children on the premises of a parochial school. In *Grand Rapids* v. *Ball*, 473 U.S. 373 (1985), it ruled that Michigan could not provide funds for remedial and enrichment programs that supplemented the core curriculum of religious schools. *Aguilar* as well as *Ball* was overturned in 1997.

76. *Witters* v. *Washington Department of Social Services*, 474 U.S. 481 (1986).

77. Ibid., at 490–92 (Justice Powell concurring).

78. *Zobrest* v. *Catalina Foothills School District*, 509 U.S. 1 (1993).

79. In *Employment Division* v. *Smith*, 494 U.S. 872 (1990), the Court ruled that a generally applicable law not directed at particular religious groups is binding even when the law conflicts with the tenets of one's faith. In *Church of Lukumi Babalu Aye* v. *City of Healeah*, 508 U.S. 520 (1993), the Court limited the reach

of *Smith* and upheld the right of Santerians to perform animal sacrifices in their religious ceremonies. See Michael McConnell, "Free Exercise Revisionism and the Smith Decision," *University of Chicago Law Review*, vol. 57 (1990); Jesse H. Choper, "The Rise and Decline of the Constitutional Protection of Religious Liberty," *Nebraska Law Review*, vol. 70 (1991). In 1993 Congress passed the Religious Freedom and Restoration Act (RFRA) in an attempt to weaken the effect of *Smith*. In *City of Boerne* v. *Flores*, 521 U.S. 507 (1997), the Court ruled that RFRA was an unconstitutional usurpation of judicial power by Congress.

80. *Bowen* v. *Kendrik*, 487 U.S. 589 (1988).

81. *Board of Education* v. *Mergens*, 496 U.S. 226, 248 (1990).

82. *Lamb's Chapel* v. *Center Moriches School District*, 508 U.S. 384 (1993).

83. *Rosenberger* v. *Rectors of the University of Virginia*, 515 U.S. 819 (1995), citing *Mergens* at 250.

84. Ibid., at 845–46.

85. "A tax exemption in many cases is economically and functionally indistinguishable from a direct monetary subsidy. In one instance, the government relieves religious entities (along with others) of a generally applicable tax; in the other, it relieves religious entities (along with others) of some or all of the burden of that tax by retaining it in the form of a cash subsidy. Whether the subsidy is provided at the front or the back end of the tax process, the financial aid to religious groups is undeniable." Ibid., at 859–60 (Justice Thomas concurring).

86. Ibid., at 861.

87. "It is clear that Title I services are allocated on the basis of criteria that neither favor nor disfavor religion. . . . The services are available to all children who meet the Act's requirements, no matter what their religious beliefs or where they go to school." *Agostini* v. *Felton*, 521 U.S. 203, 232 (1997).

88. Ibid., at 235.

89. Ibid., at 222.

90. See Rakove, *Original Meanings*, pp. 48–51, 314–16, 335.

Chapter Six

1. In terms of expenditures, education is the primary function of state government, accounting for one-third of the total. John E. Brandl, *Money and Good Intentions Are Not Enough: Why A Liberal Democrat Thinks That States Need Both Competition and Community* (Brookings, 1998), p. 17.

2. See, generally, Thomas J. Curry, *The First Freedoms: Church and State in America to the Passage of the First Amendment* (Oxford University Press, 1986); Leonard W. Levy, *The Establishment Clause: Religion and the First Amendment* (University of North Carolina Press, 1994), pp. 1–78; Michael W. McConnell, "The Origins and Historical Understanding of the Free Exercise of Religion," *Harvard Law Review*, vol. 103 (1990).

3. Carl Kaestle, *Pillars of the Republic: Common Schools and American Society, 1780-1860* (Hill & Wang, 1983), pp. 166–67.

4. Robert H. Lord, John E. Sexton, and Edward T. Harrington, *The History of the Archdiocese of Boston in Its Various Stages of Development* (Sheed & Ward, 1944), pp. 574–77.

5. David Tyack, Thomas James, and Aaron Benavot, *Law and the Shaping of Public Education, 1785–1954* (University of Wisconsin Press, 1987), pp. 90–91.

6. Lawrence A. Cremin, *The American Common School: A Historic Conception* (Teachers College, 1951). See also Os Guinness, *The American Hour* (Free Press, 1993), which highlights the character-forming and nation-building roles of the common school.

7. Nathan Glazer explains that education theorists who believed in the idea of a melting pot expected European immigrants to forsake their cultural heritage in order to become Americans. These same thinkers—including John Dewey—never considered black Americans as part of their vision. See Nathan Glazer, *We Are All Multiculturists Now* (Harvard University Press, 1997), pp. 101–02.

8. See Raymond Callahan, *Education and the Cult of Efficiency* (University of Chicago Press, 1962); David Tyack, *The One Best System: A History of American Urban Education* (Harvard University Press, 1974).

9. Horace Mann, "First Annual Report to the Board of Education" (1837).

10. See, generally, Charles L. Glenn, *The Myth of the Common School* (University of Massachusetts Press, 1988); Stanley K. Schultz, *The Culture Factory: Boston Public Schools, 1789–1860* (Oxford University Press, 1973); Frederick M. Binder, *The Age of the Common School, 1830–1865* (John Wiley, 1974).

11. Horace Mann, "Twelfth Annual Report to the Board of Education" (1848).

12. Ibid.

13. Mark DeWolfe Howe, *The Garden and the Wilderness* (University of Chicago Press, 1965), p. 31.

14. "The Bible in the Public Schools," *Common School Journal*, vol. 14, January 1, 1852, p. 9. See Thomas James, "Rights of Conscience and State School Systems in Nineteenth Century America," in Paul Finkelman and Stephen E. Gottleib, eds., *Toward a Usable Past: Liberty under State Constitutions* (University of Georgia Press, 1991), pp. 126–27.

15. Ray A. Billington, *The Protestant Crusade, 1800–1860: A Study of the Origins of American Nativism* (Macmillan, 1938) pp. 41–47.

16. See David Tyack, "The Kingdom of God and the Common School: Protestant Ministers and the Educational Awakening of the West," *Harvard Educational Review*, vol. 36 (1966), which presents a case study of Oregon.

17. Tyack, James, and Benavot, *Law and the Shaping of Public Education*, p. 164.

18. *Donahue v. Richards*, 38 Maine 376, 4409 (1854).

19. Otto Templar Hamilton, *The Courts and the Curriculum* (Teachers College, Columbia University, 1927), p. 113.

20. See James Turner, *Without God, Without Creed: The Origins of Unbelief in America* (Johns Hopkins University Press, 1985).

21. John Westerhoff, *McGuffey and His Readers* (Abingdon, 1978).

22. Tyack, James, and Benavot, *Law and the Shaping of Public Education*, p. 162.

23. "Industrial Education," *Scribner's Monthly* (March 1880), pp. 785–86, cited in Lloyd P. Jorgenson, *The State and the Nonpublic School, 1825–1925* (University of Missouri Press, 1987), p. 23.

24. See Jorgenson, *The State and the Nonpublic School*, pp. 20–158; Michael Feldberg, *The Turbulent Era: Riot and Disorder in Jacksonian America* (Oxford University Press, 1980), pp. 9–32, which discusses Philadelphia; Vincent Lannie and Bernard Diethorn, "For the Honor and Glory of God: The Philadelphia Bible Riots of 1844," *History of Education Quarterly*, vol. 8 (1968); James W. Sanders, *The Education of an Urban Minority: Catholics in Chicago, 1833–1965* (Oxford University Press, 1977).

25. This story is wonderfully told in Diane Ravitch, *The Great School Wars: New York City, 1805–1973* (Basic Books, 1974), pp. 27–76.

26. Sydney Ahlstrom, *A Religious History of the American People* (Yale University Press, 1972), pp. 563–65.

27. See J. Higman, *Strangers in a Promised Land: Patterns of American Nativism, 1860–1925* (Rutgers University Press, 1955); Billington, *The Protestant Crusade*.

28. Ruth Miller Elson, *Guardians of Tradition: American School Books of the Nineteenth Century* (University of Nebraska Press, 1964). See also Robert Michaelsen, *Piety in the Public School* (Macmillan, 1970).

29. Douglas Laycock, "Summary and Synthesis: The Crisis in Religious Liberty," *George Washington Law Review*, vol. 60 (1992).

30. Cited in Stephen K. Green, "The Blaine Amendment Reconsidered," *American Journal of Legal History*, vol. 36 (1992), p. 47.

31. See Marie Carolyn Klinkhamer, "The Blaine Amendment of 1875: Private Monies for Political Action," *Catholic History Review*, vol. 42 (1957); Green, "The Blaine Amendment Reconsidered."

32. *New York Times*, November 29, 1875, p. 2.

33. *Catholic World* (February 1876), pp. 707, 711.

34. *Nation*, March 16, 1876, p. 173.

35. Robert F. Utter and Edward J. Larson, "Church and State on the Frontier: The History of the Establishment Clause in the Washington State Constitution," *Hastings Constitutional Law Quarterly*, vol. 15 (1988).

36. Tom Wiley, *Public School Education in New Mexico* (Publication of the Division of Government Research, University of New Mexico, 1965), pp. 27–31. See also Robert Larson, *New Mexico's Quest for Statehood, 1846–1912* (University of New Mexico Press, 1968).

37. Tyack, James, and Benavot, *Law and the Shaping of Public Education*, pp. 133–53.

38. Ibid., p. 22. As early as 1785 Congress established that one parcel out of sixteen in the new territories would be set aside for educational purposes and made monies available for this purpose. "Land Ordinance of 1785," in Henry Steele Commager, ed., *Documents of American History* (Appleton-Century-Crofts, 1958).

39. Green, "The Blaine Amendment Reconsidered," p. 43. During the 1870s constitutional provisions were enacted in Missouri, Illinois, Pennsylvania, New Jersey, Nebraska, Texas, Colorado, and Minnesota. Jorgenson, *The State and the Nonpublic School*, p. 114.

40. Peter Gailie, *Ordered Liberty: A Constitutional History of New York* (Fordham University Press, 1996), pp. 183–84.

41. *New York Herald Tribune*, July 16, 1894.

42. Cited in Jorgenson, *The State and the Nonpublic School*, p. 121.

43. Henrik N. Dullea, *Charter Revision in the Empire State* (Albany, N.Y.: Rockefeller Institute Press, 1997); Lewis Kaden, "The People: No! Some Observations on the 1967 New York State Constitutional Convention," *Harvard Journal on Legislation*, vol. 5 (1968).

44. For accounts of the case, see Jorgenson, *The State and the Non-Public School*, pp. 205–15; David Tyack, "The Perils of Pluralism: The Background of the Pierce Case," *American Historical Review*, vol. 74 (1968); Thomas J. Shelley, "The Oregon School Case and the National Catholic Welfare," *Catholic History Review*, vol. 75 (1989).

45. *New Age* (October 1922), quoted in William G. Ross, *Forging New Freedoms: Nativism, Education and the Constitution, 1917–1927* (University of Nebraska Press, 1994), p. 153.

46. Luther Powell, "Preface," in George Estes, *The Old Cedar School*, cited in Tyack, "The Perils of Pluralism," p. 74.

47. Jorgenson, *The State and the Nonpublic School*, p. 206.

48. Martin J. Schiesl, *The Politics of Efficiency: Municipal Administration and Reform in America, 1880–1920* (University of California Press, 1977); Joseph P. Viteritti, *Bureaucracy and Social Justice* (Kennikat Press, 1979).

49. For a critical look at Taylor and his effect, see Robert Kanigel, *The One Best Way: Frederick Winslow Taylor and the Enigma of Efficiency* (Viking, 1996); J. C. Spender and Hugo J. Kigne, eds., *Scientific Management: Frederick Winslow Taylor's Gift to the World* (Kluwer Academic Publishers, 1996).

50. M. L. Cook, "The Spirit and Social Significance of Scientific Management," *Journal of Political Economy*, vol. 21 (June 1913), p. 493. See also W. H. Allen, *Efficient Democracy* (Dodd, Mead, 1907).

51. Jon Teaford, *The Unheralded Triumph* (Johns Hopkins University Press, 1984), and Jon Teaford, *The Municipal Revolution in America* (University of Chicago Press, 1975), which provide a critical look at the reform agenda.

52. See David Tyack and Elizabeth Hansot, *Managers of Virtue: Public School Leadership, 1820–1980* (Basic Books, 1982), pp. 129–66.

53. See Robert B. Westbrook, *John Dewey and American Democracy* (Cornell University Press, 1991), which focuses on the political relevance of Dewey's teaching and writing.

54. See Alan Ryan, *John Dewey and the High Tide of American Liberalism* (Norton, 1995); Steven C. Rockefeller, *John Dewey: Religious Faith and Democratic Humanism* (Columbia University Press, 1991). Of these two important intellectual biographies, Rockefeller stubbornly holds onto the idea that Dewey remained a religious humanist, while Ryan deals more directly with Dewey's growing contempt for religion and its adherents.

55. John Dewey, *A Common Faith* (Yale University Press, 1934), p. 7.

56. John Dewey, "Education as a Religion," *New Republic*, September 13, 1922, p. 63.

57. John Dewey, "My Pedagogic Creed," *School Journal*, January 16, 1897, p. 80.

58. Dewey, "Education as a Religion," p. 64.

59. John Dewey, "Religion in Our Schools," *Hibbert Journal* (July 1908), pp. 806–07.

60. Ryan, *John Dewey and the High Tide of American Liberalism*, pp. 339–43.

61. John Dewey, *Democracy and Education: An Introduction to the Philosophy of Education* (Macmillan, 1916).

62. National Education Association, *Report of the Commission on the Reorganization of Secondary Education* (U.S. Bureau of Education, 1918).

63. The remainder of these points were developed around a wide range of social objectives that included health, vocation, civic education, ethical character, worthy home membership, and worthy use of leisure time.

64. See Lawrence A. Cremin, *The Transformation of the School: Progressivism in American Education* (Random House, 1961); Diane Ravitch, *The Troubled Crusade: American Education, 1945–1980* (Basic Books, 1983), pp. 43–80.

65. U.S. Office of Education, *Vitalizing Secondary Education: Report of the First Commission on Life Adjustment Education for Youth* (1951).

66. See Patricia A. Graham, *Progressive Education, from Arcady to Academe: A History of the Progressive Education Association, 1919–1955* (Teachers College Press, 1967).

67. William C. Bagley, *Education and Emergent Man* (Thomas Nelson, 1934).

68. John Dewey, *Experience and Education* (Collier, 1938).

69. I. M. Kendel, *The Cult of Uncertainty* (Macmillan, 1943).

70. Robert M. Hutchins, *The Conflict in Education in a Democratic Society* (Harper, 1953).

71. Arthur Bestor, *Educational Wasteland* (University of Illinois Press, 1953).

72. Bernard Iddings Bell, *Crisis in Education* (McGraw Hill, 1953).

73. Albert Lynd, *Quackery in the Public Schools* (Little, Brown, 1953), quoted in Ravitch, *The Troubled Crusade*, p. 75.

74. Sidney B. Simon, Leland W. Howe, and Howard W. Kirschenbaum, *Values Clarification: Handbook of Practical Strategies for Teachers and Students* (A & W Publishers, 1972).

75. Frances Fitzgerald, *America Revised: History Schoolbooks in the Twentieth Century* (Little, Brown, 1979).

76. Paul Vitz, *Censorship: Evidence of Bias in Our Children's Textbooks* (Servant Books, 1986).

77. See, generally, Warren A. Nord, *Religion and American Education: Rethinking a National Dilemma* (University of North Carolina Press, 1995), pp. 138–59.

78. Cited in Stephen V. Monsma and J. Christopher Soper, *The Challenge of Pluralism: Church and State in Five Democracies* (Rowman & Littlefield, 1997), p. 31.

79. Nat Hentoff, "Bible Lessons," *Washington Post*, November 14, 1998, p. A23.

80. The Pew Research Center for the People and the Press, *The Diminishing Divide . . . American Churches, American Politics* (June 25, 1996). See also *Americans Rate their Society and Chart Its Values, The Public Perspective: A Roper Center Review of Public Opinion and Polling*, vol. 8 (February/March 1997).

81. Stephen L. Carter, "Evolutionism, Creationism, and the Treating of Religion as a Hobby," *Duke Law Journal* (1987). See also Stephen L. Carter, *The Culture of Disbelief: How American Law and Politics Trivialize Religious Devotion* (Anchor Books, 1994).

82. Richard J. Neuhaus, *The Naked Public Square: Religion and Democracy in America* (Eerdmans Books, 1984). See also Frederick Mark Gedicks, *The Rhetoric of Church and State* (Duke University Press, 1995).

83. Alan Wolfe, *One Nation after All* (Viking, 1998).

84. Bruce Ackerman, *Social Justice in the Liberal State* (Yale University Press, 1980), p. 103.

85. See Stephen L. Carter, *Civility: Manners, Morals and the Etiquette of Democracy* (Basic Books, 1998), pp. 249–76; Stephen L. Carter, *The Dissent of the Governed* (Harvard University Press, 1998).

86. See Barbara B. Gaddy, T. William Hall, and Robert J. Marzano, *School Wars: Resolving Our Conflicts over Religion and Values* (Jossey Bass, 1996); and, more generally, James Davidson Hunter, *Culture Wars: The Struggle to Define America* (Basic Books, 1991).

87. "Parents of Jewish Children Sue Alabama School System," *Education Week*, September 10, 1997.

88. Stephen Bates, *Battleground: One Mother's Crusade, The Religious Right, and the Struggle for Control of Our Classrooms* (Poseidon Press, 1993).

89. Rosemary C. Salomone, "Struggling with the Devil: A Case Study of Value in Conflict," *Georgia Law Review*, vol. 32 (1998).

90. Stephen Arons, *Compelling Belief: The Culture of American Schooling* (McGraw Hill, 1983).

91. Amy Gutman, *Democratic Education* (Princeton University Press, 1987), p. 121. See also Ackerman, *Social Justice in the Liberal State*, pp. 160–63; Steven Macedo, "Liberal Civic Education and Religious Fundamentalism: The Case of God v. John Rawls?" *Ethics*, vol. 105 (1995). For an excellent critique of Gutman's and the liberal position, see Stephen Gilles, "On Educating Children: A Parental Manifesto," *University of Chicago Law Review*, vol. 62 (1995).

92. John C. Goodlad, "Education and Community," in Roger Stone, ed., *Democracy, Education, and the Schools* (Jossey-Bass, 1996), p. 92.

93. National Center for State Courts, *State Court Organization* (1993).

94. Frank R. Kemerer, "State Constitutions and School Vouchers," *Education Law Reporter*, October 2, 1997.

95. For an analysis of how judicial federalism influences litigation concerning the First Amendment, see Joseph P. Viteritti, "Choosing Equality: Religious Freedom and Educational Opportunity under Constitutional Federalism," *Yale Law & Policy Review*, vol. 15 (1996).

96. See William J. Brennan Jr., "The Bill of Rights and the States: The Revival of State Constitutions as Guardians of Individual Rights," *New York University Law Review*, vol. 61 (1986); John Kinkaid, "Foreword: The New Federalism Context of the New Judicial Federalism," *Rutgers Law Journal*, vol. 26 (1995).

97. Note, "Beyond the Establishment Clause: Enforcing Separation of Church and State through State Constitutional Provisions," *Virginia Law Review*, vol. 71 (1985).

98. *Visser* v. *Noosack Valley School District No. 506*, 207 P.2d. 198, 205 (Wash. 1949).

99. Opinion of the Justices to the Senate, 514 N.E.2d. 353, 356 (Mass. 1987).

100. Opinion of the Justices (Choice in Education), 616 A.2d. 478, 480 (N.H. 1992).

101. Alan Tarr, "Church and State in the States," *Washington Law Review*, vol. 64 (1989).

102. Joseph E. Bryson and Samuel H. Houston, *The Supreme Court and Public Funds for Religious Schools: The Burger Years, 1969–1986* (McFarland, 1990).

103. *Koytterman* v. *Killian*, Supreme Court of Arizona, 972 P.2d 606 (Arizona, 1999).

104. For an analysis of the case law in Wisconsin, Ohio, and Vermont, see Joseph P. Viteritti, "Blaine's Wake: School Choice, the First Amendment, and State Constitutional Law," *Harvard Journal of Law & Public Policy*, vol. 21 (1998).

105. Institute for Justice, *Liberty & Law*, vol. 7 (May 1998)

106. *Warner* v. *Benson*, 578 N.W. 2d. 602 (Wis. 1998)

107. *Wisconsin Industrial School for Girls* v. *Clark County*, 103 Wis. 651, 668-69, 79 N.W.2d. 422 (1899).

108. *Jackson* v. *Benson*, no. 95 CV 1982, slip op. at 17 (Wis. Cir. Ct., January 15, 1997).

109. *Jackson* v. *Benson*, no. 96 CV 1889, slip op. at 28.

110. *Jackson* v. *Benson*, 1997 WL 476290 at 12 (Wis. Ct. App., August 22, 1997).

111. *The Milwaukee Sentinel*, June 12, 1998.

112. Ohio Constitution. art. I, sec. 7.

113. *Gatton* v. *Goff*, no. 96APE08-982 and 9610308-991 (Ohio Ct. App., May 1, 1997).

114. Ibid., at 1576.

115. *Simmons-Harris* v. *Goff*, _____ Ohio St. 3d (1999).

116. It reads, "Laws for the encouragement of virtue and the prevention of vice and immorality ought to be kept constantly in force, and duly executed; and a competent number of schools ought to be kept in each town unless the general assembly permits other provisions for the convenient instruction of youth. All religious societies, or bodies of people that ought to be united or incorporated for the advancement of religion and learning, or for other pious or charitable purposes, shall be encouraged or protected in the enjoyment of privileges, immunities and estates, which they in justice ought to enjoy, under such regulations as the general assembly of the state shall direct." Vermont Constitution, art. II, sec. 68.

117. *Campbell* v. *Manchester Board of School Directors*, 641 A.2d 352 (1994).

118. *Chittenden Town School District* v. *Vermont Department of Education*, No. SO478-96 RcC (Rutland County Superior Court, June 27, 1997).

119. Ibid., at 41.

120. Ava Harriet Chadbourne, *History of Education in Maine* (Lancaster, Pa.: The Science Press Printing Co., 1936), pp. 31–39.

121. Maine Constitution, art. VIII, sec. 1. See also William Wallace Stetson, *A Study of the History of Education in Maine* (State Department of Education, 1902).

122. *Bagley* v. *Maine Department of Education*, Docket no. CV-97-484, April 20, 1998.

123. *Bagley, et al.* v. *Raymond School District*, Maine Judicial Court, Docket Cum-98-281 (1999).

124. See Edwin S. Corwin, *The "Higher Law" Background of American Constitutional Law* (Cornell University Press, 1955).

125. For a useful analysis of the issue, see Warren A. Nord and Charles C. Haynes, *Taking Religion Seriously across the Curriculum* (First Amendment Center, 1998); Charles C. Haynes and Oliver Thomas, *Finding Common Ground* (First Amendment Center, 1996).

Chapter Seven

1. The research literature on the subject is voluminous. See Paul Lazarsfeld, Bernard Berelson, and Hazel Gauzet, *The People's Choice: How the Voter Makes Up His Mind in a Presidential Campaign* (Columbia University Press, 1944); Bernard R. Berelson, Paul F. Lazarsfeld, and William N. McPhee, *Voting: A Study of*

Opinion Formation in a Presidential Campaign (University of Chicago Press, 1954); Robert E. Lane, *Political Life: How and Why People Get Involved in Political Life* (Free Press, 1959); Angus Campbell, Philip E. Converse, Warren E. Miller, and Donald E. Stokes, *The American Voter* (John Wiley, 1964); Lester W. Milbrath, *Political Participation* (Rand McNally, 1965); Raymond E. Wolfinger and Steven J. Rosenstone, *Who Votes?* (Yale University Press, 1980); Margaret Conway, *Political Participation in the United States* (Congressional Quarterly Press, 1991).

2. Seymour Martin Lipset, *Political Man: The Social Bases of Politics* (Doubleday, 1960); Gabriel A. Almond and Sidney Verba, *The Civic Culture: Political Attitudes and Democracy in Five Nations* (Princeton University Press, 1963); Robert A. Dahl, *Polyarchy: Participation and Opposition* (Yale University Press, 1971); Robert A. Dahl, *On Democracy* (Yale University Press, 1998).

3. Norman H. Nie, Jane Junn, and Kenneth Stehlik-Barry, *Education and Democratic Citizenship in America* (University of Chicago Press, 1996).

4. Jefferson also believed that an educated citizenry was the hallmark of a strong democracy. See Thomas Jefferson, "A Bill for More General Diffusion of Knowledge," in Saul Padover, ed., *The Complete Jefferson* (Duell, Sloan & Pearce, 1943).

5. Michael J. Sandel, *Democracy's Discontent: America in Search of a Public Philosophy* (Harvard University Press, 1996), p. 3. See also Michael J. Sandel, *Liberalism and the Limits of Justice* (Cambridge University Press, 1982).

6. Mary Ann Glendon, *Rights Talk: The Impoverishment of Political Discourse* (Free Press, 1991). See also Alasdair MacIntyre, *After Virtue: A Study of Moral Theory* (University of Notre Dame Press, 1981), which is written from the perspective of the classical republican tradition; Lawrence M. Mead, *Beyond Entitlement: The Social Obligations of Citizenship* (Basic Books, 1986), which is written from a policy perspective.

7. See Morris Janowitz, *The Reconstruction of Patriotism* (University of Chicago Press, 1983).

8. See Diane Ravitch, *The Troubled Crusade* (Basic Books, 1983), pp. 3–42.

9. Stephen V. Monsma and J. Christopher Soper, *The Challenge of Pluralism: Church and State in Five Democracies* (Rowman & Littlefield, 1997), p. 39. See, generally, Stephen V. Monsma, *When Sacred and Secular Mix: Religious Nonprofit Organizations and Public Money* (Rowman & Littlefield, 1996).

10. See Ronald J. Sider and Heidi Rolland Unruh, "No Aid to Religion? Charitable Choice and the First Amendment," *Brookings Review*, vol. 17 (Spring 1999).

11. Andrew M. Greeley, *The Catholic Myth: The Behavior and Beliefs of Catholic Americans* (Scribner, 1990); Peter Rossi and Andrew M. Greeley, *The Education of Catholic Americans* (Aldine Press, 1966); Jay P. Green, "Civic Values in Public and Private Schools," in Paul E. Peterson and Bryan C. Hassel, eds. *Learning from School Choice* (Brookings, 1998).

12. Robert D. Putnam, "Bowling Alone: America's Declining Social Capital," *Journal of Democracy*, vol. 6 (January 1995).

13. Ibid., p. 68.

14. Robert D. Putnam, "Turning In, Turning Out: The Strange Disappearance of Social Capital in America," *PS: Political Science and Politics*, vol. 28 (December 1995); Robert D. Putnam, *Making Democracy Work: Civic Traditions in Modern Italy* (Princeton University Press, 1993). The latter is an extensive empirical study of local regional governments in Italy, where the concept of social capital was developed and applied.

15. Sidney Verba, Kay Lehman Schlozman, and Henry E. Brady, *Voice and Equality: Civic Voluntarism in American Politics* (Harvard University Press, 1995), pp. 76, 83. See also Robert Wuthnow, *Loose Connections: Joining Together in America's Fragmented Communities* (Harvard University Press, 1998).

16. William A. Galston and Peter Levine, "America's Civic Condition: A Glance at the Evidence," in E. J. Dionne Jr., ed., *Community Works: The Revival of Civil Society in America* (Brookings, 1998), p. 31.

17. Everett C. Ladd, "The Data Just Don't Show Erosion of America's Social Capital," *The Public Perspective* (June–July 1996).

18. Joseph S. Nye, Philip D. Zelikow, and David C. King, *Why People Don't Trust Government* (Harvard University Press, 1997).

19. Gary Orren, "Fall from Grace: The Public's Loss of Faith in Government," in Nye, Zelikow, and King, *Why People Don't Trust Government*, p. 82.

20. Robert J. Blendon and others, "Changing Attitudes in America," in Nye, Zelikow, and King, *Why People Don't Trust Government*, pp. 206–07.

21. Orren, "Fall from Grace," p. 81.

22. Joseph S. Nye, "Introduction: The Decline of Confidence in Government," in Nye, Zelikow, and King, *Why People Don't Trust Government*, p. 1.

23. Ibid. See also Seymour Martin Lipset and William Schneider, *The Confidence Gap: Business, Labor and Government in the Public Mind* (Johns Hopkins University Press, 1987).

24. See also Joseph N. Cappella and Katherine Hall Jameson, *Spiral of Cynicism: The Press and the Common Good* (Oxford University Press, 1997); Ronald Inglehart, *Modernization and Postmodernization: Cultural, Economic, and Political Change in 43 Societies* (Princeton University Press, 1997); Martin Wattenberg, *The Decline of American Political Parties* (Harvard University Press, 1994).

25. Tom Loveless, "The Structure of Public Confidence in Education," *American Journal of Education*, vol. 105 (February 1997).

26. Blendon and others, "Changing Attitudes in America," pp. 206–07.

27. See, generally, Charles Beitz, *Political Equality: An Essay in Democratic Theory* (Princeton University Press, 1989).

28. See Sidney Verba and Gary Orren, *Equality in America: The View from the Top* (Harvard University Press, 1985); Jennifer L. Hochschild, *What's Fair? American Beliefs about Distributive Justice* (Harvard University Press, 1981).

29. See Chandler Davidson, "The Voting Rights Act: A Brief History," in Bernard Grofman and Chandler Davidson, eds., *Controversies in Minority Voting:*

The Voting Rights Act in Perspective (Brookings, 1992); Chandler Davidson, "The Recent Evolution of Voting Rights Law Affecting Racial and Language Minorities," in Chandler Davidson and Bernard Grofman, eds., *Quiet Revolution in the South: The Impact of the Voting Rights Act, 1965–1990* (Princeton University Press, 1994); Joseph P. Viteritti, "Unapportioned Justice: Local Elections, Social Science and the Evolution of the Voting Rights Act," *Cornell Journal of Law and Public Policy*, vol. 4 (1994).

30. Sidney Verba and Norman H. Nie, *Participation in America: Political Democracy and Social Equality* (Harper & Row, 1972); Sidney Verba, Norman H. Nie, and Jae-on Kim, *Participation and Political Equality: A Seven Nation Comparison* (Cambridge University Press, 1978); Verba, Schlozman, and Brady, *Voice and Equality*.

31. Robert Pear, "Black and Hispanic Poverty Rate Falls, Reducing Overall Rate for Nation," *New York Times*, September 25, 1998.

32. Saul Alinsky, "The War on Poverty: Political Pornography," *Journal of Social Issue*, vol. 21 (1965).

33. John R. Hibbing and Elizabeth Theiss-Morse, "Civics Is Not Enough: Teaching Barbarics in K–12," *PS: Political Science and Politics*, vol. 29 (1996).

34. Michael X. Delli Carpini and Scott Keeter, *What Americans Know about Politics and Why It Matters* (Yale University Press, 1996).

35. Richard G. Niemi and Jane Junn, *Civic Education: What Makes Students Learn* (Yale University Press, 1998).

36. Benjamin Barber, *A Place for Us: How to Make Society Civil and Democracy Strong* (Hill & Wang, 1998), p. 4.

37. Michael Walzer, "The Idea of Civil Society," *Dissent* (Spring 1991), p. 293.

38. Francis Fukuyama, *Trust: The Social Virtues and the Creation of Prosperity* (Free Press, 1995), pp. 4–5.

39. See, especially, Alexis de Tocqueville, *Democracy in America*, vol. 2 (Random House, 1945), pp. 114–29.

40. Alexis de Tocqueville, *Democracy in America*, vol. 1 (Random House, 1945), p. 316. See also Tocqueville, *Democracy in America*, vol. 2, pp. 129–36, 152–7. For further elaboration on the theme, see William A. Galston, *Liberal Purposes: Goods, Virtues, and Diversity in the Liberal State* (Cambridge University Press, 1991), pp. 257–89.

41. Almond and Verba, *The Civic Culture*. See also Robert N. Bellah, Richard Madsen, William M. Sullivan, Ann Swidner, and Steven M. Tipton, *Habits of the Heart: Individualism and Commitment in American Life* (University of California Press, 1985).

42. James S. Coleman, "Social Capital in the Creation of Human Capital," *American Journal of Sociology*, vol. 94 (1988). Although Coleman popularized it, the term "social capital" was first used in Jane Jacobs, *The Death and Life of Great American Cities* (Random House, 1961), p. 138.

43. Galston, *Liberal Purposes*, pp. 251–52.

44. See Robert A. Dahl, *Democracy and Its Critics* (Yale University Press, 1989).

45. Peter Berger and Richard John Neuhaus, *To Empower People* (AEI Press, 1977). See also E. J. Dionne Jr., "Introduction: Why Civil Society? Why Now?" in Dionne, *Community Works*.

46. See Alan Wolfe, *Whose Keeper? Social Science and Moral Obligation* (University of California Press, 1989); Alan Wolfe, "Is Civil Society Obsolete? Revisiting Predictions of the Decline of Civil Society," in Dionne, *Community Works*.

47. Tocqueville was also aware of the kinds of conflict that voluntary associations could provoke in society. While wary of the danger, however, he finally concluded that the effect would eventually strengthen democracy. See Michael W. Foley and Bob Edwards, "The Paradox of Civil Society," *Journal of Democracy*, vol. 7 (July 1996); Michael W. Foley and Bob Edwards, "Escape from Politics? Social Theory and the Social Capital Debate," *American Behavioral Scientist*, vol. 40 (March–April 1997).

48. See, generally, Charles L. Glenn, *Educational Freedom in Eastern Europe* (Cato Institute, 1995).

49. Ibid., p. ix.

50. See Monsma and Soper, *The Challenge of Pluralism*; Charles L. Glenn, *Choice of Schools in Six Nations* (Department of Education, 1989); John E. Chubb and Terry M. Moe, *A Lesson in School Reform from Great Britain* (Brookings, 1992); Jan De Groof, "The European Model: Life without the Wall of Separation," paper presented at the Conference on Faith and Public Policy, Ethics and Public Policy Center, Washington, D.C., February 5, 1999.

51. Miron Gray, "Free Choice and Vouchers Transform Schools," *Educational Leadership* (October 1996).

52. See Monsma and Soper, *The Challenge of Pluralism*, pp. 16–17.

53. Galston and Levine, "America's Civic Condition," in Dionne, *Community Works*.

54. Mark Schneider and others, "Institutional Arrangements and the Creation of Social Capital: The Effects of Public School Choice," *American Political Science Review*, vol. 91 (March 1997).

55. C. Eric Lincoln and Lawrence H. Mamiya, *The Black Church in the Afro-American Experience* (Duke University Press, 1990), p. 8.

56. Verba, Schlozman, and Brady, *Voice and Equality*.

57. Ibid., p.18.

58. See Robert Booth Fowler, Allen D. Hertzke, and Laura R. Olsen, *Religion and Politics in America: Faith, Culture and Strategic Choices* (Westview Press, 1999), pp. 157–58.

59. Verba, Schlozman, and Brady, *Voice and Equality*, p. 519.

60. E. Franklin Frazier, *The Negro Church in America* (Schocken, 1964); Norval D. Glenn, "Negro Religion and Negro Status in the United States," in Louis Schneider, ed., *Religion, Culture and Society* (Wiley, 1964).

61. Norval D. Glenn and Erin Gotard, "The Religion of Blacks in the United

States: Some Recent Trends and Current Characteristics," *American Journal of Sociology*, vol. 83 (1977); Christopher G. Ellison and Darren E. Sherkat, "Patterns of Religious Mobility among Black Americans," *Sociological Quarterly*, vol. 31 (1990); Darren E. Sherkat and Christopher G. Ellison, "The Politics of Black Religious Change: Disaffiliation from Black Mainline Denominations," *Social Forces*, vol. 70 (1991).

62. See Robert L. Woodson, *The Triumph of Joseph: How Today's Community Healers Are Reviving Our Streets and Neighborhoods* (Free Press, 1998); Robert D. Carle and Louis A. DeCarlo, eds., *Signs of Hope: Ministries of Renewal* (Judson Press, 1997); Nancy Tatom Ammerman, *Congregation and Community* (Rutgers University Press, 1997); J. M. Thomas and R. N. Blake, "Faith Based Community Development in African American Neighborhoods," in W. Dennis Keating, Norman Krumholz, and Philip Star, eds., *Revitalizing Urban Neighborhoods* (University of Kansas Press, 1996); Fredrick C. Harris, "Religious Institutions and African American Political Mobilization," in Paul E. Peterson, ed., *Classifying by Race* (Princeton University Press, 1995); Andrew Billingsley, "The Social Relevance of the Contemporary Black Church," *National Journal of Sociology*, vol. 8 (Summer 1994).

63. See Cornel West, *Race Matters* (Vintage Books, 1994); Cornel West, *Prophetic Thought in Postmodern Times* (Common Courage, 1993). See also William Julius Wilson, *The Truly Disadvantaged* (University of Chicago Press, 1987); Meredith Ramsey, "Redeeming the City: Exploring the Relationship between Church and Metropolis," *Urban Affairs Review*, vol. 33 (May 1998).

64. See David B. Larson and Byron R. Johnson, "Religion: The Forgotten Factor in Cutting Youth Crime and Serving At-Risk Urban Youth" (Manhattan Institute for Policy Research, 1998); B. Benda, "The Effect of Religion on Adolescent Delinquency Revisited," *Journal of Research on Crime and Delinquency*, vol. 32 (1995); D. Brownfield and A. M. Sorenson, "Religion and Drug Abuse among Adolescents: A Social Support Conceptualization and Interpretation," *Deviant Behavior*, vol. 12 (1991).

65. John J. DiIulio Jr., "The Lord's Work: The Church and Civil Society, in Dionne, *Community Works*.

66. Eugene F. Rivers, "High-Octane Faith and Civil Society," in Dionne, *Community Works*, p. 60.

67. Kent E. Portney and Jeffrey M. Berry, "Mobilizing Minority Communities: Social Capital and Participation in Urban Neighborhoods," *American Behavioral Scientist*, vol. 40 (March–April 1998).

68. Ramsey, "Redeeming the City," p. 608.

69. Somini Sengupta, "Meshing the Sacred and the Secular: Floyd Flake Offers Community Development Via Church and State," *New York Times*, November 23, 1995.

70. Anemona Hartocollis, "In a Religious Model, Seeds for a Charter School," *New York Times*, February 14, 1999.

71. Ibid.

72. Interview of the Reverend Floyd Flake by the author, April 28, 1999.

73. Joan Davis Ratteray, *On the Road to Success: Students at Independent Neighborhood Schools* (Washington, D.C., 1991, updated 1996). See also David Dent, "African Americans Turning to Christian Academies," *New York Times Education Supplement*, August 4, 1996.

74. Gail Foster and Evelyn Foster, *Directory of Historically Black Independent Schools* (New York: Toussaint Institute, 1998).

75. Jeremy White and Mary de Marcellus, *Faith-Based Outreach to At-Risk Youth in Washington, D.C.* (Manhattan Institute for Policy Research, 1998), p. 7.

76. Foster and Foster, *Historically Black Independent Schools*, p. 14.

77. Ratteray, *On the Road to Success*, p. 11.

78. James S. Coleman, "Changes in Family and Implications for the Common School," *University of Chicago Legal Forum* (1991).

79. Ibid., p. 163.

80. Gail Foster, "New York City's Wealth of Historically Black Independent Schools," *Journal of Negro Education*, vol. 61 (1992), p. 197. See also Megan Drennan, "Spiritual Healing," *Education Week*, June 5, 1996.

81. Anemona Hartocollis, "Charter School Legislator Criticizes Ministers' Plans," *New York Times*, December 30, 1998. See also Anemona Hartocollis, "Religious Leaders Plan for Charter Schools," *New York Times*, December 29, 1998.

82. Lynn Schnaiberg, "Buildings in Hand, Church Leaders Float Charter Ideas," *Education Week*, February 10, 1999.

83. See Lee Stuart, "The Bronx Leadership Academy High School," in Diane Ravitch and Joseph P. Viteritti, eds., *City Schools: Lessons from New York* (Johns Hopkins University Press, forthcoming).

84. Lee Stuart, "Redefining the Public Sphere: South Bronx Churches and Education Reform," in Carle and DeCarlo, *Signs of Hope*, p. 148.

Index